THE PSYCHOLOGY
OF RITUAL

THE PSYCHOLOGY OF RITUAL

Murry Hope

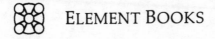

ELEMENT BOOKS

First published in 1988 by
Element Books Limited
Longmead, Shaftesbury, Dorset

Printed and bound in Great Britain
by Billings, Hylton Road, Worcester

Designed by Clarke Williams

Cover painting by Caroline Smith

British Library Cataloguing in Publication Data
Hope, Murry
The psychology of ritual.
1. Rituals
I. Title
306'.4

ISBN 1-85230-043-4

To Nurse Rhoda Adams, who was my Nanny,
with love and gratitude.

CONTENTS

Earliest records. Synonymity of religion and magic. Categorization of various types of Rites. The five Ritual Codes. Psychological classifications. Body language and mime.

The Recollective Bado Rite of the Dogons based on Sirius, re-echoed in the tribal myths of the Bambara and Bozo. Origins of Chaldean Rites and beliefs. The Oannes legend. The Horned god. The psychology of energy exchanges. An ancient Seasonal Rite.

Gnostic evolutionary classifications. How the need for an

intermediary arose. Shamanism and states of ecstasy. The shamanic role in the Sacrificial Rite. The role of the priest or hierophant in tribal and civic affairs. Social advantages of ancient rites as seen by modern psychiatrists.

The social usage of ancient Egyptian Rites. Two forms of sacred rites — religious and sensuous. The Eleusinia, or state rites of ancient Greece. Drama and the Rite. The psychological view of 'faith'. Private language of the subconscious — an anecdote. Jung on the power of the Rite to influence God.

The term 'psychism' defined occultly, psychologically and scientifically. Professor Stephen E Braude on PK and allied phenomena. Jung on mediumship and the hysterical personality-type. Brain patterns involved in psi manifestations. Channelling. The dangers of experimentation. Trance mediumship and the Rite. The role of creative imagery. Archetypes in ritual.

Freud on the libido. Jung on Tantra. Sexual expression as related to soul-age. The sublimation principle in religious orders. The redemption factor. Imbalances effected by drugs, hypnosis, deprivation. The power of repetition in unconscious programming. Yoga — its nature and discipline.

How ritual role-playing works. Archetypal identities. Hallucinations and visions. Two views — humanistic psychology and the Jungian analyst. The assumption of the archetypal role. Who or what are 'the gods'? The occult ego traps and danger zones of pride and power. Morphic resonance as applied to ritual role-playing.

Rites of birth, puberty, and death or departure. Remnants of old Rites that are still with us. The influence of the Rite on architecture and the arts. Sacred geometry. The Roman Catholic Mass as a Sacrificial Rite — its psychological effects observed. The psychology of sacrifice. Talismanic Rites.

The Book of the Dead. Ancient Egyptian Burial Rites. The Tibetan Bardo Thödol. The Requiem Mass. A Seax Wicca Rite, 'Crossing the Bridge' (at Death) and a pagan 'Rite for the Dead' reproduced in full. An old Aztec Funerary Rite. Further Rites of Departure. The psychology of the Death Syndrome.

Part II. Psychological Breakdown

The effect of certain rites on the autonomic nervous system, the brain, the mental system and the endocrine system. The relationship between the endocrine system and the chakras. The Kundalini concept. Excitatory Rites that over-energize. Psychological and somatic intolerances to psychic frequencies or resonances. The 'heat' effect. Psychedelic side-effects in ritual.

The Qabalah defined. The Tree of Life, the Double Helix and the DNA molecule. Pathworking as a legitimate occult practice. Full psychological analysis of a Qabalistic Pathworking. Jung's Qabalistic experience. Gematria.

CHAPTER 12.   *An Ancient Egyptian Rite*   124

The Book of the Dead considered. True origins of the Egyptian magical system and the philosophy behind the old Egyptian beliefs. A metaphysical consideration of the Law of Polarity and the nature of the Twinning Rite. The inherent dangers in Egyptiana and High Magic generally.

CHAPTER 13.   *A Triple Goddess Rite and an Old Celtic Healing Rite*   134

1. Moon worship and the Triple Goddess concept. The three aspects as related to the human psychological economy.
2. An old Celtic healing ceremony — a hindbrain or instinctive awareness Rite. The animistic aspects. Elemental qualities defined.

CHAPTER 14.   *Two Protection Rites*   138

1. A Jesuit ritual. The Roman Catholic attitude towards evil and a personalised devil. The delusory nature of many so-termed 'occult attacks'.
2. The Hammer Rite in the Norse/Teutonic tradition. The animus emphasis in Severity Code Rites. The nature of Runic magic and the closeness of that system to the earth-plane.

CHAPTER 15.   *An Enochian Angelic Rite*   142

The various angelic classifications and their roles in the celestial hierarchy. The *Heptarchia Mystica* of John Dee. An Enochian Invocatory Rite analysed. Left hemisphere requirements of memorization.

CHAPTER 16.   *Ritual World Tour*   148

A Shinto Harvest Festival. Aztec ceremonial bathing of the newborn. Personal Worship — *Pūja* (Tantra). Sitting and the Kōan. Aboriginal Rain Making and the Corroboree. The Great Huna *Ha* Prayer Rite. Shamanic descent to the bottom of the ocean.

Initiation — what it is and what it is not. Psychological reaction to initiation failure. Initiation Rites from the past. Ritual renaming of the novice. Shamanic Initiatory Rites. The 'berserk' factor. The heat factor. The death and resurrection syndrome or transformation principle — the alchemical inferences. The significance of trees in ancient initiation. Apuleius and the Isian initiatory scene. A Buddhic initiation. Plato and Plutarch on initiation.

The role of women in ritual. The views of Freud and Jung. Athene, Greek goddess of wisdom — her significance. Female Puberty Rites. Secret women's fraternities. Female Initiation Rituals from various parts of the world. Psychiatrist Bani Shorter on the present-day need for ritual negotiation of different thresholds. Isian Rites.

Part III. Rituals of the Nuclear Age

The astrological 'Ages'. The soul age. Inner and outer time. Aquarianism — a double-edged sword. Changes in ritual expression from Piscean to Aquarian. The resurgence of ancient religions and their associated rites. The new eco-religion. The rise of interest in occult and metaphysical studies. The cult of the guru and its dependencies. The Jungian cult. The triple programming of modern life.

The religion of alternatives. Cosmic roots. Looking forward and outward for inspiration. The role of astrology in ritual.

Channelled connections from other worlds. The nature of the Sirius ray. The current abuse of natural laws. Space, time, and the human mind.

Present-day Social Rites. The rituals of daily living. The psychology behind superstition. The power of the media in collective programming and social conditioning. Today's gods — materialism and science. Modern aspects of Dualism.

Reasons for secrecy. Ancient Secret Rites of science and knowledge. Secrecy through fear of persecution — magical and religious underground movements. The secret order as a breeding ground for spiritual and intellectual snobbery. The psychology behind the magical 'union' or select clique.

Crossing the initiatory threshold in today's world. Initiation in the trials of everyday existence. The Initiation Rites of organizations such as the Order of the Golden Dawn. The Three Degrees of Wiccan initiation. Solitary initiation. Who is or is not suited to the magical Path. The eight psychological types.

Three categories. Various rituals of healing. The Butterfly syndrome. The dangers in untrained or unprofessional diagnoses. Healing in Wiccan covens. Christian healing practices — the nature and identity of the Holy Spirit and other healing entities encountered in the Spiritualist movement. Solitary Healing Rites.

The missionary mode: social, political, religious or magical indoctrination. The psychology behind the formation of new groups or collectives. Personal power complexes. Cosmic racism. The Gaia hypothesis.

Why the need for protection and from what? The nature of evil — the misplaced energy theory. Banishment and Cleansing Rites. Exorcism. The Law of Equalities defined. Paranormal phenomena and PK. Unfounded occult attacks. The power of Egyptian talismanic magic — an anecdote.

The macrocosm/microcosm concept. The altars and sacrificial offerings of materialism and science. Employment of the Rite as part of the universal order of things. The Rite as observed in all natural cycles — death and rebirth, growth, display, maturation, withdrawal.

ACKNOWLEDGEMENTS

My gratitude and sincere thanks to my dear friend Dr John A Cosh, MA, MD, Cantab., FRCP for his invaluable assistance and medical advice.

Acknowledgements and thanks are also due to the authors and publishers who have kindly granted permission to quote from the following books:

Robert Hale Limited: *The Witches' Way* by Janet and Stewart Farrar.

Thorsons Publishing Group PLC: *The Shining Paths* by Dolores Ashcroft-Nowicki, *Sacred Geometry* by Nigel Pennick, *Futhark* by Edred Thorsson.

Harper & Row, Inc.: *Rites and Symbols of Initiation* by Mircea Eliade.

Collins Publishers PLC: *From Primitives to Zen* by Mircea Eliade, *Archaeology of Dream Time* by Josephine Flood.

Routledge & Kegan Paul Limited: *Memories, Dreams and Reflections* by C G Jung, *Alchemical Studies* by C G Jung, *Psychology and the Occult* by C G Jung, *The Limits of Influence* by Stephen E Braude.

A & C Black PLC: *The Mystical Qabalah* by Dion Fortune.

Sidgwick & Jackson Limited: *The Sirius Mystery*, by Robert K G Temple.

Llewellyn Publications, Inc.: *Enochian Magic* by Gerald J Schueler.

Samuel Weiser, Inc.: *A Book of Pagan Rituals* ed. by Herman Slater, *The Tree — The Complete Book of Saxon Witchcraft* by Raymond Buckland.

Thames & Hudson Limited: *Creation Myths* by David McLagan, *Shaman* by Joan Halifax.

Artwork by Martin Jones.

INTRODUCTION

One of the most profound observations proferred by the late Carl Gustav Jung was undoubtedly his conclusion that the human psyche accommodates an inbuilt, subliminal need to acknowledge the supramundane. Although the atheistically inclined may condemn this as irrational nonsense, experience bears out that even the most vehement unbelievers have been known to call upon some unseen power or hitherto denied force for help or comfort in times of extreme duress.

During his years as a practising psychiatrist, Jung also noted that those who embraced any form of transcendental philosophy were frequently better able to deal with the stresses, disappointments and disillusionments that life inevitably visits upon us all at some time or other during our sojourn in this time zone we call our present lives.

A belief in some form of supernatural power has been with us since the dawn of time, assuming more organized aspects as primitive peoples slowly came together to form the tribal groupings which eventually evolved into distinctive cultures. Religious credos and procedures were frequently adapted to suit the changing needs of the community, sacerdotalism being ever heedful of the advantages to be gained by convenient alliances with those in authority. The veneer of disciplined stability is easily scratched, however, and when exposed to the popular demands of the collective, or stimulated by emotionally persuasive techniques, the primitive instincts that readily surface are ripe for manipulation.

All social, religious, magical and metaphysical practices, rites and credos, both overt and covert, are therefore dictated by the psychological requirements of:

1. The collective which gives birth to them and the ethos in which they flourish.

2. The racial or group characteristics emphasized within that collective.

3. The imprint of the evolutionary cycle through which the planet is passing at the time of inception.

4. The individual psyche and its relationship to 1, 2 and 3.

The human psychological economy would appear to function at several levels, which have been given appropriate names by the different schools of psychology, religion, magic or mysticism. Jung designated them the ego or conscious mind, the personal unconscious (in which is stored all our fantasies, dreams and desires), and the collective unconscious. Another threefold reference qualifies them in terms of the natural/instinctive, rational/ intellectual and creative/intuitive, and there are numerous quaternary distinctions: logical, emotional, intellectual, spiritual; sensation, feeling, thinking, intuition; and so forth. We may approach the transcendental through any or all of these aspects, and the nature of the creed or ideology we elect to follow will proclaim all too clearly which part of our mental economy is controlling or influencing our judgement.

People have ever fashioned their tenets around their own psychological needs, or sought an existing doctrine or philosophy that will complement or accommodate their idiosyncratic or personal concept of those unseen energies to whom they feel they can turn when the need arises. Consequently, many different procedures have been adopted over the ages for the purpose of effecting a mystical communion either with the Higher Self, or with some indefinable force that is not normally perceived by way of the five senses. These have, in turn, given rise to the traditional rituals and observances, both collective and otherwise, which constitute organized social, religious and magical practices today.

Religion in its many modes, being anachronistic by nature, can both elevate and corrupt the human spirit, as the pages of history show only too clearly. It should therefore be borne in mind that much lip service has and still is being paid to established modes of idealism and belief in order to effect an air of outward respectability, or court the material favours of more prosperous members of society. Regular addiction to any Rite should, therefore, be examined psychologically for flaws in human intention, as the nature of the energy invoked, and the use made thereof, will be decided by this factor only and not by the outward display or traditional sublimity of the ceremony.

The rapid advancement of modern science and technology has had the effect of telescoping time so that the history of the human race can be viewed in *gestalt*. The past and present no longer seem aeons apart. The way that people felt, thought, acted and worshipped in say, ancient Sumeria, can be seen as little different from the way we think and act now, allowing for the more primitive social conditions that prevailed in those times. We may employ the wonders of modern science and technology to enhance our rituals and proclaim our dogmas to larger audiences, but the fundamentals would appear to be little changed. Whether or not we have arrived at a more profound understanding of the purpose of our beingness, or formulated a more sublime concept of that which transcends us, however, is for the philosophers and mystics to determine, although a few rather obvious answers to this are, I trust, to be found in the ensuing pages.

Part 1
History and Background

Chapter 1

THE BIRTH OF THE RITE

Primitive man was by no means as conditioned as his modern counterpart when it came to making use of the instinctive side of his nature. Being unlettered and unread, his practical reasoning powers had not received that emphasis which normally triggers the left hemisphere of the brain into action, inducing what we consider to be a rational way of thinking. His instinct and his intuition were therefore his only mental allies, and as these were as yet unsullied by that overemphasis of logic considered by mystics to be the cause of so many modern-day ills, he was only too aware of the life force around him and its manifestation in all that he observed. Realizing how dependent he was upon this force, he sought to communicate with it and placate it so that it would work harmoniously both with and through him, and if he could persuade it to perform according to *his* wishes, then so much the better. It was upon this premise that the Rite was born.

Evidence of the Rite has come down to us from the earliest records, and if we are to lend credence to oral and metaphysical traditions, it was in existence long before the pages of recorded history. Rites, however, cover a multitude of purposes and carry a variety of messages, as we shall see. It should also be borne in mind that in those very early days, magic and religion were synonymous, so that which might appear as impious mumbo-jumbo to the modern religious thinker was highly respectful and devotional to the participants of the time.

Some categorization will, no doubt, make it easier for the

reader to gain a clearer perspective on the nature of, and intention behind, some of the more familiar rites that we take so much for granted, as well as the lesser-known rituals that will be surfacing during the ensuing pages. I have therefore drawn up the following list, which I feel to be fairly comprehensive:

1. Recollective ceremonies — the remnants of rites of earlier, more advanced civilizations, the origins and true meanings of which have become obscured.

2. The worship or acknowledgement of cosmological or celestial influences — the sun, moon, stars, or natural phenomena, such as thunder, lightning, and so on.

3. Pantheistic, Pagan and Animistic Rites — (animism being the belief that all inanimate objects and natural phenomena have a living soul or essence) in which due deference is paid to the spirits of nature. Seasonal rituals would come under this category, also the Rites of Sympathetic Magic (invocation or evocation through mimicry).

4. Placatory or Propitiatory Rites — performed with a view to keeping the gods or spirits happy so that they do not give vent to their wrath at the population's expense.

5. Ancestral Rites - which involve making contact with, and securing the good offices of, those of the tribe who have passed on.

6. Self-Exploratory Rites — including those self-analysis techniques which project the participant back into his or her own inner resources.

7. Fertility Rites — involving the multiplication principle which, as much as it may surprise some, is *not* limited to the human reproductory system.

8. Social Rites — including those rites which greet us when we first enter life, Maturation or Puberty Rites which are designed to prepare the young people of the tribe for the step into adult life, and the Last Rites administered at the approach of death.

9. Sacrificial or Expiatory Rites — which make their appearance in both religion and magic to this very day.

10. Initiatory Rites — including Rites of Submission, many of

which originally involved physical mortification or deprivation. In this day and age, however, as with many other rites
which originated in more primitive times, these are usually
enacted symbolically.

11. Supplicatory Rites — including general unspecified collective prayer offerings and invocations which may or may not
involve energy exchanges (gifts). These can be purely
devotional, or they may include specific pleas for bounty or
guidance.

12. Rites of Protection, Purification, Banishment, Cleansing and
Healing — which naturally vary in intention according to the
persuasion of the users.

Most rites, however, are a blend of several of the above categories. For example, they nearly all include a devotional acknowledgement and/or a request of some kind. Although they may not
have started off that way, accumulated layers have frequently
been added to accommodate the faiths of conquering nations
and/or the tenets of new religions or ideologies.

The above categories could also be subdivided as follows:

(a) Public Rites, in which anyone can take part although the
quality of the energy generated will obviously affect each
participant in a slightly different way.

(b) The Solitary or Personal Rite, which can be performed by
the lone individual within his or her own space.

(c) The Secret Rites of 'closed' groups or collectives.

(d) Simple Rites that carry no great mystique, which can be
safely executed by anyone.

The latter category obviously raises the question as to whether
there are rites which are not safe for participation by all. The
answer must be 'yes'. The psychology behind this will, I trust,
become obvious in the ensuing pages.

There are also five basic codes via which the Rite may be
approached, each of which emphasizes a particular area of
human psychology:

1. *The Severity Code* — which features in Teutonic Magic, the
martial arts, warrior and heroic rites, certain African and

Amerindian rituals and the harsher Christian and Islamic practices — is of a disciplinary and sometimes punitive nature, and can involve physical mortification which may vary in intensity according to the traditions of the tribe or ethos concerned.

2. *The Emotional Code* — frequently associated with the Celtic, romantic or eco-systems of magic, reaches deeply into the feeling nature and can therefore be abreactive (inducing the release of repressed emotion). If handled in a balanced manner, however, it can supply a subconscious outlet in an otherwise emotionally arid existence.

3. *The Contemplative Code* — with its strongly mystical and ascetic undertones, is to be evidenced in many Far Eastern observances, as well as in certain Christian practices.

4. *The Intellectual or Analytical Code* — often associated with Qabalism and the Western Hermetic Tradition.

5. *The Instinctive Code* — as practised in primitive tribal rituals, sympathetic magic, some pantheistic, pagan and animistic traditions and certain branches of Wicca.

These can be classified as 'introversial' or 'extroversial', according to the overt or covert nature of the rite on the one hand, or the psychological effect it has on the participants on the other.

Some public rites may appear to involve more than one code. The Catholic Mass, for example, is a Sacrificial Rite which frequently carries an intellectual content for the clergy and an emotional one for the laity. In essence, however, it qualifies as 'Intellectual' because its content is carefully planned and rigidly adhered to.

Active/passive, patrist/matrist, animus/anima, categories can also be applied as follows:

1. *The Severity Code* — introverted, covert, active, patrist and of animus emphasis.

2. *The Emotional Code* — extroverted, overt, passive, matrist and of anima emphasis.

3. *The Contemplative Code* — introverted, covert, passive, patrist and of anima emphasis.

4. *The Intellectual Code* — introverted, covert, passive, patrist and of animus emphasis.

5. *The Instinctive Code* — extroverted, overt, active, matrist and can be of either anima or animus emphasis.

When dealing with the individual psyche, however, one should remember that these are but generalizations, as an actively inclined patrist might, on certain occasions, choose to involve him or herself in a more submissive rite. However, the overall code will usually prevail, those taking part becoming caught up in the essential nature of the ceremony.

Assuming there is a desire to participate in some rite or other, be it social, magical or religious, the general approach to life adopted by each individual will tend to point him or her, albeit unconsciously, into one or other of the aforementioned avenues of expression. For example, there is the 'thinking approach', which is usually attendant to liberalism in the broadest consideration of the term. 'Thinking' people tend to be drawn to Contemplative or Intellectual expressions of the Rite while those 'non-thinkers', who do not care for too much intellectualizing, would probably be best able to express themselves in Emotional or Instinctive liturgies.

The Severity approach attracts both thinkers and non-thinkers, leaders and followers, as may be evidenced in the national rites of the Hitler Youth and the battles and tortures that have stained the pages of history with their blood in the name of some fanatically espoused cause. I am not decrying the use of this code, however, as I know several worthy people who engage in its practices to good effect. As with everything else in life it comes down to the question of balance, and what we have to ask ourselves before we decide on a course of ritualistic action is: what is lacking in our characters? What do we need to learn? What do we need to let go of, to discover, to expiate, to *give*? If it is self-discipline that is lacking, then Severity Rites could serve us well. If our emotions are the problem, what better than the Intellectual or Analytical approach? The over-pressured city executive could benefit both physically and mentally from exposure to Instinctive ritual outlets, while those who have lost touch with nature and the eco-life with which we share this planet could gain strength and solace from the knowledge that they are not alone in the world if they participate in Emotionally coded ritual practices.

In the days when the instinctive/emotional aspects of human psychology were in ascendance, matrism dominated social life and the accent was very much on agricultural activities and the creative function at all its levels of manifestation. The classical writers tell us that in this 'Silver Age', men did not make war or kill each other, neither did they offer blood sacrifices, although they were, to a degree, subservient to their womenfolk. The Bronze Age of the classical heroes followed in the wake of this Arcadian idyll, and was in turn usurped by the Age of Iron, a period of misery, crime, treachery and cruelty 'when men respect neither their vows, nor justice, nor virtue'.[1] Our present day, no doubt.

The Rites that dominated in each respective Age can be readily fitted into the aforementioned codes, which also tells us a lot about the prevailing cultural inclinations of the time.

It is interesting to observe how each code has its own body-language. Severity Rites tend to favour physical movement of a disciplined nature, Instinctive Rites lean towards dance, mime and music frequently feature in Emotional type rituals, while in the Contemplative schools the body is positioned in ways which are calculated to trigger certain areas of the brain via the chakric system. Intellectually orientated rites frequently employ patterned movements which are felt to be based on cosmic principles.

The use of mime would appear to be common to most rites, which is understandable if one considers the intrinsic nature of this art form. As a pupil of the Royal College of Music, I underwent training in classical mime, which I have since found to be invaluable, both in ordinary person to person communication and magical workings. The arms outstretched with palms open, for example, is a receptive gesture which falls naturally into role-playing rites, while the protective personal embrace inevitably makes its appearance in rituals of protection. The psychology of gesture is a study that would benefit any student of psychology or the magical arts.

One's opinion is frequently sought regarding the efficacy of the much lauded rituals of the Order of the Golden Dawn, the beauty and theatricality of which are often mentioned by writers outside the occult field. Rites of this kind can effect combinations of codes, although their main appeal would seem to be to the intellectually or emotionally orientated among us. One psychological observation I have made is that people drawn to the

Instinctive or Emotional Rites do not appear to be as pretentious, self-opinionated and dogmatic as their more intellectual or contemplative brethren. Those who are of a basically simple psychological make-up seldom cherish ideas of self-importance or spiritual snobbery, whereas the types that lay claim to great knowledge, especially of the more 'secret' variety, could well be compensating for some psychological deficiency. But more of that in a later chapter.

The philosophers and sages of old frequently commented on the nature, meaning and efficacy of the Rite. Hsün Tzu, along with Confucius and Mencius, was one of the outstanding figures of the Chou dynasty era. He is believed to have lived between 289 and 238 BC, although his exact dates are not known. Concerning the Rite, the learned sage had this to say:

Meaning and Value of Rituals: A Confucian Appraisal

Rites (*li*) rest on three bases: Heaven and earth, which are the source of all life; the ancestors, who are the source of the human race; sovereigns and teachers, who are the source of government. If there were no Heaven and earth, where would life come from? If there were no ancestors, where would the offspring come from? If there were no sovereigns and teachers, where would government come from? Should any of the three be missing, either there would be no men or men would be without peace. Hence rites are to serve Heaven on high and earth below, and to honour the ancestors and elevate the sovereigns and teachers. Herein lies the threefold basis of rites . . .

In general, rites begin with primitive practices, attain cultured forms, and finally achieve beauty and felicity. When rites are at their best, men's emotions and sense of beauty are both fully expressed. When they are at the next level, either the emotion or the sense of beauty oversteps the others. When they are at still the next level, emotion reverts to the state of primitivity.

It is through rites that heaven and earth are harmonious and sun and moon are bright, that the four seasons are ordered and the stars are on their courses, that rivers flow and that things prosper, that love and hatred are tempered and joy and anger are in keeping. They cause the lowly to be obedient and those on high to be illustrious. He who holds to the rites is never confused in the midst of multifarious change; he who deviates therefrom is lost. Rites — are they not the culmination of culture? . . .

Rites require us to treat both life and death with attentiveness. Life is the beginning of man, death is his end. When a man is well off both at the end and the beginning, the way of man is fulfilled. Hence the gentleman respects the beginning and is carefully attentive to the end.

To pay equal attention to the end as well as to the beginning is the way of the gentleman and the beauty of rites and righteousness . . .

Rites serve to shorten that which is too long and lengthen that which is too short, reduce that which is too much and augment that which is too little, express the beauty of love and reverence and cultivate the elegance of righteous conduct. Therefore, beautiful adornment and coarse sackcloth, music and weeping, rejoicing and sorrow, though pairs of opposites, are in the rites equally utilized and alternately brought into play. Beautiful adornment, music, and rejoicing are appropriate on occasions of felicity; coarse sackcloth, weeping, and sorrow are appropriate on occasions of ill-fortune. Rites make room for beautiful adornment but not to the point of being fascinating, for coarse sackcloth but not to the point of deprivation or self-injury, for music and rejoicing but not to the point of being lewd and indolent, for weeping and sorrow but not to the point of being depressing and injurious. Such is the middle path of rites . . .

Funeral rites are those by which the living adorn the dead. The dead are accorded a send-off as though they were living. In this way the dead are served like the living, the absent like the present. Equal attention is thus paid to the end as well as to the beginning of life . . .

Now the rites used on the occasion of birth are to embellish joy, those used on the occasion of death are to embellish sorrow, those used at sacrifice are to embellish reverence, those used on military occasions are to embellish dignity. In this respect the rites of all kings are alike, antiquity and the present age agree, and no one knows whence they came . . .

Sacrifice is to express a person's feeling of remembrance and longing, for grief and affliction cannot be kept out of one's consciousness all the time. When men are enjoying the pleasure of good company, a loyal minister or a filial son may feel grief and affliction. Once such feelings arise, he is greatly excited and moved. If such feelings are not given proper expression, then his emotions and memories are disappointed and not satisfied, and the appropriate rite is lacking. Thereupon the ancient kings instituted rites, and henceforth the principle of expressing honour to the honoured and love to the beloved is fully realized. Hence I say: Sacrifice is to express a person's feeling of remembrance and longing. As to the fullness of the sense of loyalty and affection, the richness of ritual and beauty — these none but the sage can understand. Sacrifice is something that the sage clearly understands, the scholar-gentleman contentedly performs, the official considers a duty, and the common people regard as established custom. Among gentlemen it is considered the way of man; among the common people it is considered as having to do with the spirits.[2]

The Buddhist Emperor and Philosopher Ashoka (*circa* 274–232

BC), however, offers advice as far as the Rite is concerned that would not go amiss today. In discriminating between meaning-less ceremonies and the *Ceremonies of Dharma* he says:

King Priyadarshī, the Beloved of the Gods, says: People perform various ceremonies. Among the occasions on which ceremonies are performed are sicknesses, marriages of sons or daughters, children's births and departures on journeys. Women in particular have recourse to many diverse, trivial, and meaningless ceremonies.

It is right that ceremonies be performed. But this kind bears little fruit. The ceremony of Dharma* *(Dharma-mangala)*, on the contrary, is very fruitful. It consists in proper treatment of slaves and servants, reverence to teachers, restraint of violence towards living creatures, and liberality to priests and ascetics. These and like actions are called the ceremonies of Dharma.

Therefore, a father, son, brother, master, friend, acquaintance, or even a neighbour ought to say about such actions, 'They are good; they should be performed until their purpose is achieved. I shall observe them.'

Other ceremonies are of doubtful value. They may achieve their purpose, or they may not. Moreover, the purposes for which they are performed are limited to this world.

The ceremony of Dharma, on the other hand, is not limited to time. Even if it does not achieve its object in this world, it produces unlimited merit in the next world. But if it produces its object in this world, it achieves both effects; the purpose desired in this world and unlimited merit in the next.

It has also been said that liberality is commendable. But there is no greater liberality than the gift of Dharma or the benefit of Dharma. Therefore, a friend, a well-wisher, relative or companion should urge one when the occasion arises, saying, 'You should do this; this is commendable. By doing this you may attain heaven.' And what is more worth doing than attaining heaven?[3]

Need one say more!

Endnotes:

1. Hesiod, as quoted in the Larousse *Encyclopedia of Mythology*, p. 99.
2. *From Primitives to Zen* Mircea Eliade, pp. 234–236.
3. *Ibid.* p. 561.

*Dharma: Cosmic law, and the right individual conduct of conformity to this law.

Chapter 2

YESTERDAY AND TODAY

There are a formidable number of rites to choose from and making an appropriate selection for this work has been no easy task. While anthropology and ethnology can supply a wealth of ethnic material, when it comes to the magical or occult field — with the exception of a few oral traditions and fragmentary passages that have survived in such works as the Egyptian Book of the Dead — most of the ritual in use today has been rewritten in modern parlance with, no doubt, a firm belief in the new formula's power to accommodate and retain the original meaning and efficacy. There would appear to be no guarantee, however, that a ritual in itself generates the same amount or quality of energy, or effects identical results for every user. So while we may, for example, amuse ourselves with obscure Enochian angelic nomenclatures, we are not all John Dees in the making — although, if we are to believe his recent biographers, it is questionable whether these were of all that much benefit to Dee himself.

Let us commence our analysis with a more detailed examination of a Rite, the antiquity of which is unquestionable, which would definitely seem to qualify under the Recollective category. Rites of this type, if we care to view their significance through the eyes of certain seers and scholars, are suggestive of roots external to our own solar system itself and could, therefore, pertain to its original seeding and ultimate evolutionary direction.

Before embarking on the ensuing analysis, may I make known

my awareness of, and respect for, the many schools of research and inspired mysticism which accept the existence of such prehistoric civilizations as Atlantis, Lemuria or Mu, all of which must obviously have accommodated the Rite to a greater or lesser degree. In fact many of the rites that history has handed down to us neatly stamped 'primitive' can be analysed as folk memories of earlier technological achievements which have degenerated into tribal magic and myth.

Although many orthodox historians still embrace the school of thought that designates the region of the Euphrates generally known as Sumeria as the cradle of civilization, the rapid progress of modern science in the field of anthropology and archaeology is now leaning towards the idea that central Africa was possibly the mythical Garden of Eden. Since the Neanderthal/Cro-Magnon enigma does not appear to have been resolved to the satisfaction of many concerned, we will run with current opinion and make our first touch down in the region of Mali (the former French Sudan), which is home to the African tribe of the Dogon.

The whole religious system and native rites of the Dogon are based on traditions which have been handed down from generation to generation concerning the nature and energy of Sirius, a binary star in the constellation of Canis Major. The profundity of their creed may be evidenced in their rites, but in order to understand something of the nature of these we must first examine the mythological foundation upon which they are based.

The star Sirius has obviously held considerable significance for mankind since the earliest of times. The ancient Egyptians featured it in both their religion and calendar, the Dog Days being reckoned from its heliacal rising. They called it Sothis and linked it with their Goddess Isis and the Zodiacal sign of Virgo.

The Egyptians and Dogons were not, however, the only races to accord special powers to this stellar beacon. The Bambara called it 'the star of foundation' *sigo dolo*, which is the same term used by the Dogon, while like the Dogon they also referred to the companion star (known as Sirius B or Digitaria) as *fini dolo*. Jointly the two stars were called *fā dolo fla*, (the two stars of knowledge) because 'it represents in the sky the invisible body of Faro' conceived of as a pair of twins — the implication being that the star is the seat of all learning. Another African tribe, the Bozo, were also familiar with the system. They called Sirius *sima*

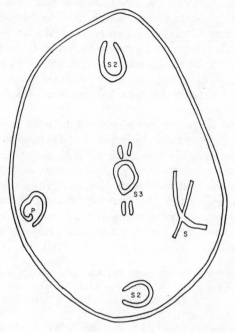

KEY : S = SIRIUS
       S2 = POSITIONS OF SIRIUS B
       S3 = ANOTHER STAR
       P = A PLANET

kayne (literally: Sitting Trouser), and its satellite *toñõ nalema* (Eye Star).[1]

Among other knowledge comparable with modern astrology and astronomy, the Dogon were aware of the four major moons of Jupiter, which they named *dana tolo unum* (children of *dana tolo* — Jupiter), and the rings of Saturn, which are only visible through a telescope. Saturn, which they associated strongly with the Milky Way, they called 'the star of limiting the place'. These are but snippets of their vast astronomical knowledge, further details of which are to be found in Robert K. G. Temple's fascinating and thought-provoking book *The Sirius Mystery*.

The Dogon also possessed a clear knowledge of the human circulatory system and accepted the existence of life in other parts of the universe. According to their tradition there were many populated 'stars', and the intelligent life-forms living thereon

were not always hominids. They say that mankind (as we know
it) lives on the Fourth Earth, but on the Third Earth there were
'men with horns', *inneu gammurugu* (satyrs?); on the Fifth Earth
'men with tails', *inneu dullogu*; and on the Sixth Earth 'men with
wings', *inneu bummo*. All this information, they claim, was
given to them by beings of superior intelligence (gods), who
arrived on Earth from the Sirius System way back in the mists of
time![2]

All Dogon Rites are connected either with Sirius, its twin
Digitaria, a third star which they believed existed in that system,
or with one or possibly two planets. The associated rituals are
complex but meaningful, and suggest a re-enacting of psycho/
cosmic drama which took place (or is currently taking place) in
our own solar system and that of Sirius. All the traditional
archetypal *dramatis personae* are present: the God (Nommo)
who will be sacrificed for the purification and reorganization of
the universe:

> . . . He will rise in human form and descend on Earth, in an ark, with
> the ancestors of men . . . then he will take on his original form, will
> rule from the waters and will give birth to many descendants . . . The
> Nommo divided his body among men to feed them; that is why it is
> said that as the universe 'had drunk of his body'; . . . He was crucified
> on a *kilena* tree which [*sic*] also died and was resurrected.[3]

Then we have Ogo, the chaotic disrupter: as he was about to be
finished (being created) he rebelled against his creator and introduced disorder into the universe. Eventually he will become 'The
Pale Fox' (le renard pâle), which is the image of his fall. The planet
in the Sirius system from which the Nommo (collectively) issued
was said to be 'pure' as against our own solar system which is,
according to Dogon teachings, decidedly 'impure', being referred
to as the placenta of the evil Ogo. Our own planet Earth is,
significantly ' . . . the place where Ogo's umbilical cord was
attached to his placenta . . . '.[4]

The best-known Dogon ritual is that of the *Bado*, which
honours the one-year axial rotation of the star Digitaria. This is a
long and complicated Rite involving several diagrams, and to
fully comprehend it would require a more than rudimentary
knowledge of the Dogon concept of the Sirius System. The
substance of the Rite is, however, summarized in the following
Dogon statement, which re-echoes the eternal search of the soul
for its twin on the one hand, and man's continual quest for

individuation (the uniting of the anima and animus) in pursuit of true knowledge and perfection, on the other. The deeply obvious alchemical inferences here speak of the wisdom of the originators of the Rite and the profundity of its accompanying metaphysical philosophy, while its similarity to certain teachings in the Gnostic *Pistis Sophia* does not go unnoticed:

> Digitaria, as the egg of the world, . . . was split into two twin placentas which were to give birth respectively to a pair of Nommo Instructors. What happened, however, was that a single male being emerged from one of the placentas; in order to find his twin, this being tore [sic] off a piece of this placenta, which became earth. This intervention upset the order of creation: he was transformed into an animal, the pale fox, *yuruga*, and communicated his own impurity to the earth, which rendered it dry and barren. But the remedy to this situation was the sacrifice, to the sky, of one of the Nommo Instructors which had issued from the other placenta, and the descent of his twin to earth with life-giving, purifying rain. The destiny of Yourougou is to pursue his twin to the end of time — the twin being his female soul at the same time. On the mythical level, Digitaria is thus considered to be the Yourougou held in space by Nommo, relentlessly revolving around Sirius, or Yasigui in other words, and never capable of reaching it.[5]

The Dogon were fully aware that Sirius B (Digitaria) took fifty years to orbit the larger Sirius A, and as a consequence the number fifty became sacred to them. The significant emphasis of this number also makes its appearance in many other, seemingly unrelated beliefs and magical systems that followed through the pages of history. Seven times seven being forty–nine, the fiftieth day was believed to have great magical and spiritual significance, and rituals associated with the 7:49:50 numerology may be noted in both occult practices and orthodox religious observances to this day. For the benefit of those who might care to pursue this study, a simple map of the Sirius System according to the Dogon tradition is included.[6]

The Dogon were by no means the only race who built their rites around 'extra-terrestrial' phenomena. The Chaldeans, who are often described as the fathers of astrology, also laid claim to being taught by beings who, if we are to believe the myths, were decidedly not of hominid form. In Berossus' account of the Chaldean Creation myth we read of primitive man:

> At first they led a somewhat wretched existence and lived without rule

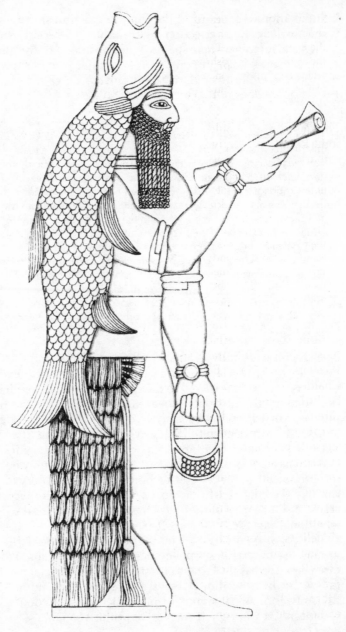

The Chaldean God Oannes

after the manner of beasts. But, in the first year, appeared a monster endowed with human reason, named Oannes, who rose from out of the Erythraean sea, at the point where it borders Babylonia. He had the whole body of a fish, but above his fish's head he had another head which was that of a man, and human feet emerged from beneath his fish's tail; he had a human voice, and his image is preserved to this day.[7]

The description would seem to fit a being who was garbed in some kind of protective suit and mask. As I have no intention of embarking on a discussion concerning the origins of civilization at this point, I will leave my readers to decide for themselves from which direction (east, west or above!) our Babylonian visitor hailed. What we do know about him, however, is that:

He passed the day in the midst of men without taking food; he taught them the use of letters, sciences and arts of all kind, and rules for the founding of cities, and the construction of temples, the principles of law and surveying; he showed them how to sow and reap; he gave them all that contributes to the comforts of life. Since that time nothing excellent has been invented.[8]

We must therefore assume that all Chaldean Rites may be attributed to his influence and this would include, of course, those astrological data that are the basis of much magic both in Western and Near Eastern traditions to this day. That the Chaldeans possessed a great knowledge of the heavens there can be little doubt. Later centuries of studied observations and carefully kept records obviously added to this pool, but as far as its origins are concerned — as in the case of the Dogon — we are left with anthropological and psychological enigmas; that is, of course, if we limit our study of intelligent life to the hominid species and this planet in particular. Surely, the student of psychology who is hidebound by the dogmas formulated by earlier researchers and practitioners is just as blinkered as the fanatical religious fundamentalist; so while we all need the guidelines with which the great minds of the past have supplied us, the human spirit must ever press forward in its quest for knowledge — for such is the path of evolution.

Some of the oldest known rites are those associated with the 'Horned God', much beloved of pagans to this day. One of the earliest representations of this deity is to be found in the *Caverne des Trois Frères* in Ariége. It shows a man clothed in the 'skin of a stag with antlers on his head' and has been dated to the Palaeolithic (Old Stone Age) period. Here we have some of the first evidence of ritual role-playing — the celebrant, shaman or participant assuming the shape or appearance of the animal or god in order to partake of its prowess, strength or divine guidance. This was sometimes effected more for the benefit of the observer than that of the actor, however, a typical example being the wearing of the Anubis head masks by the Egyptian Priests who administered anaesthetics or effected the rites which prepared the body of the deceased for mummification. (For the nature and role of Anubis, see *Practical Egyptian Magic* and *The Way of Cartouche*.)

Many of the peoples of earlier races and times possessed a more accurate concept of mankind's true role on earth than we have today in that they had an instinctive understanding of the ecological nature of things and the part they needed to play in order to maintain that delicate balance. The 'exchange of energies' concept has existed in both magic and religion since the dawn of time. People gave of what they had to the gods, nature entities, ancestral spirits and celestial deities in exchange for their bounty, the nature of which, although not fully understood by all, was considered a necessary prerequisite for the functioning of a balanced social and religious life. Failure to comply with this natural state of equipoise was guaranteed to bring down the wrath of the deities concerned.

Translated into a modern setting this could be seen to relate to the chaos which has resulted through mankind's misuse of nature's many bounties: 'deforestation', dust bowls, the problem of nuclear waste, exploitation of natural resources and so on. As though the eco-related aspect of the human psyche is being awakened from its sleep or being re-educated following a period of regression, instinctive rites are slowly surfacing from the collective unconscious in the form of a resurgence of old beliefs and religions which accommodate the Exchange of Energy Principle, that is, that one must always give in order to receive.

At the purely personal level this is abundantly clear, a fact that many psychiatrists will, I am sure, be happy to endorse. Those who are essentially 'takers', who give nothing in return either spiritually, emotionally or practically, are more inclined to neuroses and psychoses than people who are more generously inclined. The eventual disenchantment with each new acquisition, be it personal or inanimate, is inevitably followed by boredom as the psyche convolutes inwards in ever-decreasing spirals until the back-up of accumulated energies manifests as antisocial behaviour, psychosomatic illness or mental imbalance. Thus, many of the ancient Pantheistic and Animistic Rites, both collective and personal, which involve the act of giving out before one takes in, could alleviate some of the suffering and tension of modern-day living and engender a respect for and a need to communicate with the eco-environment by rendering a clearer comprehension of the life force in all things.

One very old rite which is still observed today is the Padstow 'Obby Oss' Festival in Cornwall, a public Seasonal Rite of Spring which was probably inherited from our Celtic ancestors, although there is also evidence that rites of this nature existed in these Isles prior to the Celtic invasion. The psychology behind this Seasonal Rite carries far deeper connotations than the simple fertility emphasis, however, as it also serves to programme the subconscious and its somatic resonances to adapt to the ensuing weather conditions or elemental qualities that will dominate the oncoming cycle. Its preparatory nature is, therefore, highly beneficial if viewed in this particular light.

As far as the Padstow Rite is concerned, it may be argued that the text of the May Song has doubtless undergone so many changes over the centuries as to render it unrecognizable to its originators. In spite of this it would still appear to carry that underlying psychic charge, the nature of which relates directly to the collective unconscious. I was able to observe at first hand the effect of the constant drum beat and repetitive chanting on both those who threw themselves heart and soul into the Rite and the curious bystanders who attended purely for the entertainment value. Evidence of the surfacing of some archaic Group Soul was abundantly clear to the experienced observer, the energies emitted reaching far deeper into the unconscious than the generally assumed fertility connotations. In fact, my dialogues with several of the local people highlighted this only too clearly, one Padstonian remarking to me that she felt as though something touched her very soul, although she could not find the right words to express the true nature of the experience.

Primordial contacts of this nature are not so rare as we might imagine, and as far as the people of Padstow are concerned, the experience appears to benefit them considerably, bringing enjoyment and relaxation and cementing their link with the Group Soul. For the benefit of those who might care to make a more comprehensive study of this ancient festival, full details of the

Rite and its accompanying pageantry are given in a booklet entitled *Padstow's 'Obby 'Oss and May Day Festivities*, by Donald Rawe.

Endnotes:

1. *The Sirius Mystery* Robert K G Temple, p. 48.
2. *Ibid*. pp. 20–30.
3. *Ibid*. p. 216.
4. *Ibid*. p. 32.
5. *Ibid*. p. 48.
6. *Ibid*. p. 20.
7. *The Dawn of Civilization* Professor Gaston Maspero, p. 546.
8. *Ibid*. p. 546.

Chapter 3

ENTER THE INTERMEDIARY

There have long been those individuals gifted with a profound metaphysical awareness. This innate sensitivity may cause them to undergo inner experiences of a transpersonal nature, or enable them to effect a union with those subtle energies which appear to influence our lives, a subjective reality denied to the rest of us. The less gifted among us may, however, be just as eager to contact our higher selves or have the will of the gods made known to us, so we naturally turn to whoever can provide the required service or teach us the know-how.

It has been said in the past that ritual exploits man's collective need for dialogue with his Creator, which is true to an extent. However, while it may be argued that many rites are simple paradigms for the emulation of cosmic principles, these rituals are, after all, mankind's own creation. In all creativity there is the inevitable gap to be bridged between the inspired concept and its practical realization, and it is into this gap that the shaman, priest or intermediary has conveniently stepped.

The late G R S Mead tells us that it was the custom among the Gnostics to divide mankind into three classes:

(a) the lowest, or *hylics*, were those who were so entirely dead to spiritual things that they were as the *hyle* or unperceptive matter of the world; (b) the intermediate class were called *psychics*, for though believers in things spiritual, they were believers simply, and required miracles and signs to strengthen their faith; (c) whereas the *pneu-*

matics or spiritual, the highest class, were those capable of knowledge of spiritual matters, those who could receive the Gnosis. [He continues:] It is somewhat the custom in our days in extreme circles to claim that all men are 'equal'. The modern theologian wisely qualifies this claim by the adverb 'morally'. Thus stated the idea is by no means a peculiarly Christian view — for the doctrine is common to all great religions, seeing that it simply asserts the great principle of justice as one of the manifestations of the Deity. The Gnostic view, however, is far clearer and more in accord with the facts of evolution; it admits the 'morally equal', but it further asserts difference of degree, not only in body and soul, but also in spirit, in order to make the morality proportional, and so to carry out the inner meaning of the parable of the talents.[1]

As it would appear that most of us fall into the two aforementioned categories, it is little wonder that the intermediary made a very early appearance in the history of Homo sapiens. The first priests or shamans may well have been absolutely genuine (as indeed many still are today), but as time advanced and it became all too obvious to the less scrupulous that there was a lot of temporal power in this quarter available for the taking, the baser instincts soon surfaced and the darker face of sacerdotalism was born.

Shamanism pre-dates the earliest recorded civilizations by thousands of years and it is just as prevalent in the modern world, albeit under titles that are more acceptable to the prevailing tenets of religion or humanism than 'witch doctor' or 'medicine man'. In his recent BBC series *Exploring Human Consciousness*, Dr Nicholas Humphrey referred to shamanism as having become 'democratized'. He recalled how in the past, society would train the shaman through a series of complicated initiatory rites so that he or she might undergo ordeals not normally available to the masses, whereas nowadays everyone is exposed to a wider gamut of experience through the media, the arts and by psychological experimentation. The artist, novelist and popular personality have become today's shamans; non-parochial, international, 'inter-time', 'inter-cosmic'. Dr Humphrey's appropriate cliché was: 'The artist is the midwife to the birth pangs of human experience.'

While there is certainly a strong degree of truth behind these observations, it is really only half of the picture, Mead's three classes being as much in evidence today as they were in the time of the early Gnostics. So we need to take a deeper look at the ritualistic role played by the intermediary and its effect on the individual psychology.

In spite of cultural diversities, shamanic knowledge and procedures are reasonably consistent across our planet, the overlays of the ethos which mark the ethnic stamp being fairly obvious. Although the origins of the shamanic mode were closely allied to the hunt, the shaman was metaphysically aware of the life force in all creation. While the killing of animals for food and clothing, or the cutting of trees for fuel and shelter was an acknowledged necessity, it was also of cardinal importance that the spirits of these lifeforms should be placated, in case they took their revenge by removing those physical bodies upon which humans relied for survival. The shaman was adept at communicating with the unseen, and his aid was sought to ensure the maintenance of that essential balance. Those employing his services being naturally anxious to have some visible evidence of what they were getting for their method of exchange, a series of rites, mini-dramas or dances, with accompanying paraphernalia appropriate to the request, were enacted to the satisfaction of all concerned.

Shamanic dances were always associated with the state of ecstasy which, states Eliade, is a 'timeless primary phenomenon'. He continues, 'psychological experiences of rapture are fundamental to the human condition, and hence known to the whole of archaic humanity.'[2] In spite of parochial interpretations which tend to glorify the tribe or those for whom the specific rite has been performed, there is doubtless a uniformity in the visionary content of shamanic ecstatic enlightenment.

A deep comprehension of the psychology of all life is to be found in the esoterica of many earlier races. A drawing from a fresco in the Palaeolithic cave of Lascaux (France), for example, depicts an entranced shaman and the sacrifice of a bull bison (wisent). The spirit of both bison and shaman are liberated, one through trance and the other through death. Thus a communication between both entities is effected at a transcendental level, and their earthly functions and territories are established and agreed.[3]

Although the more sensitive and enlightened among us may decry the necessity for the sacrifice in the first place, it would appear that each time zone, or evolutionary epoch, is subject to the rules effected by the stage of advancement of the majority. And who are we to pass judgement? The shamans of old (unlike some 'enlightened' clerics of today who regularly participate in their own special brand of sacrificial rite) were at least aware of the existence of the souls of animals and tried to make their peace with them through their rites. It is a great pity that much of the wisdom of the past has become obscured by the dark mists of prejudice and bigotry. When it comes to a deeper comprehension of the complexities of the human condition, we are often unable to see the wood for the proverbial trees! If we are to make contact with the deeper, underlying aspects of our own psychology, and in so doing realize our true *raison d'être*, we must surely lower the barriers between past and future, and view the human experience and its eco-relationships in *gestalt*.

Modern occultism tends to see the role of the Ritual Celebrant or Hierophant as different from that of the mystic, psychic or scryer; the distinction lying in the positive/directive/extroverted expression as against the receptive/submissive/introverted mode. Apologies for these classifications are borrowed from past traditions: 'Zadok the Priest, and Nathan the Prophet, anointed Solomon King', the inference being that the two roles were not interchangeable. Shamanism disregards these distinctions totally, traditional shamans being the embodiment of both principles, and nothing if not good channellers. Had they been unable to make contact with the spirits of animals, ancestors, gods or natural phenomena, and convey comprehensible messages from these to the members of the tribe, their purpose would have been defeated.

It is surely to the shaman that all ritual owes the concept of role-playing, or the temporary assumption of the nature of the divinity whose good offices are being sought through the energies of the rite. Role-playing in ritual is, of course, an integral part of sympathetic magic, although many may not see it this way. Psychologically, it evokes the particular aspect of the representative god-essence within the self. In other words, by undertaking, for example, the role of Nephthys in an Egyptian Rite, the player is searching for correspondences hidden deeply within his or her own subconscious, and submitting the appropriate archetypal figure for conscious scrutiny by both the self and the group.

Sometimes this soul search proves highly rewarding, as in the case of a gentleman whom I talked to recently, who had participated in an Egyptian group working in which he had been allotted the role of Thoth. Unfortunately for him, on that particular evening he had come down with a severe toothache resulting from an oncoming abcess. He decided to try to forget his discomfort and participate fully in the spirit and devotion of the Rite, and in spite of his physical discomfort all went well. The following day he found to his amazement that the toothache had disappeared and the anticipated abcess miraculously had dispersed. The penny did not drop until a week or so later, when he related the incident to me and I reminded him that in addition to being scribe to the gods, Thoth was also god of medicine. He had, in his sincerity, invoked the Thoth (healing) essence within his own unconscious and healed himself or, as others might believe, been healed by the god by allowing entry to his energies.

There is more to be said about shamans alone than this book could accommodate. These gifted mystics — who are frequently fine healers and counsellors, and whose knowledge of the human condition and its accompanying psychology is of a high order — represent but one class of intermediary, however. Better known in the Western world are the priest, the priestess, and the psychic, the latter being the popular term for prophet.

History is littered with tales of dominant priesthoods which have altered the course or destiny of nations through their political machinations. The Roman historians, and Caesar in particular, frequently commented on the destructive nature of Celtic sacerdotalism. The question inevitably arose as to why a people so able to create a civilized society and defend itself in war should have fallen to its less cultured adversaries who later rent its peoples apart.

It was noted that most civilizations that have conquered, risen and stayed in a position of power for any period, have relied to a great extent on loyalty to the state or patriotism, doubtless engendered by the concept of racial supremacy. While the Celts did not dismiss this idea, there was a force in their society that dominated the civic-cum-political inspiration that was the unifying power behind most of the classical nations; this was their sacerdotalism. The Druids were the sovereign power in Celtica, a fact confirmed from both Roman and Irish sources. All affairs of state were subject to their office and they ruled with a rod of iron. Their priests drew their authority from supernatural sanctions which, in the eyes of the more materially inclined Romans, constituted Celtica's undoing.

Whether, in fact, temporal rulership does constitute a disaster area in the power of national politics must surely be re-evaluated in the light of modern events. The Romans certainly thought this way, but today we appear to be faced with a situation where the balance of world power is, to an extent, in the hands of religious and idealistic fanatics, and one wonders what Caesar would make of that!

There have been other equally powerful ecclesiastics who have left their mark across the globe. Ignatius Loyola's Jesuits are a good example of a far-seeing sect whose disciplinary codes (Exercises) are re-echoed in several highly questionable modern mind-programming systems. Discipline, when self-imposed is nothing if not valuable, but conditioning techniques which do not allow for the freedom of the human spirit are definite 'no-nos'. In his recent novel, *Contact*, astronomer Carl Sagan wrote of the priesthood: 'The first priest was the first rogue who met the first fool.' A somewhat sweeping statement, I feel, but nevertheless one which contains a grain of truth.

A similar standard also applies to ritual generally, especially in cases where the experience appears to take priority over the result. Dehumanization is likely to result when the Rite becomes an end in itself, and those rituals which are performed only for their poetic beauty are simply titillating the egos of the participants, while defeating the Rite's traditional objectives. Of course, a balance is called for between dangerously absurd hedonism and extreme standards of discipline in any Rite, social or otherwise.

Those participating in Rites of Banishment, Cleansing or High Magic, for example, must be careful not to break the circle or protective cover, for in so doing they are likely to endanger not only themselves but others present. I had some experience of this myself some years ago when I officiated at a private Lodge. Certain ladies present were more concerned about the doings of their prodigies than the work on hand, to the extent that the opening and closing of the Rite was being dictated by these external demands. This lack of discipline was causing considerable concern to the more dedicated members, myself included, and in the end I was obliged to withdraw as the true significance of the Rite was slowly giving way to maternal priorities. Fortuately, I have now left those days behind me, although they have probably placed me in a better position from which to adopt the role of observer, for had I not tried out these various systems about which I am now writing, I would have been as guilty as those armchair psychologists who would surely qualify for Newton's remark to Halley: 'Sir, I have studied it, you have not.'

One thing to be said in favour of the Rite is that when it is correctly orientated and well performed it can aid the expansion of human consciousness at both the personal and the collective levels.

Psychoanalysts, for example, are coming to realize that a degree of preparation for the contingencies of adult life is decidedly advantageous. The repeated use of certain rituals, both religious and secular, encourages psychological integration, mental stability and social responsibility, while exercising a binding factor which has proven helpful to many people who are in an early stage of spiritual development. There would appear to be more mental stability among those who are committed to a given faith or ideal, and as long as the principle does not develop into hysterical fanaticism, the benefits are much in evidence.

Endnotes:

1. *Fragments of a Faith Forgotten* G R S Mead, pp. 139–140.
2. *Shaman* by Joan Halifax, p. 6.
3. *Ibid.* p. 11.

Chapter 4

MAGICAL AND SECULAR RITES IN HISTORY

The Rite in its many forms has been in existence since man first organized himself into distinct groups and cultures. The Elders of the tribe, or those who exerted authority over the populace at large, were quick to realize both the coalescing effect of the public rite and its possibilities as a tool of central control. The early priesthoods, and those ecclesiastics that followed in their footsteps down the pages of history, were only too well aware of the power to be gained by subjecting the people to the kind of mass rites which either gave access to the racial collective unconscious, rendered the mind vulnerable to auto-suggestion, or simply encouraged the release of corporeal emotions.

That the leaders and scholars of old were aware of the psychology behind these planned occasions is well attested to in Porphyry's letters to Anebo. These dialogues were faithfully recorded by Iamblichos in a work entitled *Theurgia*, or *The Egyptian Mysteries*, in which the inner meanings of certain Egyptian rites are fully explained to the logically minded Greek sage. The text is at times obscure, but in essence the reason given for the encouragement of controlled public orgiastic rites is, simply the release factor, which allows the rougher elements to rid themselves temporarily of pent-up aggressions or sexual inhibitions (subconscious or otherwise). This book is a gold-mine of information on the order and nature of the Egyptian rites of the period, Iamblichos himself is said to have lived between AD 255 and 330. Of Anebo we know little, although he is referred to as a Priest of Anubis, while Porphyry (*circa* AD 232–304) was a native of Tyre.

Particularly relevant to the subject matter of this book is, I feel, the reference to two kinds of sacred rites, the text of which runs as follows:

Let us next consider what is in harmony with the sentiments which have been uttered, and without twofold constitution. For when we become entirely soul and are outside of the body, and soaring on high with all the gods of the non-material realm, we occupy ourselves with sublime visions. Then again, we are bound in the oyster-like body and held fast under the dominion of matter, and are corporeal in feeling and aspiration. There comes, accordingly, therefore, a twofold form of worship. For the one which is for unstained souls will be simple, free of the body and pure from every condition of generated existence; but the other, which is accommodated to souls that are not pure and liberated from the conditions of generated existence, is filled with corporeal things and everything that relates to the world of matter.*

I admit therefore that there are two forms of Sacred Rites. The one, those for individuals who are entirely purified. Such rarely happen, as Herakleitos affirms, beyond a single person at one time or a few that may be easily counted. The other class, such as are yet held by the body, consists of those who are of the realm of matter and of corporeal quality, sustaining themselves through change.

Hence, unless such a form of worship shall be instituted for cities and peoples that are not relieved from the hereditary allotment, and that hold tenaciously to the communion with the body, they will fail utterly of both kinds of good, that which is superior to the realm of matter, and that which is of the world of matter. For the former they are unable to receive, and to the latter they bring nothing of kindred nature. At the same time everyone performs his service according to what he is, and certainly not with reference to what he is not. For it is not proper for it to exceed the worshipper's own condition. I have the same thing to say also in respect of the intimate union which joins together the men who are worshipping and the powers that are worshipped as members of a family. For I desire the same unity, that the usage of religious worship which is homogeneous with it shall be chosen, namely: not only that which is non-material being com-

*This twofold phase of religious customs — the religion of the right hand and that of the left — still exists with the worshippers of Siva and the Sakti in India. It was exhibited in the Orphic and Dionysiac worships of Greece, and in several Oriental Rites. So the ascetic and the freer religionist alike were treated according to their respective dispositions.

mingled in the manner accordant with itself, and joining the incorporeal natures in a pure manner with themselves, with pure incorporeal
powers, but also uniting the corporeal natures after a corporeal
manner with corporeal essences, commingling with the bodies the
superior essence that pervade them.

[*Why worship is of a sensuous character*]

We shall not, therefore, think it unworthy of us to treat also of matters
of such a lower character. Thus in respect of the needs of the body, we
also perform some office to the guardians of the corporeal nature, the
gods and good demons; such as purifying it from old stains, or freeing
it of diseases, and making it abound with health, or taking away from
it heaviness and torpor, and imparting to it lightness and activity
instead — or if nothing else, procuring for it all manner of benefits.
We do not, therefore, in any way treat it as though it was of mental
quality or even as though it was not corporeal. For the body is not
constituted to participate in such modes of proceeding. But when it
participates in modes of a nature corresponding to itself, a body is
healed and purified by bodies. From necessity of such a kind,
therefore, the institution of Sacred Rites will be of a corporeal ideal;
on the one hand pruning away what is superfluous in us and on the
other supplying whatever in us is wanting, and also bringing into
order and proportion in so far as it is disordered. We often make use of
sacred ceremonies, beseeching from the superior races that they do for
us many things of importance to the human life. These, doubtless, are
for the beings that take care of the body, or have charge of those
things which we procure for the sake of our bodies.*

The 'superior races' preferred to relate to spirits of a higher order
and not to people, while the term 'demon', which was in general
usage in those times to denote another order of tutelary essences,
did not carry its Christian connotations.

It is interesting to observe how familiar the sages of that period
were with the psychological and physical needs of their charges.
Every man and woman was allowed to draw from the Rite
according to his or her own nature and stage of transpersonal
comprehension, from the most highly spiritual state in which
direct communion was sought with the gods, to the purely
physical, as manifest in the orgiastic activities of the Korybantes,
or the practices peculiar to Sabazian worship which served as a
preparation for the Bacchic Rites. Things do not change, only our

---

*In the Egyptian system, the human body was apportioned into thirty-two regions,
each of which had its own overlord or presiding divinity in charge of it, and its own
class of physicians at the different temples.[1]

outward pretences mask our true thoughts when we partake of the public ritual experience.

At least these aforementioned rites did not encourage the double standards of morality that exist in some of the more rigid religious societies of today although, as Professor of Psychiatry Hans Eysenck believes, we need to strike a happy medium between permissiveness and repression, a fact which was perhaps better understood and observed in some of the older cultures.

Probably the most famous and best-recorded rites in history were those of the Eleusinia, which constituted the public and private State Rites of classical Greece. So closely were its inner secrets guarded, that Athenian law punished by death anyone who tried to probe them, whether out of sheer curiosity, rebelliousness or egotism. (For those interested in the finer magical and esoteric detail I can recommend the following books: *Eleusis and the Eleusinian Mysteries* by George E Mylonas, and *The Mysteries of Eleusis* by Goblet d'Alviella.)

In order to evaluate the psychological nature of the rites however, a cursory examination of their content is essential, so I shall make use of my own commentary from a previous work:

When the mysteries were at their height, three grades were involved: the Small Mysteries, the Great Mysteries, and Epoptism. Every respectable citizen of Athens endeavoured to become initiated at the higher or more secret levels, but there was also a public side in which glorious pageantry and outward display served to keep the man in the street happy. The Priestly or Inner ceremonies were administered by two families: the Eumolpides and the Kerykes, whose offices extended throughout the whole period of early paganism until the eventual triumph of Christianity.

Obviously, one had to pass through the Lesser Mysteries before the doors to the inner *sanctum sanctorum* were opened. These were celebrated towards the end of winter, in the month of *anthesterion*, just after the flower festivals or Anthesteria which were sacred to Demeter and Dionysus. The Great Mysteries were celebrated in September in the month of *boedromion*, between the time of harvesting the grain and sowing the new seeds. However, there was often a repeat of the Lesser Mysteries held at the end of summer to spare the beginners — many of whom had travelled from afar to witness the rites and become initiated into them — a second and perhaps costly journey.

The Small or Lesser Mysteries were also known as the Mysteries of Agra as they were celebrated in Agra, a suburb of Athens, and not Eleusis. Anyone could attend these, it appears, even foreigners.

Among the scant fragments of archaeological information available is a painted vase which shows the divinites involved in the ceremony. Demeter is seated in the centre with the traditional calathus head-dress; Aphrodite is at her right hand and Eros at her feet. On the left is Persephone, torch in hand, and the young Iaccus holding the cornuco-pia. Also present were Dionysus, complete with magical thyrsus, and Hercules armed with a club. The officiating priest and those under-taking the initiatory rites were also in evidence.

The Great Mysteries commenced on the thirteenth day of *boedro-mion* when the young men left for Eleusis to fetch certain sacred objects which were then placed in the care of the high priest. On the fifteenth day of the month there was a general gathering of the neophytes of both sexes, which did not always end in an orderly or spiritual manner — the servants of the Bacchanalia making sure of that. The sixteenth day saw the mystics setting out for the sea-shore, each bringing a sacrificial piglet to offer to Demeter, with men and piglets together entering the waves for purification.

The seventeeth day involved floral tributes to Dionysus and a wake in honour of Asclepios who, like Persephone and Dionysus, had also spent a period in the Underworld. Day eighteen saw everyone assembling to carry the statues of the goddesses to the temple of Asclepios for the Epidaurean celebrations.

On the nineteenth day the procession assembled in front of the Eleusinion (at one period it was the Pompeion). A statue of the young god Iaccus, crowned with myrtle and holding a torch, was borne ahead. Iaccus would appear to be no more than the personification of some local tutelary spirit, who was granted the right to serve Demeter and later became fused with Dionysus the child. Various fetishes were also carried, each object holding a deeply mystical or magical signifi-cance. The remaining first fruits of the harvest, supplied by the general populace, were placed in pots and carried on the heads of the Kernophores, or white-robed priestesses. Four white horses carried the call calathus basket containing the sheaves of corn.

The long procession covered some twenty kilometers leaving Athens via the Dipylon gate. All along the way there were chapels, shrines and short stays for rest and worship. And, of course, the usual gathering of fortune-tellers, artists, purveyors of magical parapherna-lia, and the inevitable ladies of easy virtue . . .

Needless to say, the final stages ended in a giant orgy with everyone over-imbibing, so it is little wonder that the satyrs and their friends also appeared in this light. When the necessity for public celebrations of an orgiastic nature come[s] up for discussion, we are reminded of the dialogues between Anebo, priest of Anubis, and Porphyry. That these revelries relieved public tension was one explanation, the inference being that the ordinary people were presented with an opportunity to work something out of their system, after which the streets were safer for gentler folk to walk during the ensuing weeks (see page 33).

On the twentieth day the neophytes engaged in solemn sacrifice to the gods. From then until day twenty-three there would appear to be a degree of conjecture as to what actually took place, but it is generally agreed that at some point the story of Demeter must have been enacted, accompanied by some form of ecstatic meditation which was guaranteed to put the neophytes in touch with those who dwelt either in Hades or the Elysian Fields.

Epoptism was considered the highest and most secret initiation to be undergone. Plutarch assures us that one could not hope to penetrate such Mysteries until late in life, but there were no doubt exceptions.

There is much disagreement among historians and scholars regarding the days of these final ceremonies and what actually took place. But, from a study of the aforegoing, it might seem logical to assume that the twenty-fourth and twenty-fifth were days of importance. All we do know is that those initiates who passed their tests received a medal inscribed with the head of Demeter, an ear of corn, a poppy and the word 'ἐποψ, several of which have been discovered in the Eleusis area.

As with most systems of ceremonial magic, drama also featured strongly in the initiatory rites, with the stories of Demeter, Persephone and those other divinities who had at some time paid a visit to the regions of Hades playing a prominent part. In the *Thesmophoria*, which was celebrated in Attica in the month of October, the absence and return of Persephone was dramatically commemorated, although it is generally agreed that the public Eleusinian rites were by no means confined to the enactment of this legend.

Although ancient Greek magic featured a degree of role-playing ritual, which it no doubt inherited from earlier times, after the onset of the cult of the Hero a gradual transformation took place with logic assuming the reins that had previously been held by intuitive promptings and the need for overt devotional expression. In other words, that very Aquarian thing — individual responsibility — experienced its birth throes in the heroic deeds of the classics.

In his book *Fragments of a Faith Forgotten* the Theosophical scholar G R S Mead insists that the open state Eleusinia, with its processions and public participation, was tainted at the inner levels by the disorderly elements of the undisciplined oriental cults that had fused with it over the years, while its outer show was purely political. The real Mysteries, we are informed, belonged to the Orphic tradition.[2]

The Eleusinia, however, were not the only popular Rites of those times. There were Dionysian, Sabazian and Orpheun ceremonies, to name but three more, each differing in purpose and profundity. The populace were therefore able to choose which avenue of public or private expression they might care to espouse in order to fulfil their physical, emotional or spiritual needs and/or aspirations.

There is little doubt that these rites exerted a considerable influence upon both the governing bodies of the time and the people who looked to them for leadership and guidance. One could presuppose, of course, that as most of those of exalted status were able, by virtue of their rank, to gain entry into the deeper mysteries and therefore partake of the higher aspects of the Rites, wise and just leadership would be the natural outcome. As history ceaselessly reminds us, however, this is not necessarily the case. Temporal rank and authority would not appear to be synonymous with either wisdom or spirituality, the id* being ever ready to surface when the stresses of power or mass adulation nudge the human consciousness out of balance.

Perhaps, however, the ancient rites did contribute something to the mental equilibrium of the heroes of the day. According to the classics it was the custom to prepare for approaching periods of trial or stress by participating in rites of cleansing, mortification and submission to the divine will. In modern psychological parlance, it could be described as self-discipline or self-programming (if one considers the 'gods' in terms of aspects of the psyche which need to be contacted and tamed by the will).

Religious and magical credenda and their accompanying rites have ever been adapted to suit state policies or political expediencies, the original source being either denigrated or unacknowledged. The Romans borrowed from the Greeks, the Celts from the Neolithic peoples and the Christians from the pagans, while religious bets were equally hedged! The Emperor Constantine, who is credited with installing Christianity as the state religion of Rome, instructed the makers of his tomb to place among its stones offerings and prayers to the old gods, just in case he had made a mistake!

Christianity itself has done much to influence, and been much influenced by, world power politics. The Justinian–Irenaeus controversy, for example, set the pattern of ethical thinking which ultimately divorced man from the concept of individual responsibility and deprived him by dogma of knowledge of his

*See Glossary

place in the cosmic framework of the creative whole. The doctrine of reincarnation was readily accepted by Christianity until its expurgation by the Second Council of Constantinople in AD 553, when it was declared heretical. This assembly was, in reality, only the last phase of a violent ten-year conflict inaugurated by the edict of the Roman Emperor Justinian in AD 543 against the teachings of the Church Father Origen. Justinian had assumed the leadership of the Church to the extent that imperial edicts regulated public worship, directed ecclesiastical discipline and even dictated theological doctrines. The Church was obliged to submit to a period of Caesaro-papism.

One teaching that did worry Justinian was that of reincarnation, the idea that an Emperor could be anything less exalted proving something of an anathema to him. Finding an ally in Irenaeus, Bishop of Gaul, he strove to bring about the change in doctrine that was ultimately effected by the Second Council of Constantinople. We are told, however, that this occasion was attended by very few bishops and was presided over by Eutychius, Patriarch of Constantinople, rather than Pope Vigilius himself. Apparently the Pontiff, although in that city at the time, refused to attend and add his 'ex cathedra' touch to the proceedings. History is littered with similar instances which have resulted in the minds of future generations being programmed into erroneous concepts of our role in the universe.

In *Creation Myths*, David Maclagan writes:

> The ecological vision of the Whole Earth is only the most recent image of a long tradition which reaches back through the Hermetic teachings to the idea of a world soul, an *anima mundi*. Plato's *Timaeus* showed that the entire cosmos must, by virtue of its order and harmony, possess intelligence and be 'in very truth a living creature with soul and reason.' The cosmos of the *Timaeus* is framed by the Creator; but in many myths the creator dissolves into his creation, in nearly all cases through death or self-sacrifice. After the Norse giant Ymir was slain by the first three gods,
>
> > From the flesh of Ymir the world was formed.
> > From his blood the billows of the sea.
> > The hills from his bones, the trees from his hair,
> > The sphere of heaven from his skull.
>
> In Hindu cosmology Purusha, the Primal Man, is dismembered and the universe formed of all his parts (hence to recognize the essential unity of macrocosm and microcosm was to lose one's particular identity in that of Purusha). In some cases, such as the Egyptian

Memphite creation account the creator god is identified with the first
appearance on earth: one of Ptah's names is 'Uprising Earth'.[3]

Where, but in certain sacred rites that have been secretly conveyed down the ages, have these truths survived, and how much
suffering has been caused to the many who have been deprived of
their sublime content?

Just as we have today, all the early nations and cultures of the
world had their public and private rites, the nature of which were
determined by the prevailing national ethos. Anglo-Saxon rituals
naturally differed in form and content from those favoured by the
Latin peoples, while the Eastern Schools tended more towards
abstract mysticism than the overt magical exercises of the
Western Traditions. These could be monotheistic, polytheistic,
animistic or pantheistic in essence, but this mattered little as far as
the participants were concerned. Although the conscious mind
may reject this statement, the human psyche is not, in fact,
selective when it comes to an understanding of the nature of, and
belief in, a superior force or deity. In other words, the psychological advantages of 'faith' to the individual are the same regardless of whether the chosen god form is called Jesus, Jehovah, Isis,
Zeus, Aradia, the star Sirius or the West Wind. From the occult
viewpoint it is only intention that decrees the nature of the
attracted energies (like attracts like!), while the student of the
human mind would view it in terms of that aspect of the
psychological economy with which contact is effected (the transpersonal or higher self, or the id).

Viewing the matter objectively, as far as human psychology is
concerned, there is little difference in essence between the old
pagan Celtic, Roman, Egyptian or Greek rites and beliefs and the
rituals of today's popular mass state religions. All rest to some
degree on scientifically questionable hypotheses, mythological
inconsistencies, the lionization of figures from past history, the
acceptance of a supernatural force or forces superior to man and
the continuance of the ego* or psyche after death. The procedures
adopted by some Christian fundamentalist evangelical movements, for example, are calculated to induce mass abreaction by
effecting those altered states of consciousness which render the
unconscious mind totally open to auto-suggestive reprogramming (although they would doubtless not view it in that light). In
other words, in common with many religious and idealistic

*See Glossary

collectives they are not averse to using psychological techniques to effect their ends. But surely this is nothing new. St Paul, no doubt, used similar tactics on his travels, as did Apollonius of Tyana and a string of earlier mystics and teachers extending back into the mists of time. The essential nature of man would not appear to change very much, but then we might well be viewing the situation from a very small time sector, as compared to the whole evolutionary pattern of the genotype we call Homo sapiens.

While psychiatrists of the humanistic schools might disagree, there are many practitioners and students of the human condition who do recognize the psychological advantages to be gained from adherence to one or other of the aforementioned premises. What we are or are not able to prove within our lifetimes assumes a lesser relevance when viewed against the sociological and spiritual integration and stability which frequently goes hand in hand with adherence to a philosophy, creed, *Anschauung* or ethical code that is not tainted by hysterical fanaticism.

The subconscious mind would not appear to be hidebound by dogma, as many hypnotherapists have discovered, ardent adherents to one particular belief having been known to confess total disinterest in that same faith when questioned under third degree hypnosis. The subconscious mind also has a language of its own which it uses to communicate with both the collective unconscious and its own rational counterpart. In some people its only avenue of expression is through dreams, while with others the connecting link between the right and left hemispheres of the brain, being less rigid, allows for an easier flow of communicatory symbols between the conscious and unconscious states. Ritual addresses the human psyche at all of its levels through the language of symbology. This language is by no means limited to any one creed or ideology. Anyone who has led a meditative rite at which members of the general public have been present will attest to this.

On one occasion I was asked to lead a meditation at a major London psychic festival. Realizing that I was faced with an audience of mixed faiths, I chose a general pathworking based on the single archetypal figure of Isis as the Mother Goddess, a picture of whom I projected mentally. I took great care not to give any clues as to whom I had in mind when I asked those present to 'take the hand of a gentle figure who will approach you'. When asked to recount their impressions and experiences at the end of the session, the participants more than confirmed the totally transcendental nature of the archetype which they each saw in the light of their own belief. Thus we had numerous Virgin Marys, a couple of Aradias and Artemises, three who 'saw' Isis in her Egyptian form, a Crone aspect of the Triple Goddess, a Shekinah, three Kwan Yins, someone's own deceased mother, one Sarasvati, and a few who fell asleep and 'didn't get anything'! Not a single person present admitted to having 'seen' a male figure. I made a particular note of what happened as I felt it might come in handy one day for a study of this nature.

The efficacy of any rite will be dependent upon several factors:

1. the collective thought force of the chosen school of belief to which the participant adheres
2. the energy overlays accumulated by the particular rite over long periods of use
3. the wisdom and soul age of the originators of that rite, or the ethos which gave it birth
4. the degree of commitment and mental state of the participants

Although the outcome may afford the sincere believer a temporary feeling of elation and mystical fulfilment, it is as well to bear in mind that the power will be limited to that particular manifestation of faith, and will not necessarily offer anything like the potential available to those who can work through independent imagery.

Religious and occult systems of the past have usually made their appearance at times in the evolution of the planet when it has been necessary for the minds of people to be drawn into a particular avenue of discipline. They therefore carry the stamp or hallmark of the age in which they were first made manifest. Evolution, both spiritual and somatic, would appear to move on, although this linear concept of progression depends very much on one's view of the nature of time itself.

It would therefore appear that although each of us receives from the Rite according to our individual needs, stage of awareness and inner comprehension of the transcendental — at the unconscious level the message is the same for us all! Underlying insecurity is demonstrated by the closed mind, while the inferiority complex loudly proclaims itself in those who feel the need to impose their views on others in order to prove themselves in some way. The missionary mode frequently lends its garb to the ego-conscious, whether the message be a social, religious, magical or philosophical one. Emotional dependencies always constitute a danger, the nature of life and experience being what it is. So, although we may gain much from participation in this or that secular, magical or religious practice, ultimately we must each look to the Temple that is the Self, wherein is performed that sacred rite of mental control which will eventually enable us to overcome the id and transcend those barriers of the material world which separate us from the Cosmic Whole.

As to the question of whether the Rite does have the power to actually influence God or whichever force is being addressed, I can do no better than quote the thoughts of Jung, formulated during his travels in America:

If for a moment we put away all European rationalism and transport ourselves into the clear mountain air of that solitary plateau, which drops off on one side into the broad continental prairies and on the other into the Pacific Ocean; if we also set aside our intimate knowledge of the world and exchange it for a horizon that seems immeasurable, and an ignorance of what lies beyond it, we will begin to achieve an inner comprehension of the Pueblo Indian's point of view. 'All life comes from the mountain' is immediately convincing to him, and he is equally certain that he lives upon the roof of an immeasurable world closest to God. He above all others has the Divinity's ear, and his ritual act will reach the distant sun soonest of all. The holiness of mountains, the revelation of Yahweh upon Sinai, the inspiration that Nietzsche was vouchsafed in the Engadine — all speak the same language. The idea, absurd to us, that a ritual act can magically affect the sun is, upon closer examination, no less irrational but far more familiar to us than might at first be assumed. Our Christian religion — like every other, incidentally — is permeated by the idea that special acts or a special kind of action can influence God – for example, through certain rites or by prayer, or by a morality pleasing to the Divinity.

The ritual acts of man are an answer and reaction to the action of God upon man; and perhaps they are not only that, but are also intended to be 'activating,' a form of magic coercion. That man feels capable of formulating valid replies to the over-powering influence of God, and that he can render back something which is essential even to God, induces pride, for it raises the human individual to the dignity of a metaphysical factor. 'God and us' — even if it is only an unconscious *sous-entendu* — this equation no doubt underlies that enviable serenity of the Pueblo Indian. Such a man is in the fullest sense of the word in his proper place.[4]

Endnotes:

1. *The Egyptian Mysteries* Iamblichos, pp. 204–206.
2. *Practical Greek Magic* Murry Hope, pp. 63–66.
3. *Creation Myths* David Maclagan, pp. 25–26.
4. *Memories, Dreams and Reflections* C G Jung, pp. 237–238.

Chapter 5

PSYCHISM AND THE RITE

Is psychism, or that which comes under the broad heading of 'psychic gifts', necessary to the effective workings of magical or occult rituals? Well, it all depends on one's definition of the word, as it is all too frequently used to describe a whole range of preternatural activities such as extra-sensory perception, altered states of consciousness, out of the body experiences, prescience, psychometry, clairvoyance, astral projection, trance medium-ship and several other modes of paranormal perception which are known collectively to the psychologist as 'cryptaesthesia'. The recent addition of semantics from the various schools of psychology and parapsychology has added to the confusion, with the result that many of these terms have come to mean different things to different people.

Stephen E Braude, Associate Professor of Philosophy at the University of Maryland has recently made an intensive study of parapsychology and ESP. In his book *The Limits of Influence* he writes:

> The empirical part of this book deals primarily with a rather restricted portion of the total evidence for psychic (now called 'psi' or 'paranor-mal') phenomena — namely, the evidence from physical mediumship. A *medium* is an ostensible psi agent who purports to be an intermedi-ary between the spirit world and this world. A *mental* medium is a medium who apparently transmits and receives communications from the world of spirits. A *physical* medium is a medium in whose presence psychokinesis (PK) is observed.[1]

To the occultist, however, there are some finer distinctions, and over my many years of studying that broad spectrum of mystical pursuits which shelter under the metaphysical umbrella, I have arrived at three basic definitions (which can, in turn, be subdivided):

1. The psychic or mediumistic person who is telepathically receptive, inasmuch as he or she has the ability to tune in to other minds, energies or frequencies which could be totally alien to his or her immediate environmental programming. Genuine psychics are also able to tap the collective unconscious which exists interdependently of time and space, hence the ability to 'see' the past and future.

2. The occultist or magus, who strives to manipulate cosmic forces or subtle energies by using mind or will-power, which skill is slowly (and ofttimes painfully) mastered by way of a series of disciplines known as initiations.

3. The mystic, who is frequently of religious leanings, who extends his or her faith a step or more beyond the accepted dogmas of orthodox teachings, choosing to seek both within and without for the answers to life's enigmas. Illumination may be experienced during this observatory process, but the knowledge gained is not necessarily employed in the practice of either psychism or occultism.

The occultist or magus represents the active/directive aspect of the metaphysical polarity and the medium or psychic, the passive/receptive side — the yang and yin respectively. An occultist may be lacking in psychic gifts, while an excellent clairvoyant might be insufficiently skilled in the control of his or her own mind and will-power to become a magus. Dr John Dee, the famous Elizabethan magus, always chose to work with mediums, notably the somewhat suspect Edward Kelley. Whether, in fact, the illustrious doctor doubted his own psychic abilities, or whether he simply felt safer in the officiating role, is open to speculation.

This arrangement was also used with considerable success at the Oracle of Delphi, when the Pythoness (the Priestess of the Oracle) would enter a state of trance and make a series of symbolically obscure utterances which the presiding priest would then translate for the benefit of the enquirer. A similar procedure was adopted at several other of the famous Oracles of the past, notably that of Zeus at Dodona.

No doubt in the fullness of time, science will effect a standardization of metaphysical parlance, as the validity of supernormal claims are either proven or disproven methodologically and an acceptable standard of evaluation arrived at. Terms such as 'morphic resonance' are already creeping into the psychic vocabulary as the gap between physics and metaphysics is slowly closing.

We would not be fulfilling our task, however, if we failed to consider what has already been discovered by psychologists and psychiatrists concerning the nature of psychism. During his long life Jung investigated a considerable amount of psychic phenomena, and mediumship in particular. His findings were far from conclusive and it was only his own subjective experiences that eventually convinced him of both the existence of a superior creative force and the right of every individual to approach the transcendental in a way best suited to his or her individual psychological make-up, environmental programming and national ethos.

After an intensive investigation into mediumistic phenomena, Jung concluded that many people who exhibited psychic gifts were slightly abnormal mentally and had hysterical tendencies; he conceded, however, that there were an equal number of hysterics amongst the rank and file of the ordinary populace, so the two conditions were not necessarily synonymous.[2] Symptoms of hysteria can, however, afflict anyone in circumstances of stress, heightened emotion or inner conflict.

This hysterical personality-type is also believed to be more prevalent in some races than others — the Celts, for example, about whom physicist Danah Zohar comments:

> 'Second sight' was also attributed to the ancient Celts. With them, prevision was often described as just another racial peculiarity, like their red hair and moon-shaped faces. Their Druid priests were said to find prophecy so easy and natural that they had no recourse to the drugs or ecstatic states which were commonly employed by other people to enhance this faculty.[3]

Celts are to this day noted for their artistic gifts and associated temperament which could, in the eyes of some, appear as a form of hysteria.

In the light of these comments one is tempted to suggest that the hysterical personality might well be prone to strong psychosomatic tendencies, as in cases of stigmata, which would surely indicate a closer than normal link between the two hemispheres of the brain on the one hand, and easy access to alpha and theta brain patterns on the other. In commenting on the phenomena of 'heightened unconscious performance', as exhibited in mediumship, somnambulism, thought-reading and similar phenomena, Jung wrote:

> Here I will mention only Binet's experiments, . . . On the basis of these experiments he comes to the following conclusion: 'According to the calculations that I have been able to make, the unconscious sensibility of an hysterical patient is at certain moments *fifty times* more acute than that of a normal person.' Another example of heightened performance that applies to our case and to numerous other somnambulists is the process known as cryptomnesia. By this is meant the coming into consciousness of a memory-image which is not recognized as such in the first instance, but only secondarily, if at all, by means of subsequent recollection or abstract reasoning. It is characteristic of cryptomnesia that the image which comes up does not bear the distinctive marks of the memory-image; that is to say, it is not connected with the supraliminal ego-complex in question.
>   . . . *The image enters consciousness without the mediation of the senses, intrapsychically.* It is a sudden idea or hunch, whose causal nexus is hidden from the person concerned. To this extent cryptomnesia is an everyday occurrence and is intimately bound up with normal psychic processes. But how often it misleads the scientist, author or composer into believing that his ideas are original, and then along comes the critic and points out the source!
>   Footnote 119: Cryptomnesia should not be confused with hypermnesia. By the latter term is meant the abnormal sharpening of the powers of memory, which then reproduce the actual memory images themselves.[4]

I will leave the master at that point, but his words surely caution us to bear certain factors in mind when assessing the validity or otherwise of psychic claims — his observations being particularly worthy of note concerning clairvoyance and trance-mediumship. Although much of what is served up as clairvoyance can be said to come from either telepathizing with the enquirer, common observation or simple psychology, there is at times the odd flash of genuine inspiration which homes onto a particular target with uncanny accuracy, but which does not necessarily appear on command.

Some occultists tend to look askance at what is popularly called 'channelling' on the grounds that either the imagination can play too active a part, or that the practice can be conducive to possession or psychic fragmentation. But while these are perfectly valid objections as seen through the eyes of the cautious, what about the old adage with which the neophyte is invariably confronted sooner or later in his or her magical career: 'To Dare; To Will; To Know; To Keep Silent'. How else can one comprehend an experience unless one partakes of its content? In his *VII Sermones ad Mortuos*, Jung unashamedly admits to being overshadowed by a force he identified with Basilides the Gnostic. Nor was this his only brush with the psychic during his long and varied life.

To these considerations must also be added that a great deal of what is given out as words of enlightenment, teachings or the promptings of essences or intelligences external to the psyche of the medium, are nothing more than contacts with an inner aspect of his or her own personal psychological economy. In other words, the audience is being presented with a philosophic or metaphysical summary of views held by either: (a) the transpersonal or higher self (one well-known medium actually admitted this to me in confidence); (b) the alter-ego, or a suppressed aspect of the psyche which has failed to find an outlet for its views in the normal channels of life; (c) a fragmented section of the mind bordering on the schizophrenic; or (d) a convenient way of putting across that which the deliverer would dearly love to express openly but dare not for fear of ridicule. 'It wasn't me, of course, so don't anyone take offence!'

Does the role-playing Rite, therefore, constitute even the slightest danger to the participants, and should the shamanic approach be included in the enactment or not? This question inevitably leads us into the turgid waters of mental stability and ethics, both highly charged subjects which need careful handling.

We live in an age where it is the fashion to 'have a go' regardless of the consequences and the suffering that might be caused, both to the self and to those around who might catch the stray flak. The picture is an all too familiar one, the self-justifying rhetoric of the 'all equal' school neatly packaged in the clichés of humanistic psychology, the old dichotomies of right and wrong having conveniently collapsed beneath the rubble of hedonism. Pro-

fessor Hans Eysenck, writing in *The Mail on Sunday* (7 July 1985)
commented:

> We have been conned by the pseudo-psychological teaching of
> speculative psychoanalysts warning us against inhibiting our baser
> instincts. We have been pushed in the wrong direction by pseudo-
> liberal tolerance that is tolerant even of intolerance.

Which leads us back to that eternal dualistic conflict between
discipline and chaos, light and darkness, love and hate — which
Jung was most certainly acknowledging when he wrote:

> Only here, in life on earth, where the opposites clash together, can the
> general level of consciousness be raised. That seems to be man's
> metaphysical task — which he cannot accomplish without 'mytholo-
> gizing'. Myth is the natural and indispensable intermediate stage
> between unconscious and conscious cognition. True, the unconscious
> knows more than consciousness does; but it is knowledge of a special
> sort, knowledge in eternity, usually without reference to the here and
> now, not couched in the language of the intellect.[5]

Whether or not one subscribes to the existence of supernatural
forces of evil intent is purely academic at this point. What we do
know for sure is that the fragmentation of the human psyche can
be the cause of great personal suffering, in addition to being a
burden on society. And when this destruction could have been
avoided by the application of a little cold water on an overheated
ego, then there is undoubtedly cause for concern.

From an ethical standpoint, 'goodness' is not the prerogative of
any one religious persuasion — orthodox or otherwise — regardless of the numerical superiority of its adherents, any more than
the other side of the coin belongs to unpopular minority groups
which do not conform to the standards of current collectives. As
history will bear honest witness, all creeds have at some time
spawned both saints and sinners.

The ultimate aim of all magical and alchemical rites and
practices should be spiritual transmutation, born of the realization of the true and full mental powers which are the natural
heritage of the human psyche incarnate within this time frequency we call 'material existence'. The achievement of this
realization serves to open the universal doors through which the
Initiate may then pass in his or her unending quest for knowledge,
enlightenment and love. Should the intention behind this quest be

anything less than the ideal, the Initiate will fall victim to the wiles of his or her own ego or desire-nature and become lost in the maze of personal illusion. Or in psychological terms, the delusion effectively masks reality to the extent that paranoic schizophrenia, in the guise of sanctity on the one hand, or evil hedonistic adepthood on the other, slowly depersonalizes and disintegrates the psychic fabric until the visible signs of inner decay outwardly declare the extent of the destructive process. In plain words, not everyone is psychologically suited to handle those mental stresses that are peculiar to the genuine occult path on the one hand, or sufficiently strong-minded to cope with shamanic altered states of consciousness on the other — genuine priests, mediums and shamans being few and far between. When the chiefs vastly outnumber the braves the chances of winning the battle are scant, so for the sake of our own mental health it is far better that we make an honest assessment of our talents and employ them accordingly.

The established churches constantly decry 'questionable occult practices' on the grounds that these represent a communion of sorts with what are felt to be demoniacal forces. That is, of course, with the exception of those carried out under their own auspices. Those dialectical materialists who dismiss this as pure superstition may well concede that said 'devils' are only hidden aspects of the darker side of our own nature, and in many cases they will probably be right. The medical profession tends to discourage occult experimentation because experience has shown that mental illness often results from its misuse. Having worked in a mental healing group for many years, I can sympathize with those psychiatrists, psychotherapists and professional counsellors who have the task of re-cementing the personality fragments of ill-informed dabblers, as there is no doubt that the energies generated or liberated by certain rites can adversely affect both the mental state of the participant and his or her somatic balance. However, I shall be dealing with this aspect in some detail in Chapter 10.

If you, the reader, however, are a sincere believer in the validity of extra-sensory perception and allied manifestations of the paranormal then take heart; even science is slowly coming to the conclusion that there is something in it. A recent article in the *Guardian* entitled 'Quantum Leap from Science to the Supernatural' carried some encouraging words from Cambridge Professor of Physics, Brian Josephson, yet another highly respected scientist to join the growing ranks of those who are striving to close the gap between physics and metaphysics.

Having played devil's advocate against a background of healthy scepticism, however, one must admit that there are incidences of genuine trance or clairvoyance. These are usually discernible by other psychics present, who are themselves able to effect a degree of prescience which gives them a sight of, or access to, the waveband to which the medium is attuned. None of us being exempt from the pitfalls of self-delusion, I was trained to consider this possibility and advised never to trust my own psychic judgement completely, but always seek confirmation from another or others who were used to working on similar frequencies to those with which I was accustomed.

Let us return once more to the role, if any, to be played by the psychic faculty in the enactment of the Rite. From my own experience I would say that trance-mediumship in occult ritual is a definite 'no-no', as far as most Western Tradition rites are concerned. I was once invited to a Lodge working at which a lady of supposed mediumistic talents was also a guest. The Celebrant handled the opening perfectly and all went well until the allotted roles were assumed, whereupon the said lady immediately slipped into trance and commenced to take over the proceedings, much to the consternation of everyone else present! Besides being an incorrect magical procedure, this is also the height of bad manners, as anyone who has been well-trained in the magical arts will know.

What made matters worse was that the entrancing entity (whose supposed presence I seriously doubted) was not on the same wavelength as the rest of us, so the Celebrant motioned me, as the other occultist present, to help him either remove the intruder (if there was one), or bring the lady out of the hypnotic state, as the case might be. This we achieved, much to the annoyance of the medium, who protested that her guide had been interfered with by evil forces! The Lodge Master was obliged to bring the proceedings to an early close, and as the atmosphere was disturbed a good clearance was needed.

What can help in magical workings is either controlled imagery/creative imagination, or the genuine clairvoyance which the ancients referred to as 'the sight'. The former can play a very positive part in the transference of the ego-consciousness and identification with the Principle represented in role-playing magic. Ancient Egyptian rites frequently included a scryer who employed either a crystal or a bowl of clear water. Creative imagery should function on alpha rather than theta brain rhythms, giving the sort of controlled psychism that is essential to good ritual discipline. This may not be as spectacular or pheno-menal as those trances in which the consciousness is relinquished to the deeper hypnotic state, but in group workings it is far more reliable.

Another danger in too deep a relinquishment of consciousness in magical rites lies in the possibility of transference (see Chapter 6), which could result in the construction of emotional dependen-cies. Complexes resulting from interchanges of this sort can be damaging to both the dependant and the object of his or her dependency — the altered state of consciousness being ever a revealer of the kind of vulnerability that inevitably acts as a magnet to the ego-dominant (usually animus-accentuated) psyche!

This brings us to the inevitable question: why do the members of so many metaphysical groups of all kinds frequently fall out amongst themselves? This, I fear, is a somewhat disturbing psychological phenomenon to which there must obviously be an answer. It would appear to require a very stable and well-integrated person to cope with the stresses and personality clashes which inevitably rear their ugly heads at some time or other during group proceedings. These days in particular, psychic groups, lodges and covens appear to mushroom over-night. The initial enthusiasm, however, eventually gives way to dissatisfaction, personal sniping, behind the back planning and eventual disintegration — which usually involves a few partner-ship musical chairs, and one or more of the disenchanted leavers starting up another group on their own. This behavioural pattern is, of course, by no means limited to those who follow the esoteric path. Jockeying for position is a pastime indulged in by members of most collectives, religious or secular.

As related to the psychic or occult group, however, the problem as I see it resides in two factors. Firstly, the true reason for the initiation of the venture; and secondly, the intentions of those who have elected to participate in the Rite through that particular avenue of expression. The sad but unmistakable truth which must be faced is that lonely, frustrated and/or emotionally unstable people who are looking for a social outlet, a partner or a prop, are frequently attracted to occult or mystically orientated groups or movements. While this can equally be said of orthodox religious and social collectives, the latter are shielded, to a degree, by the establishment and the sheer weight of their numbers.

Before my readers despair of the human condition it must be emphasized that there are some very stable groups whose members have been working happily and harmoniously together for many years. These may not make the headlines, but when it comes to the 'nitty gritty' of occult power, it is they who hold the real reins — as mental stability that is borne out of strength of purpose will always triumph.

Recent discoveries in the field of astrophysics suggest the nature of what we understand as 'chaos' to be something of an anomaly in that it is eventually self-organizing. An interesting psychological corollary may be observed in the fact that many of those who display chaotic or antisocial behavioural patterns in youth frequently mature into highly disciplined pillars of society, converts of any kind generally tending towards over-zealousness if not actual fanaticism!

A well-attuned and balanced psychic faculty can definitely aid ritual identification of (and with) the archetypal energies invoked. In all role-playing and pathworking rites, it does help to know what or whom one has contacted, as the demon of self-delusion is ever lurking at the outer portals of the mind.

The type of heightened consciousness which frequently occurs during participation in a correctly balanced and well-orientated rite will automatically grant access to the archetypal world. A study of the archetypes and those aspects of the mind to which they relate therefore merits consideration. Jung's 'Philemon', for example, had a lame foot. So did the Fisher King of the Arthurian cycle and Hephaestus of Greek mythology, both of whom are associated with the Foundation Principle, or the abstract made manifest. All the 'smith' gods fall into this category, notably Ptah of Memphis, who was recognized by the ancient Egyptians as being the Creator of the World of Matter or — to employ the semantics of angelology — Lord of the Kingdom of the Archons (those beings who manipulate the subatomic world). There is more to be learned from the archetypal presences that manifest during the Rite than might at first be suspected. This is equally true, whether one cares to limit them purely to corresponding aspects of the human psyche, or accept their existence in broader, more cosmic terms.

Those who follow the Western Tradition are to a great extent, influenced by left hemisphere logic, the tendency being to create numerous categories into which their archetypal contacts can be pigeon-holed. Now while this is all very neat and tidy, there are many who believe that it can also constitute a limiting factor. Shamanism's apparent disregard of Western ritual discipline, for example, is deceptive, and before one condemns the shamanic codes as pure hysteria, an examination of their Initiatory Rites is advised, some of which would sorely test the physical and mental endurance of many a Western practitioner. In Chapter 17, which deals specifically with Rites of Initiation, I shall be discussing and comparing some of the methods mankind has devised over the ages to test his or her right to call him or herself 'shaman', 'priest' or 'priestess', initiate or magus in the truly metaphysical meaning of those terms.

Endnotes:

1. *The Limits of Influence* Stephen E Braude, p. xii.
2. *Psychology and the Occult* C G Jung, p. 101.
3. *Through the Time Barrier* Danah Zohar, p. 16.
4. *Op. cit.* Jung, pp. 83–84.
5. *Memories, Dreams and Reflections* C G Jung, pp. 288–289.

Chapter 6

DISCIPLINE OF THE RITE

Does the enactment of physical and mental disciplines within the framework of the Rite serve as a genuine aid to the raising of consciousness? If so, to what ultimate effect as far as the human condition is concerned?

In his efforts to attain some form of spiritual realization or subjective awareness of the transcendental, man has devised many strange and sometimes alarming techniques, some of which apply more to the private than the public rite. These can only be classified approximately under physical and mental headings, because there is frequently a combination factor involved.

There would appear to be two distinct schools of thought regarding the type of experience necessary to spiritual ascent or subliminal attainment. The one favoured by several Eastern schools — as well as amongst the more instinctively inclined races — is concerned with the expression of the libido via the reproductory organs or sexual chakra, the idea being that it is essential to experience fully the chthonic before the supraphysical can be approached. In contrast, the ascetic mysticism which flavours the rites and ethics of both East and West demands a tight control of the lower chakric functions, and often involves vows of chastity and/or total abstinence. An analysis of both approaches is essential if we are to fully understand the true nature of the Rite, so let us commence with the former.

Sigmund Freud's views on the nature and functions of the libido are probably the best-known of all his studies. Jung, speaking of his early friendship with Freud, wrote:

> In retrospect I can say that I alone logically pursued the two problems which most interested Freud: the problem of 'archaic vestiges', and that of sexuality. It is a widespread error to imagine that I do not see the value of sexuality. On the contrary, it plays a large part in my psychology as an essential — though not the sole — expression of psychic wholeness. But my main concern has been to investigate, over and above its personal significance and biological function, its spiritual aspect and its numinous meaning, and thus to explain what Freud was so fascinated by but was unable to grasp. My thoughts on this subject are contained in the *Psychology of the Transference* and the *Mysterium Coniunctionis*. Sexuality is of the greatest importance as the expression of the chthonic spirit. That spirit is the 'other face of God', the dark side of the God-image. The question of the chthonic spirit has occupied me ever since I began to delve into the world of alchemy. Basically, this interest was awakened by that early conversation with Freud, when, mystified, I felt how deeply stirred he was by the phenomenon of sexuality.[1]

As regards the nature of the libido, Jung conceived of this as 'a psychic analogue of physical energy, hence as a more or less quantitative concept, which therefore should not be defined in qualitative terms'.[2] One is reminded of Anebo's 'corporeal necessities'!

In the light of earlier remarks concerning the hysterical nature of psychism, it should be borne in mind that Freud himself was no stranger to this phenomenon. The Akhnaton incident related by Jung serves to remind us that although Freud's doctrines were overtly terrestrial, there was a compartment of his subconscious or superconscious which he suppressed.[3] An examination of the contents of his home (which has now become a museum) will more than satisfy the occultist or transcendental psychologist as to the area of subjective subliminal reality involved, his collection of magical and mythological *objet d'art* being the envy of your author, for a start!

During his travels in India, Jung was shown a pagoda in Konarak (Orissa), which was covered from base to pinnacle with explicit sexual sculptures. Seeing a group of young peasants admiring the same, Jung took issue with the pandit regarding the possible dangers of the fantasy-inducing aspects of the display, to which the guide replied: 'But that is just the point. How can they ever become spiritualized if they do not first fulfil their karma? These admittedly obscene images are here for the very purpose of recalling to the people their dharma (law); otherwise these unconscious fellows might forget it.' As the two men continued their exploratory walk, the guide added: 'Naturally this does not apply to people like you and me, for we have attained to a level of consciousness which is above this sort of thing.'[4]

Are we then to assume that those rites which have a more sublime and less carnal content are for the evolved or mature souls, or those who see themselves in that light? If this be the case, is there not a psychological danger lurking within this assumption which could have formed the basis of many of Freud's conclusions? If we hold such an exalted view of ourselves that we fail to come to terms with our essential nature or expression of the libido, we fall into just as deep a trap as the hedonist whose abandonment to personal gratification precludes him or her from fulfilling a karmic potential.

Surely it all comes down to why we may or may not feel the way we do about chthonic expression. To suppress the sexual function deliberately because of a guilt complex or moral confusion as to its correct use, is just as damaging to the psyche as the overuse of the faculty. The former can result in severe repression which can either be directed inwards, causing psychosomatic illnesses — or outwards, when it can manifest as blatant aggression. In view of the current epidemic of sexually transmitted diseases which have resulted from unbridled hedonism, I hardly think the latter calls for comment.

To known oneself is to be absolutely honest about one's needs (as distinct from one's wants), both spiritual and corporeal. Tantra and similar rites may well be suitable modes of expression for the many who are still coming to terms with their bodies, but once again we are faced with the question of intention. If the motivation is sincere, but the aspirant feels that he or she simply cannot cope with the more transcendental disciplines until the pent-up need for physical expression has been expunged from his or her system, then fair enough. If, however, the sexually orientated rite is used purely for self-indulgence and titillation, then intention decrees the level of the energies that will be attracted, and the Kundalini or serpent power of the participants will proceed no further than the lower chakras, which are liable to become effectively blocked. Moral issues I will not comment upon, as I consider these to be a matter for the conscience and karma of the individual.

On the other side of the coin, there are many aspiring mystics who do have a preference for sublimating their natural physical urges, not because they necessarily feel guilty about them or regard them as being of a lower order or 'dirty', but simply because they know, albeit unconsciously, that they have probably worked through all that before and are therefore at the limit or threshold of more edifying or spiritually uplifting pursuits. It is at this point that we enter the field of emotional transference, which is ever spiked with hidden thorns.

Originally conceived of in Freudian psychology as relating to the patient/analyst relationship, the transference principle would appear to have wider connotations within the framework of human experience, especially in relationship to the fields of metaphysics and mysticism. Jungian analyst Bani Shorter says of it:

> The term 'transference' refers to a natural psychological tendency to project and 'transfer' the dependency of psychic growth onto someone else at a time of crisis and change. What is transferred is, in its most basic definition, the inability to transform as needed. And the projection, for so it is, is of two kinds, one material and the other spiritual.[5]

Those who have by choice elected to serve their deity in Orders of any kind, are often referred to as being 'wedded to Christ' (or the Church) to the extent that participation in the rites of the respective faith in itself constitutes a form of sublimated orgasmic consummation. While emotional transference is not necessarily the designated outcome of this experience, it can occur and with very strange results. The case of Ignatius Loyola, founder of the Society of Jesus, is one that springs to mind.

Born in Spain in 1491, the young Ignatius was something of a gallant at the Spanish Court, However, he sustained a severe leg wound which was badly set, as a result of which he felt his appearance to be too grotesque to merit the further attentions of the ladies of the Court. The story of his earlier masochistic leanings and pendulous swing between sanity and insanity is too long to recount, but suffice it to say that it concluded in a fanatical sublimatory emotional transference to the Virgin Mary archetype, whom he swore to serve for the rest of his days. The fanaticism of this idealized devotion, and the tortured mind of the man himself, may be evidenced in his famous Spiritual Exercises, which are as psychologically valid today as they were when he first introduced them. In fact, the Calvinistic preachers of the time referred to them as being of a magical formulae which induced states of openness and susceptibility to the devil! Powerful rites indeed!

Transferences only constitute a danger if they become out of balance to the degree that the object or ideal with which the dependency is formed assumes responsibility for the actions, thoughts and logic of the transferer. Utopian concepts, for example, have ever constituted a psychological pitfall, although it could equally be argued that they offer a sustaining ray of optimism in a world far removed from their probability. If we live in the perpetual hope of the next plane (wherever or whatever that might be) being better than the one in which we exist, we are bound to lose out on our karma, the sounding-board of experience being ever the spring-board to evolutionary progress. The ancient Celts, who were reputedly of Indo-Aryan origin, were so convinced of a heavenly Utopia that they were known to leap onto the funeral pyres of their deceased relatives in order to arrive there more quickly, a similar practice being re-echoed in the Hindu Rite of Suttee.

Expiation rites in which the *mea culpa* syndrome receives unnatural emphasis should also be watched, the Confessional being a classic example which has survived to this day. The psychology behind confessing one's sins involves a transference of the guilt or responsibility for one's actions onto some convenient scapegoat, the repetition of a few ritual phrases, accompanied by a short admonition and suggested penance, removing the weight from the confessee's shoulders.

Enter the redemption factor. Apologetics for or against established doctrines are not part of my task in this book. However, it should be borne in mind that the 'scapegoat' is essentially a totem of sympathetic magic — so has our cultural advancement really changed the nature and emblems of our rites?

Somatic and liminal side-effects frequently result from disciplines undertaken during the performance of certain rites. These states can be either hypnotically self-induced, activated by the nature and intensity of the Rite or influenced by rhythmical movements, drum beats, vocal chants, and special breathing techniques calculated to affect the autonomic nervous system to the extent that the normal pain threshold is either extended or by-passed completely (See Chapter 10).

While masochistically induced states of ecstasy may appear mystically impressive to the untutored, the true nature of their pleasure content would be obvious to the trained observer. What needs to be asked is: are pain-inducing practices, such as the 'Sun Dance' of the Dakota and Cheyenne Indians and rites of a similar nature which mutilate the human form in the extreme, truly an aid to the alchemical ideal? Also, can such phenomena be considered as valid mystical experiences? For those at a given stage of evolutionary development, it must be supposed that they are — or they would not indulge in them. To many, however, they constitute an effrontery to the beauty of the created form and those elemental essences that contribute to its growth and structure. As the achievement of many of these phenomena would appear to be dependent upon somewhat questionable ecstatic or paraphronesic states artificially induced by hypnosis, drugs or deprivations, one cannot help asking why it is necessary to effect these imbalances in order to attain to a supposed degree of enlightenment?

The energy generated by mindless repetition is known to react on the unconscious mind to the extent that a reprogramming is effected at the logical or left hemisphere level. That same depth can, of course, be plumbed by the hypnotist or psychotherapist with similar results. Taken in this context, there is little difference, if any, between the ecstatic chanting of the dervishes and the alleluias of the Christian evangelical fundamentalists, while the utterances of the entranced shaman could be equated with glossolalia (speaking in unidentified tongues). It can be argued that those who indulge in this exercise, either under the auspices of certain branches of Christianity or in the psychic trance state, are grasping at collective unconscious race memories of earlier cultures. The psychologist, however, would no doubt prefer Jung's diagnosis of cryptomnesia as the more logical explanation, as his research did reveal that among the gibberish which normally passes as the 'gift of tongues', there was the odd word from another language which was probably registered subconsciously at some earlier point in life.

Xenolalia, or paranormal speaking in real languages, has apparently yet to be proven. However, not a single case has been recorded since the advent of tape recorders or computers. In 1926, Teresa Neumann, a famous Christian sensitive, allegedly cried out in Aramaic as she re-enacted Christ's passion, and in the 1930s an English medium known only as Rosemary was reputed to have spoken in ancient Egyptian during seances. As no living scholar would appear to know how the ancient Egyptian language was pronounced, the performance of the latter is obviously questionable.[6]

Yoga must surely qualify for inclusion under the heading of this chapter as one of the best-known solitary disciplinary rites, although it can also be experienced in the group situation. I have no intention of embarking on a treatise on this subject, as it is adequately covered in other publications. There are, however, various types of yoga which are designed to produce different effects — some physical, others devotional, ecstatic or sublime:

1. Hatha Yoga   Control of the body.'

2. Raja Yoga   Connects or links the mind with the spirit and the spirit with the Absolute.

3. J'nana Yoga   The pursuit of wisdom.

4. Mantra Yoga   Which is concerned with sound.

5. Bhakti Yoga   The love of God and religious devotion.

6. Karma Yoga   Concerned with action and service.

7. Laya Yoga   Pertains to the chakric centres.

There are also other forms of yoga that are not so well-known or easily recognizable to the Western novice.

The word 'yoga' means 'union' and the practice of yoga is believed to advance the student towards a state of union with his or her higher self. Some schools of mysticism recommend that the ideal path to transcendental attainment is via the mastery of the body through Hatha Yoga, and advancing from there to the more abstract spiritual modes. Others disagree, saying that if Raja Yoga is practised, the mind and spirit will be controlled and the body will respond naturally as a result.

In the East, the more spiritual forms of yoga are usually passed on to a student or 'chela' by a teacher or 'guru'. Westerners, however, are frequently left to their own devices, and not always with satisfactory results. There are schools of thought which designate that the ways of East and West are basically different, and that the systems associated with each should remain that way. On the other hand, one has to consider the karmic background of the individual who might well have experienced several Eastern lives before electing to be born into Western society. So in the final analysis, it is very much a personal matter.

Yogis have demonstrated palpably to science their ability to control the autonomic nervous system. According to yogic teaching there are two nerve currents in the spinal column called *Pingala* (masculine/positive) and *Ida* (feminine/negative), which are believed to coil and cross each other. Between these two is *Sushumna* in the semblance of a tube, at the lower extremity of which is the *Kundalini* or potential divine energy. Special breathing techniques have been adopted to activate or re-balance these. As the student slowly gains control and his or her consciousness expands through meditation and the assumption of the required postures, the Kundalini rises up the Sushumna or Tree of Life, passing through each of the chakras as it does so. (For more details of the chakric system see Chapter 10.) The diaphragmatic breathing advocated by the yogis is known to induce a general calming effect, which accounts for its use as a prophylactic. Yogic breathing is not, however, a panacea for all ills and it is erroneous to assume that because one has effected an excellent control over one's body via the practice of Hatha Yoga, that one is necessarily mentally strong.

Some years ago a gentleman of considerable prowess in Hatha Yoga sought my help. He was on the verge of a nervous breakdown due, he claimed, to someone in India having put a 'hex' on him and his family. So utterly had he convinced himself of the efficacy of the supposed spell, that he had programmed his own path of self-destruction. My difficulty lay in persuading him to convince himself that the problem could be overcome. This I was able to achieve by effecting what he believed to be a genuine exorcism, carried out according to a Rite acceptable to his own ethos, utilizing the nomenclatures of deities with whom he was familiar and felt safe. Fortunately for both of us it worked!

One final note upon which to end this chapter. The human mind is greatly affected by symbols, especially if these contain subliminal overtones. A friend once approached me regarding the meaning of a Rite in which she had been asked to participate, which involved her handing a clean, white handkerchief over to another in exchange for a flower. 'What did it all mean?' she asked.

Let us put it this way. If you were an army officer engaged in a battle which you and your men were rapidly losing to the enemy and you wished to avoid further bloodshed, what would you do? Assuming that the 'other side' was civilized enough to observe the statutes of the Geneva Convention, you would hoist a white flag, a symbol of *surrender* since the earliest of times. Need I say more!

Endnotes:

1. *Memories, Dreams and Reflections* C G Jung, p. 163.
2. *Ibid.* p. 199.
3. *Ibid.* p. 153.
4. *Ibid.* p. 259.
5. *An Image Darkly Forming – Women and Initiation* Bani Shorter, p. 106.
6. *Mysteries of the Church* Edited by Peter Brookesmith, pp. 70–75.

Chapter 7

TO PLAY OR NOT TO PLAY?

We all play roles, at least that is the opinion of American psychologist Eric Berne, of Transactional Analysis* fame. In his book *Games People Play* he sees us effecting the roles of Child, Parent or Adult in the drama of everyday existence, moving from one to another to accommodate our prevailing moods or the situations in which we find ourselves.

In the ritual context, however, the term 'role-playing' is used to describe the assumption of a character or *dramatis personae* identifiable to the participant as an aspect of the deity, natural force or archetypal principle which is being invoked or evoked within the context of the ceremony. But not all rites involve the function of role-playing. The private rituals of Greek magic, for example, are simply concerned with an approach to and dialogue with the tutor or god-form to whom the Rite is addressed, so that although the essence (or essences as the case may be) is fully acknowledged and due deference paid to it, no effort is made to assume its identity.

While the secular rites of Celtic magic are not strictly of the role-playing variety, its Initiatory Rites are decidedly so, since they involve a blending with not only the archetypal god-forms, but also the essences of nature, the elemental forces and the animal kingdoms, as may be evidenced in the Bardic *Song of Amergin.*[1]

*See Glossary

Although some practising Qabalists role-play, assuming the archetypal identities of the Sephirotic essences as they move through the Tree, I am given to understand that many prefer the Pathworking method, so for those who would like to see how this is done, I have featured an excerpt from a classical Qabalistic pathworking in Chapter 11. Egyptian rites are probably the best examples we have of ritual role-playing amongst the earlier races, since their *modus operandi* can be traced back to antiquity through the *Book of the Dead*.

The fact that one is allotted a role to play or an archetypal identity to assume is no guarantee, however, that one will be blessed by an actual visitation or overshadowing of the kind guaranteed to produce the ecstatic state or a degree of transcendental reality. The principle involved was explained to me thus: in the drama of life, all levels of existence from the most humble to the most exalted are basically contained within the 'Eternal Now', time having no relevance within the context of the more exalted frequencies. What we, as individual essence fragments encapsulated in a state of matter, are able to perceive of these states of 'outer time' is dictated entirely by the extent to which we are capable of expanding our perceptive awareness.

As a child at boarding school I was told, 'God is everywhere, watching you all the time,' so no matter what I was doing or where I was hiding He could see me! As I recall, this caused me much consternation at the time, and I was obliged to rationalize it by telling myself that if He really was as good a God as they said, then He would surely understand that having given me a body which required attending to from time to time, no offence would be taken when I undertook this necessary ritual. With this thought firmly fixed in my mind (I was about nine years old at the time), I dismissed my embarrassment and forgot about it.

Simplistic though this concept of an ever-watchful deity might sound, there is a grain of truth in it. As we slowly progress from initiation to initiation, so the breadth of our visionary awareness expands, allowing us a slightly wider view of the universe with each painful step. We may not see a figure of Isis when we perform our Egyptian Rite, or the Archangel Mikaal in his shining glory waiting to greet us as we enter the Sephira of Tiphareth. Then one day — when we think we are a total failure and never likely to see anything, having participated in our Rite with patient regularity — the warmth of a presence will make itself felt, and we will know that we have finally opened a chink in our psychic vision of sufficient size for us to be truly aware of the nature and energies of the essence we have invoked. Of course, Isis, Mikaal, Odin or the Christos are always there, but it appears that we need a little spiritual maturation before we can view them with objective reality. Or is this, in fact, really the case? At which point we come to a psychological consideration of the value of role-playing and what actually takes place during its enactment.

Visions would appear to be part of our natural heritage as members of the hominid species. People have experienced them since the beginning of time, a fact which history has made no effort to conceal. Nor is the visionary influence limited to followers of religious or transcendental systems. Under certain conditions, such as those involving extreme stress or great relief, atheists have encountered it, as have hardened explorers and warriors who might normally consider things of that nature as belonging exclusively to the world of women. Such people might well prefer to accept the clinical explanation that their hallucinatory experiences are attributable to changes in body chemistry brought about by prolonged stress or extreme conditions of endurance. And why not? After all, this is a perfectly valid assessment since, as we have already discussed, rites which demand physical extremes tend to produce similar results — the ecstatic state being known to effect dramatic changes in breathing, pulse rate and body temperature.

Is the Rite's power to affect our body chemistry then, in the nature of a somatic mismanagement, so that our participation in the ecstatic venture is in fact, a form of madness? Or is the whole mystical procedure a momentary glimpse ahead to a time when we will be able to effect these changes at will (as true Adepts are supposed to do anyway), without exhibiting the symptoms of mental illness (hysteria) which have become associated with certain altered states of consciousness? Time alone will tell.

There is yet another point to take into consideration: not all transcendental experiences are necessarily of a similarly charged content. In contrast to the highly energetic nature of certain physically orientated ritual practices, the heightened state of spiritual transcendence which is attained when the Kundalini makes contact with the Sahasrara (or Crown) chakra is said to effect an utter stillness and peace, which is accompanied by *a slowing down of the pulse rate and similar autonomic functions!*

Having accepted role-playing as a valid contribution towards the efficacy of the Rite, the question naturally arises: with whom or what (if anything) is the ritual performer actually making contact? As there are obviously several approaches to this question which range from the strictly empirical to the emotionally illogical, it is as well to take a few factors into consideration before selecting a conveniently comfortable camp over which to hoist one's pennant.

We are all programmed from birth, both genetically and environmentally. While it is not impossible to break the code of that conditioning and re-programme ourselves (or be subtly re-programmed by others), with the majority of people the original pattern stays for the duration of a particular lifetime. So unless we have made a thorough study of the mind, were born psychically aware or are what is popularly termed in metaphysical parlance an 'old soul', our answers to the aforementioned question will be coloured by the religious, humanistic or philosophic doctrines in which we have been raised or which we have chosen to adopt in our maturity.

Humanistic psychology would no doubt view the magical role-playing experience as self-delusion or pure escapism, born of a need to create an imaginary environment which, unlike the real world in which we live, is subject to our will and therefore gives the illusion of dancing to our commands. The Jungian analyst, on the other hand, might view the drama in the archetypal context — the respective overshadowing representing an aspect of the self which has been thrown into relief by the unconscious — either as a compensatory factor or as an aid to a more efficient overall functioning of the psyche.

The assumption of the archetypal role is sufficiently rooted primordially to place a purely instinctive emphasis upon it, which firmly removes it from the realms of either emotion or pure reason. Primordial impulses are believed by some researchers to emanate from the hindbrain along with other instinctive awareness patterns which link it with the collective unconscious. Role-playing is, therefore, more complex than may at first be evidenced. Its somatic implications, as connected with the functioning of the hindbrain, allows it at least a glimmer of empirical credence.

The archetypal world, however, does not consist purely of shadows or the phantoms released by the unconscious mechanisms of the mind. It has both a deeper relevance and a subjective reality which can constitute a powerful manipulatory factor in mental programming. Viewed in this light, its effect on the psychology of Homo sapiens — and therefore its power to change the course of events — becomes frighteningly obvious. Place this observation in the context of the Rite and we start to get somewhere.

Our next consideration must apply to the views of those who do accept the existence of the archetypal world and its manifestation through the processes of the mind, and the beliefs of the many who espouse the magical concept that gods, nature entities, spirits, demons, angels and so on, do personalize and make their presence felt during the Rite.

Let us analyse one particular example — an Egyptian Propitiatory Rite in which the Horus role has been allotted to a young man who is undergoing his first experience of role-playing. The usual ceremonial is carried out, the cleansing completed and due deference paid by the Celebrant to the Elemental Kingdoms. The Rite itself has been dedicated to Isis, so after the appropriate invocations have been made, the Celebrant hands the proceedings over to the Priestess who will take on that role. Being very experienced, she has no difficulty in assuming the archetypal identity or 'making contact'. The others present are then invited by the Goddess to assume their respective roles. Our young man is apprehensive at first, but the Rite has been correctly organized and well run, so the energies generated commence to take their effect on him.

Subconsciously, his brain switches from left to right hemisphere to allow access to the archetype, and slowly the gentle strength and radiance of Horus starts to permeate his beingness; his breathing pattern changes from the shallow phase of initial nervousness to the deeper, diaphragmatic mode of serenity. He feels himself encompassed by a warm, sunlit glow, and the sheer beauty of the experience brings tears to his eyes. The correct balance is gradually achieved and he is able to proceed with the ceremony in the Horus role, being addressed by Isis as her son. When the essential content of the Rite has been completed, the archetypal entities take their leave of their temporary hosts, the Celebrant effects all the necessary thanksgivings and dismissals, the participants are 'earthed', auras are sealed, and the proceedings are drawn to a close.

What exactly happened to our young friend? Did the Egyptian God Horus really overshadow him, and if not, which cerebral mechanisms afforded him the temporary elation, cosmic understanding and emotional release which he experienced?

First questions first. The fact that someone feels they have been overshadowed by a 'god' — be that in the form of Jesus, Odin, Keridwen, Isis or whoever — is no guarantee that they have actually been contacted by the finer essence of that god-form. What has probably taken place is: (a) they have absorbed the essential nature of the archetype, Horus for example, which may or may not play a regular role in their daily lives; (b) the energies of the Rite have liberated a related aspect of their own psyche, so that emotions that have lain dormant — probably as a result of early sexual role-playing programming — have been released, allowing the Horus attributes of gentle strength, beauty, warmth and love to pass from the unconscious to be savoured by the conscious rationale; and (c) pure auto-suggestion. They have heard about or read somewhere what was expected of them and subconsciously performed accordingly. In most cases (b) and (c) are probably the truth.

Ardent ritualists who read this may well protest: 'Are you then saying that none of us every really makes contact with anything or anyone outside of our own subconscious minds?' No, I am not, but then that surely is what Initiation and Adeptship are all about. Real contact does not happen at the drop of a hat or because the participant felt that the Rite would provide better entertainment than the current evening's television. When we role-play we get exactly what we deserve, no more and no less. Should your psyche deem it necessary to make use of the energies of the Rite to evict the odd psychologial bogey, then you may well undergo the abreactive experience (especially if you are cast in a role such as Kali, Sekhmet or the Morrigan!) which will be cathartic if nothing else, and could put you off magic for a while to come. On the other hand, you may be an 'old time-travelled soul', in which case you will have no trouble contacting the loftier transpersonal levels. And how can one tell which is which? To borrow an old phrase from the Scriptures: 'By their deeds shall ye know them!'

Sadly, as is sometimes the case, an occultist may start off with good intentions, but pride and power are nothing if not good travelling companions, and the archetype is slowly forced to one side to make way for the inflated ego. Such egos feed from other egos; genuine archetypal energies or god-forms do not. If, therefore, the proceedings are correctly orientated, the participants in any Rite who give liberally of themselves in an unselfish way will in return receive blessings which are in proportion to their personal output on the one hand, and their individual state of spiritual development on the other. Should they find this not to be the case, however, they would be well advised either to question their own motives or to move on — for the compatibility factor exists at all levels. While it is conceded that will-power is involved in the manipulation of magical energies, this should be achieved through the Love Principle rather than the Might Principle, while the magically ambitious should beware of *the Law of Equalities!*

When considering the many nomenclatures assigned to the numerous archetypes, it is as well to respect the beliefs of others that may not always accord with one's own chosen creed. There are still people around who, for example, conceive of the Greek Pan or the Celtic Cernunnos as manifestations of the Christian devil. What nonsense! These deities were worshipped long before the advent of Christianity and to consider them in such a light is pure ignorance. Many people still mistakenly equate a Black Mass with the practices of certain pre-Christian religions. The Mass being essentially a Christian ceremony, a degree of belief in Christianity is necessitated to lend logic to its defacement, and as most practising pagans are not of Christian persuasion, the credulity is somewhat strained! Care should be taken to distinguish mentally unbalanced hedonists seeking sexual 'kicks' from those participating in the genuine rites of minority faiths.

Thankfully, a belief in the existence of interrelated intelligences which inhabit the 'unseen' universe is no longer limited to those of metaphysical inclination. It has been some years now since physicists Einstein, Podolski and Rosen produced the revolutionary theory which was subsequently expressed mathematically by Dr J S Bell of CERN laboratory in Geneva. The theory known as the 'EPR Paradox' claims that subatomic particles which have been in contact continue to influence each other long after they have been moved apart. Likewise, the magical Law of Contact (or Contagion) has always held that contacts once established continue to interact long after separation. So what else is new?

The Law of Hermes — God of Learning, Medicine, Science and Keeper of the Akashic Records (the connecting thread between all sympathetic or imitative magical systems) — has also emphasized the closely interrelated nature of all things — the Oneness of All Life. How this phenomenon is achieved is still being debated by science. Professor Fritjof Capra tells us that the physicist is fully aware of the essential unity of all things and events.[2] Research reports on this study are now becoming quite common. Dr Evan Harris Walker — quoted by Dr Lyall Watson in his book *Gifts of the Unknown* — is a ballistics expert and quantum theorist who, in spite of his empirical training, does not find it difficult to conceive of space as inhabited by an unlimited number of interconnected conscious entities who are responsible for the orderly running of the universe. In fact, he concedes that there is consciousness everywhere, which says something for the old scientific statement that nature abhors a vacuum!

While it has been scientifically established that minute particles can communicate with each other over vast areas of space, Rupert Sheldrake (PhD Cambridge, former Frank Knox Fellow at Harvard University, and Research Fellow of the Royal Society), who specializes in biochemistry, cellular biology and philosophy, has recently observed that this phenomenon is by no means limited to the subatomic world. Random groupings of cells, he notes, appear to communicate between themselves for the purpose of organizing into distinct colonies for specific tasks. Nor are communications between fish, birds and animals subject to sidereal or spatial limitations, many species being capable of effecting instantaneous telepathic contact over immense distances. To these phenomena Sheldrake has applied the term 'morphic resonance'. In his book *A New Science of Life* he also postulates the theory of morphogenetic (form-creating) fields which, though invisible, shape a growing animal or plant (and humans too, perhaps!).[3]

Of the concept of transcendent reality Dr Sheldrake writes:

> The universe as a whole could have a cause and a purpose only if it were itself created by a conscious agent which transcended it. Unlike the universe, this transcendent consciousness would not be developing towards a goal; it would be its own goal. It would not be striving towards a final form; it would be complete in itself.
>
> If this transcendent conscious being were the source of the universe and of everything within it, all created things would in some sense participate in its nature. The more or less limited 'wholeness' of organisms at all levels of complexity could then be seen as a reflection of the transcendent unity on which they depended, and from which they were ultimately derived.
>
> Thus this fourth metaphysical position affirms the causal efficacy of the conscious self, *and* the existence of a hierarchy of creative agencies immanent within nature, *and* the reality of a transcendent source of the universe.[4]

This whole idea seemed to incense the critic writing for *Nature* whose review of the book included the statement: 'Infuriating . . . the best candidate for burning there has been for years.' Obviously a dialectical materialist!

When it comes to the question of whether these archetypal forces, gods or discarnate energies which play so important a role in the Rite really do exist, or whether they are simply the product of centuries of mankind's over-active imagination, we may now turn to science for confirmation. In the light of recent theories and discoveries, especially in the field of subatomic physics, it is not so illogical to conceive of the existence of orders of intelligent essences that organize the universe, to whom we may address ourselves either mentally or via the Rite. Numerous names have been allotted to these over the aeons which differ with each race, culture or ethos, but this should in no way detract from the reality of their existence. Perhaps it will be to science that the role of highlighting the sheer folly of the bigotry involved in denigrating or despising the esoterica of diverging creeds will finally fall. One cannot help feeling that the scientist might eventually prove a better ally to the occultist than those emotionally, orientated faiths that stifle freedom of thought, and in so doing restrict the evolutionary progress of the soul.

Endnotes:

1. *Practical Celtic Magic* Murry Hope, p. 225.
2. *The Tao of Physics* Fritjof Capra, pp. 141–157.
3. *A New Science of Life* Dr Rupert Sheldrake, pp. 199–208.
4. *Ibid.* pp. 206–207.

Chapter 8

RITUAL HERITAGE

There is little doubt that the Rite has left its distinctive stamp on both history and culture. Much of that which we take for granted in our ordinary, everyday lives had its origin in early channels of ritualistic expression. For example, after we are born many of us are subjected to the rites of one or other of the popular religions. Baptism is, after all, a Rite of Birth, and the custom of immersing the newborn child in clear water is by no means limited to Christianity. Then there are the Maturation or Puberty Rites, such as the Jewish bar mitzvah and bas mitzvah, and their equivalents in other cultures which lead us into adulthood.

The marriage ceremony re-echoes past Bonding Rites, and when we finally leave this world the Funerary Rites we engage in differ little from those employed by our distant ancestors. Old Healing Rites are fast reappearing, albeit garbed in the modern semantics of alternative therapies. The Morris Dancers who make their colourful appearance in our towns and villages can trace their steps back to ancient rites, while many an old pagan custom, such as Well Dressing, is still kept alive by the Christian Church in parts of England to this day. Nothing really changes.

Ritual has also left its indelible impression on all art forms, its emphasis obviously being coloured by the relative ethos through which it finds expression, so that the principle remains intact and only the detail differs. Let us take architecture, for example, as a manifestation of the masonic energies of Ptah, Master Architect of the Universe. How many structures across the length and breadth of this planet have been erected ostensibly for the performance of the Rite? Too many to include in a single tome, but for a start we could try Stonehenge, Karnac, the Potala at Llasa, the Parthenon, the temples of the East, and the churches and cathedrals of the West.

Even the sacred caves of the ancients and holy places of the Australian Aborigines and Amerindians merit consideration in this context. Early man may have built dwelling places to shield himself and his family against the elements and other hostile environmental factors, but side by side with these structures of convenience he also erected others to accommodate the Rite. In his cave-dwelling days, his shamans performed their sympathetic ritual dances which were dutifully recorded on the walls of his caves — his first attempt at art. Sometimes these temples to the deity or deities were simple groves or open-air affairs; some sacred rock, for example, or a particularly meaningful stream or waterfall. These may not qualify for inclusion in the architectural category, but they are nevertheless a significant heritage of the Rite and their power to influence our lives exists to this very day, even if only as tourist attractions.

Ritual ornamentation of the kind which is shown on many old buildings, churches and castles is now being restored and the property listed. A prime example of an old ritual practice pre-served in stone may be observed in the Sheela-na-gigs or female exhibitionist figures which still adorn churches and castles in the British Isles. While their origins are still debated, they are generally believed to have been associated with the old matrist cults which were prevalent in these Isles prior to the Celtic and later invasions. Zodiacal signs are also to be found amongst the carvings on many early churches, while the ritual of laying a cornerstone (like launching a ship with a bottle of champagne) is still observed to this day.

Many of the great cathedrals were, like the Parthenon, erected according to the Golden Section Order, which is defined by one dictionary as:

> A ratio between two dimensions of a plane figure or the two divisions of a line such that the smaller is to the larger as the larger is to the sum of the two, roughly a ratio of three to five. The proportion, which is used in the fine arts, is considered particularly aesthetically pleasing. Also called 'golden mean'.

Expert Nigel Pennick adds:

> The Golden Section is a ratio which has been used in sophisticated

artwork and in sacred architecture from the period of ancient Egypt.
In ancient Egypt and Greece, there occurred an extensive use of what
the early twentieth-century geometrician Jay Hambidge dubbed
'dynamic symmetry'. Both Egyptian and Greek sacred objects and
buildings have geometries based upon the division of space attained
by the root rectangles and their derivatives. The root rectangles are
produced directly from the square by simple drawing with compasses,
and thus come into the category of classical geometry, produced
without measurement.[1]

Sacred geometry was always considered as part of the secret
knowledge of the older orders of Freemasonry, as it lent concrete
form to the overt expression of the abstract. As such, it constitutes an important aspect of arcane knowledge which is closely
connected with the Rite, and temples and places of magical
significance were erected according to its mathematical rules. I
could not hope to effect a more appropriate appraisal of its
metaphysical influence and the effect it has exerted on the magical
and mystical growth of civilization than to refer once more to
Pennick, who, in the Introduction to his book *Sacred Geometry*,
says of it:

> Geometry exists everywhere in nature: its order underlies the struc-
> ture of all things from molecules to galaxies, from the smallest virus to
> the largest whale. Despite our separation from the natural world, we
> human beings are still bounded by the natural laws of the universe.
> The unique consciously-planned artefacts of mankind have, since the
> earliest times, likewise been based upon systems of geometry. These
> systems, although initially derived from natural forms, often
> exceeded them in complexity and ingenuity, and were imbued with
> magic powers and profound psychological meaning.
>
>   Geometry, literally 'the measuring of the earth', was perhaps one of
> the earliest manifestations of nascent civilization. The fundamental
> tool which underlies all that is made by the hands of people, geometry
> developed out of an even earlier skill — the handling of measure,
> which in ancient times was considered to be a branch of magic. At that
> early period, magic, science and religion were in fact inseparable,
> being part of the corpus of skills possessed by the priesthood. The
> earliest religions of humanity were focussed upon those natural places
> at which the numinous quality of the earth could be readily felt:
> among trees, rocks, springs, in caves and high places. The function of
> the priesthood that grew up around such sites of natural sanctity was
> at first interpretative. Priests and priestesses were the specialists who
> could read meaning into auguries and oracles, storms, winds, earth-
> quakes and other manifestations of the universe's energies. The arts of

shamanism that the earliest priests practised gave way with increasing sophistication to a settled ritual priesthood that required outward symbols of the faith. No longer were unhewn boulders and isolated trees the sole requirement of a place of worship. Enclosures were laid out, demarcated as special holy places separate from the profane world. In the ritual required by this laying-out, geometry became inseparably connected with religious activity.

The harmony inherent in geometry was early recognized as the most cogent expression of a divine plan which underlies the world, a metaphysical pattern which determines the physical. This inner reality, transcendent of outer form, has remained throughout history the basis of sacred structures. Hence, it is just as valid today to construct a modern building according to the principles of sacred geometry as it was in the past in such styles as Egyptian, Classical, Romanesque, Islamic, Gothic, Renaissance or art nouveau. Proportion and harmony naturally follow the exercise of sacred geometry, which looks right because it *is* right, being linked metaphysically with the esoteric structure of matter.

Sacred geometry is inextricably linked with various mystical tenets. Perhaps the most important of these is that attributed to the alchemists' founder Hermes Trismegistus, the Thrice Great Hermes. This maxim is the fundamental 'As above, so below', or 'that which is in the lesser world (the microcosm) reflects that of the greater world or universe (the macrocosm)'. This theory of correspondences underlies all of astrology and much alchemy, geomancy and magic, where the form of the universal creation is reflected in the body and constitution of man.[2]

In the light of the aforesaid the influence of more than one ancient rite on the architecture of those structures which have come to add meaning to our historical and cultural heritage becomes blatantly obvious.

Not all rites are esoterically orientated, however. Secular rituals such as the coronation ceremony, Lord Mayor's shows, race meetings and other sporting functions, are all ritual expressions of the racial or group collective. As there are far too many of these to include in this work, I intend to concentrate on those rites we have inherited from the past which continue to exert an important psychological or mystical influence on our lives to this day.

Music is another avenue of artistic expression which certainly owes much to the Rite. The earliest recorded dance forms may be evidenced in shamanism; and anthropology and ethnology are generous with their material when it comes to the music and ritual movements of earlier races, much of which has survived to this day. The folk music of all countries also carries a thread of the Rite, as do those secular tribal practices which are inevitably performed for the benefit of visiting dignitaries from other countries.

It is with the world of classical music, however, that the Rite has effected a real alliance. More obvious examples of this harmonious partnership are to be found in Mendelssohn's incidental music *A Midsummernight's Dream*, Stravinsky's *The Rite of Spring* and Tippett's *The Midsummer Marriage*. There are, however, less overt and more potent examples of ritual power concealed within the scores of many musical works if one takes the trouble to search for them.

Both Mozart and Beethoven were Freemasons who made a point of injecting the essence of the rituals into their music. The key of E flat, for example, which has great Masonic significance, is featured in the Beethoven *Missa Solemnis*, while Mozart went so far as to unashamedly expose certain Masonic mysteries to the gaze of the musical public in his opera *The Magic Flute*, which deals with the evolutionary journey of the soul and its final Initiation into the Temple of Light.

Many people who attend this opera fail to understand the full significance of what they are being shown and conceive of the proceedings as some kind of fairy tale. And yet the archetypal characters are all present: the Three Ladies who also appear in the Norse, Greek, Teutonic and Arthurian cycles, and the three genii who counteract their moves; the evil temptress and her willing slave who does her every bidding; the prince and princess, as representing the animus and anima who, in the process of coming together, undergo a series of initiations including trial by the four elements, before they can be united in the Temple of the Sun. The simple figure of the Bird Catcher, with his propensity for chatter and his sole request for a mate, steps right out of the drama of evolution. There are strong magical undertones throughout this work, the original 'catcher of birds' being a cat, the animal held in esteem by the Order of Knights Templar on account of its connection with the Egyptian Cat Goddess Bast and her mother, the great Isis. The sistrum was sacred to both Isis and Bast, and it is this instrument and not the peal of bells that should really be used in the opera.

More familiar, however, will be the great Masses which have added so much to our musical culture. These are, thankfully, no longer performed only in the strictly religious context and may be heard in concert in most cities in the civilized world. The Mass is basically a Sacrificial Rite, and the version which has received the most musical emphasis is the Tridentine. This was in common use prior to the Second Vatican Council (1962–1965) which effected alterations in the structure and language of the original rite. It is the opinion of many, including Catholic priests and members of the Ecclesiastical Roman Catholic hierarchy, that this was a grave mistake, the power and essence of the Rite which had been built up over centuries of enactment having been altered or lessened as a result.

The old Tridentine mass was always performed in Latin which gave it a universal touch, inasmuch as one could enter a Catholic Church in any part of the world and participate in the Rite, language offering no barrier. Although I am not a Catholic, I thought this was rather a good idea as it reminded me of the universal language of symbology so beloved by the unconscious mind. When a professional classical singer, I was frequently employed as both chorister and soloist in Catholic and other churches and cathedrals. With the Catholics, however, it was always High Mass which was sung, with fully accompanying ceremonial. I was therefore afforded a first-hand opportunity to observe the Rite and the effect it had upon those present. The liturgy of Roman Catholicism can be profoundly moving at the emotional level, and therein lies a clue to that Church's hold on its members. People are wide open to auto-suggestion when their emotional centres (or their auras) are opened, as may be evidenced in those enormous gatherings of Protestant evangelical fundamentalists and charismatics, where mass abreactions are commonplace.

The Tridentine ritual resembled other magical rites in that there was a degree of role-playing, although this was sadly limited to members of the male sex. In the celebration of High Mass the role of the Celebrant was usually undertaken by the most senior ecclesiastic available, so in the normal Sunday ceremony it would fall to the parish priest, with his second in command playing the part of 'deacon' and his curate that of sub-deacon. The sub-deacon always intoned the Epistle, and the deacon the Gospel, *'In illo tempore . . . '*

As to the psychological effects of the Mass as a ritual, one particular incident comes to mind. I was one of a small group of music students who were engaged to back up the resident choir for a performance of the Palestrina *Missa Papae Marcelli*. The occasion was the visit of a Cardinal, who naturally assumed the role of Celebrant, his attendant monsignor taking on the part of deacon and the parish priest that of sub-deacon. The effect of the Cardinal's rank and bearing, both on the energies of the Rite itself and the emotions of the laity was electric, many of those present, including the menfolk, being moved to tears.

Transubstantiation, or the changing of the *substance*, constitutes the basis of the Eucharistic Rite. In other words, the normal essences of the bread and wine are removed and replaced by energies representative of the body and blood of Christ, so that those who partake of communion from these consecrated emblems also absorb something of His Nature and Beingness. A similar rite took place in the old Egyptian, Greek and Roman Iseums (Temples of Isis) when special cakes were baked and offered to the goddess in the belief that she would cast an aspect of her essence therein, so that those who latterly ate of this blessed repast would experience the touch of her divinity. Several other older rites were not dissimilar — those of Mithras, in particular, spring to mind.

Of course, if one analyses the Mass from an occult standpoint one can find all sorts of interesting pieces which originated elsewhere — the *Lavabis me* (I will wash my hands) for example, which was a regular feature in the initial cleansing invocations of many pre-Christian rites, while the old canon simply bristles with magical innuendos. It is little wonder, therefore, that the Mass tends to emphasize the liminality of those who attend the Rite.

Mircea Eliade also views the Eucharistic Rite in an Initiatory light. He comments:

> Another cult act whose structure is initiatory is the Eucharist, instituted by Jesus at the Last Supper. Through the Eucharist the Christian shares in the body and blood of the Lord. Ritual banquets were frequent in the mysteries, but the historical precedents for the Last Supper are not to be sought so far away. The Qumran texts have shown that the Essenes regarded meals taken in common as an anticipation of the Messianic Banquet. As Krister Stendhal points out, this idea is also found in the Gospels: 'Many will come from the east and west and sit at table with Abraham, Isaac and Jacob in the Kingdom of Heaven.' (Matthew 8:2). But here there is a new idea: the Christians regarded Jesus as already risen from the dead and raised to Heaven, whereas the Essenes awaited the resurrection of the Teacher of Righteousness as priestly Messiah together with the anointed of

Israel. Even more important is the fact that, for the Christians, the Eucharist depended on a historical person and a historical event (Jesus and the Last Supper), but we do not find in the Qumran texts any redemptory significance accorded to a historical person.

Thus we see in what sense primitive Christianity contained initiatory elements. On the one hand, baptism and the Eucharist sanctified the believer by radically changing his existential status. On the other hand, the sacraments separated him from the mass of the 'profane' and made him part of a community of the elect. The initiatory organization of the community was already highly developed among the Essenes. Just as the Christians called themselves saints and 'the chosen', the Essenes regarded themselves as initiates. Both were conscious that the virtue of their initiation set them apart from the rest of society.[3]

In his book *Alchemical Studies* Jung has a great deal to say concerning the psychology of the sacrifice. Commenting on the life and works of Paracelsus he states:

> We have never seriously considered the fact that for the medieval investigator the redemption of the world by God's son and the transubstantiation of the Eucharistic elements were not the last word, or rather, not the last answer to the manifold enigmas of man and his soul. If the *opus alchymicum* claimed equality with the *opus divinum* of the Mass, the reason for this was not grotesque presumption, but the fact that a vast, unknown Nature, disregarded by the external verities of the Church, was imperiously demanding recognition and acceptance.[4]

The same work contains 'The Visions of Zosimos', a commentary which Jung originally gave as a lecture at the Eranos Conference at Ascona, Switzerland, in August 1937. Of particular interest is 'The Sacrificial Act', which commences with the paragraph:

> The central image in our dream-vision shows us a kind of sacrificial act undertaken for the purpose of alchemical transformation. It is characteristic of this Rite that the priest is at once the sacrificer and the sacrificed. This important idea reached Zosimos in the form of the teachings of the 'Hebrews' (i.e., Christians). Christ was a god who sacrificed himself. An essential part of the sacrificial act is dismemberment. Zosimos must have been familiar with this motif from the Dionysian mystery-tradition. There, too, the god is the victim, who

was torn to pieces by the Titans and thrown into a cooking pot, but
whose heart was saved at the last moment by Hera.[5]

The Osirian myth would also appear to reiterate this observation.

Sacrificial rites have been around for a long time. The Old
Testament is full of them and there is scarcely a creed which
does not employ them either actually or symbolically in
some form or other. There were times (thankfully in the distant
past) when the King, as representing the most valued or highly
esteemed person in the community, was ritually sacrificed as a
gift to the gods. Sometimes this sacrifice was by way of an
appeasement; at others a request for bounty. The Sacrificial Rite
is closely allied to the phoenix theme which embodies the eternal
drama of death and resurrection. The kings and rulers eventually
became wise to the fact that their exalted position would most
certainly merit them the role of sacrificial victim, and so, after
conferring with their wise men, the idea of a substitute was
suggested and the 'symbolic sacrifice' was born. This frequently
involved the death of an animal or bird, as in the case of the Celtic
'Wren Hunt'.

The gentler creeds, however, even in earlier times eschewed
blood sacrifice, their adherents preferring to offer gifts of
produce, seeds, fruits of the earth and even works of art. Such
cults, Homer informs us, were frequently matrist, so it was
probably easier for the people to conceive of the spirit of the
Divine Mother, or some tutelary goddess, entering into food-
stuffs or domestic artefacts than the fresh blood of some poor
animal. The significance of blood as the life force has ever excited
certain chthonic elements in the make-up of mankind, and while
one can appreciate why, one cannot help asking if we will ever
grow out of this sufficiently to drop it once and for all and
acknowledge the Deity with more civilized votive offerings.

The Catholic Church, in keeping with other branches of
Christianity, is careful not to allow women to participate in its
most sacred rites although there are a few of a lesser order which
are designated for women only. I have frequently pondered on
the psychology of this irrational distinction and arrived at the
conclusion that it all results from a subconscious fear complex,
the female sensitivity posing some kind of a threat, although the
male rationale will find every logical excuse under the sun to
convince one otherwise.

Intermediaries are acknowledged in Catholicism in the form of saints, angels, apostolic personages and church doctors from the past. The Litany of the Saints, for example, lists quite a number of these. Different saintly personalities are imbued with certain qualities, the natures of which are usually described by their earthly activities. St Thomas Aquinas, a doctor and scholar, is invoked for help with examinations or difficult studies; St Anthony for lost property; St Christopher, formerly patron saint of travellers, lost his job at the Second Vatican Council, however, in company with several other old favourites. These beliefs in no way differ from the occult concept of intermediaries, and many of the angelic personages accepted by the Roman Church are identical to those used in magical practices.

The question is bound to arise as to whether the high rites of the Roman Catholic, Anglican, Greek or Russian Orthodox Churches carry more power or exert a stronger effect on the human psyche than the simpler services of the 'low' churches. The answer to this must lie in the psychology of the individual, as there are people who are easily moved by religious sentiments no matter under which banner they might choose to march. Overt emotion, as dictated by the solemnity of the occasion, may be witnessed at times in all congregations.

High Church rites are not dissimilar to those of ceremonial magic in the employment of elaborate vestments, altar pieces, incense, bells, candles and other regalia — so in this sense they do tend to engender a degree of magical power. At the other extreme, many of the evangelical, charismatic and fundamentalist churches indulge (albeit perhaps subconsciously) in instinctive rites which, as we have already discussed, could be seen to have a shamanic content.

Islam also has its rituals, most of which, in keeping with the meaning of its title, to 'submit' or 'obey', are collective rites in the Severity Code. Here again we are dealing with a religion which is totally male-orientated, so that the imbalance caused by the lack of anima emphasis is bound to take its psychological toll somewhere along the line.

As recent research has lent credence to the belief that the life force permeates all things, animism can finally be removed from the category of pure superstition; and just as we human beings can absorb energies external to our own psyches, so it is possible for amulets, icons or any objects in fact, to be supercharged either consciously or unconsciously. (One cannot help wondering where the 'transubstantiation' theory begins and ends.) Holy relics have, of course, been venerated within the religious context since the beginning of time and many miraculous occurrences accredited to their powers.

It is also possible to imbue an object with energies of a specific nature, as in the case of talismans. Talismanic rites, which are a study in themselves, are adequately covered in A E Waite's book *The Occult Sciences*. On the other hand, it is possible to effect this energizing process without having recourse to long and complicated rituals purely by the power of the mind, as long as one understands the infusion principle and the nature of the energies involved.

In the same way, symbols inherited from the past exert just as great an influence on us today. Ancient Egyptian symbology, for example, is certainly subliminally charged. I have made a special study of this, and incorporated it into a system of twenty-five cards which have become known collectively as 'Cartouche'. The word *cartouche* is of French origin and represents an oval or oblong box which contains the name of a sovereign, or a person of rank or note. As several of these symbols are keys to strong and benign archetypal contacts, my idea was to present them in a form which could easily be used by people in our present time, Letters I have received from all over the world confirm that this does indeed work, so we have much to thank the ancient Egyptians for, while also acknowledging their profound insight into the workings of the human mind. Long before I realized the subliminal significance of early Egyptian symbolism, Jung and other psychiatrists had also noted that it accorded with the universal language of the unconscious. Chalk one up for the ancient Egyptian Rite!

Who then, if anyone, actually programmed the archetypal symbology which is the silent language of the unconscious? Minds more advanced than our own, would be my reply, and as this can be taken in any number of ways according to the nature of one's persuasion, I will gracefully withdraw at that point.

Endnotes:

1. *Sacred Geometry* Nigel Pennick, p. 25.
2. *Ibid.* pp. 7-8.
3. *Rites and Symbols of Initiation* Mircea Eliade, pp. 116–117.
4. *Alchemical Studies* C G Jung, pp. 159–160.
5. *Ibid.* p. 70.

Chapter 9

RITES OF DEATH AND DEPARTURE

Death Rites have exerted a profound influence on mankind since the earliest recorded times, the actual burial itself often being preceded by the Rite of Departure, which is re-echoed in our present-day ceremony of the Last Rites. All burial or last rites are, of course, based on the concept of an afterlife, or a continuation of the conscious ego after it has been liberated from its physical shell — the nature of each rite being naturally coloured by the beliefs of those who employ it.

The ancient Egyptians, for example, were convinced that the soul of the deceased, upon death, would be escorted through the Underworld either on a special barque, or by Anubis in his role of psychopompus (conductor of the souls of the dead). It would then be required to appear before the Judgement Seat of Osiris, where the weighing of the Heart against the Feather of Truth would take place. The *Papyrus of Nebseni* gives a fine example of the famous judgement scene in which the soul of the departed is required to give forty-two statements of all the merits it has achieved, or the wrongs it did not commit during its lifetime. These were known collectively as the Negative Confession.[1]

Egyptian Funerary rites were highly complicated affairs, however, involving the chanting of long prayers and litanies which the priests undertook on behalf of the deceased. All the necessary passwords, actions and responses were vividly displayed on the walls of the tomb itself, in case the deceased might forget what to do or say and become lost in some dreadful limbo. The walls of the passages leading up to the final resting place were covered with happy scenes from everyday life, to remind the soul of what it had known and might yet experience in another dimension if it performed the After Death Rite according to the priest's instructions.

Other early Funerary rites involved the burying of all the deceased's possessions along with the corpse, the idea being that he or she would continue to live in the same way in the next world and would therefore need all the paraphernalia of rank, plus the entourage necessary to maintain the accustomed lifestyle. A royal personage or great warrior for example, would be laid to rest with all the emblems of his or her rank and power; gold, jewellery, artifacts, weapons, and in some cases even servants and animals. This custom may be observed in ritual burials as far apart as China and the British Isles.

The Tibetans, like the Egyptians, also had their own Book of the Dead, the *Bardo Thödol*, a guide for both the dead and the dying. The first part, called *Chikhai Bardo*, describes the moment of death. The second part, *Chonyid Bardo*, deals with the states which supervene immediately after death. The third part, *Sidpa Bardo*, concerns the onset of the birth instinct and pre-natal events.[2] These also involved long and complicated sets of instructions and verses to be memorized, which were designed to guarantee safe entry into the ensuing life or next incarnation.

Some Funerary rites involved the element of fire. In Scandinavia, for example, the body of the deceased was placed in a boat which was then set alight and turned out to sea, while in India corpses are still being burned publicly.

The shamans were ever aware of the journey to be undertaken by the soul after death. They therefore made a point of spending some time with the person who was dying, circumstances permitting of course, so that they could counsel them and allay their fears regarding what could be waiting for them on the 'other side'. Having close contact with the next dimension, and therefore the spirits of the ancestors, the shaman could convey messages of hope and assure the dying person that he or she would be greeted on arrival. This practice is not dissimilar to that of modern spiritualism, adherence to which is frequently adopted by those nearing the twilight of life.

Christian last rites vary with each denomination, the depth and extent of the ritual being dependent upon so-called high or low liturgical procedures. The relative of someone I know, an aetheist who had no time at all for Christianity in any form, was earnestly prayed over by a lay Methodist Preacher just prior to his death. As a result he experienced a state of ecstasy quite out of keeping with his normal cynical character and was fortunately able to mention this to those around his bedside before he took his final breath.

The Catholic Sacrament of Extreme Unction involves both Absolution and Holy Communion, the idea being to cleanse the dying person of his or her sins so that he or she will be welcomed into the Kingdom of Heaven after perhaps a short but uncomfortable stay in Purgatory. In the Catholic doctrine, if one dies in a state of mortal sin then it is hell and damnation for evermore, whereas venial sins, which are not considered in such a serious light, must be paid for in the purgatorial state. One is never quite clear (your author included) as to the demarcation line between mortal and venial sin, intention perhaps playing some role in the final judgement. The belief is, however, that the soul can be assisted out of its purgatorial sufferings through the intercession of the faithful, to which end candles are burned and prayers and novenas offered for it after it has effected its departure.

A Requiem Mass may also be said to aid the soul's adjustment to whichever state it might find itself in as a result of its sins. The Requiem Mass is much loved of classical composers, most of the 'greats' having produced one at some time or other. The music of the *Dies Irae* is usually written to portray the supposed fear and awe experienced by the soul when confronted with the hereafter and the inadequacies of the life it has just vacated, while the final invocation is by way of a request for peace, perpetual light and eternal rest for the deceased: *Requiem aeternam dona eis dominum, et lux perpetua luceat eis.*

All religions do not adopt such a gloomy view of passing into the afterlife, however. Here are two short Pagan rites which acknowledge the joy of the transition, while also recognizing the natural grief of those who have sustained the loss. The first of these comes from Saxon Wicca sources:

[Crossing the Bridge (At Death)]

Since the Seax-Wica, in company with other traditions, believe in reincarnation, death is a time for celebration rather than grief. Death signifies the completion of a learning period — the individual has 'graduated' and will be going on to other things. This, they feel, should be celebrated. Sorrow, then, is a sign of selfishness. We are sorry for *ourselves*, that we have been left behind without the love and company of one dear to us.

As with other aspects of the religion there are no hard and fast teachings on what should be done with the body at death. It was but a shell for the spirit, or soul, that inhabited it and has now gone on . . .

This rite may be performed at any of the other rituals, prior to the *Ceremony of Cakes and Ale*, or it may be done as a rite in itself, preceded by *Erecting the Temple* and followed by the *Ceremony of Cakes and Ale* and, of course, *Clearing the Temple*.

(*The Erecting the Temple* is performed. Priest and Priestess kiss. Thegn sounds a long note on the Horn.)

Thegn:	The Horn is sounded for _____ (Name of the Dead Witch) . . .
All:	So be it!
Priestess:	That today _____ (Name) is not with us, here in the Circle, saddens all. Yet let us try *not* to feel sad. For is this not a sign that he/she has fulfilled this life's work? Now is he/she free to move on. We shall meet again, fear not. And that will be a time for further celebration.
Priest:	Let us send forth our good wishes to bear him/her over the Bridge.* May he/she return at any time to be with us here.
	(All take their Seaxes and point them at a spot behind the Altar, facing the Priest and Priestess. They imagine the dead Witch standing in that spot, looking as they best remember him/her. They concentrate on sending Love, Joy, Happiness, from their bodies, along the line of the Seax, into the imagined body. This continues for a few moments. The Priestess signals the end by replacing her Seax and saying:)
Priestess:	We wish you all the Love and Happiness we may. We will never forget you: Do not you forget us. Whenever we meet here, you are always welcome.
All:	So be it!

(All now sit, and if any present wish to speak of the dead they may do so. If no one else, then at least the Priest or Priestess should speak

---

*As the Romans believed themselves ferried across the River Styx by the ferryman Charon to Hades — their land of the after-life — so the Seax-Wica believe themselves to cross a (perhaps metaphorical) Bridge to Drëun. They send forth their 'wishes', that is, 'power', not because the dead could not cross without it, but to let the dead know that they are not forgotten.[3]

reminiscently of the dead Gesith. Then shall follow the *Ceremony of Cakes and Ale*.)

Our next Funerary Rite is one of a collection of pagan rituals which has been conveniently translated into the everyday language of today:

[*Rite for the Dead*]

If one has lost a member of his or her family and desires a Pagan ceremony at the interment, this rite may be performed.

As the coffin is carried to the burying-ground, four torchbearers should accompany it — one before the pallbearers, one behind and one on either side. The priestess and priest shall walk at the head of the procession of mourners. The nearest of kin should walk with them. The priestess should carry three boughs of evergreen, and flowers; others in the procession should be encouraged to carry flowers also. The priest should have placed a net over the coffin.

As the coffin is placed in the grave the priest shall place one torchbearer at the foot of the grave, one at either side, and one behind the priest, priestess and family who all do stand at the head. When all is in readiness, the priest will hold both hands aloft and say:

We gather here now
To bid farewell to a friend
Who must travel far.
The blessings of the Goddess,
Of the God, of the Old Ones
And of good friends
Are with you
As you travel beyond.

If it is so desired by friends and family, the priestess or priest, or others, may at this time give a brief eulogy for the departed. If singing is desired it, too, should be done at this time. The priest shall say, then:

There is a reason for being here
In this world and this life.
There is a reason for leaving,
When the purposes of this life are done.
The soul must journey beyond
To pause, to rest,
To wait for those who are loved.
For the world beyond is a land
Of eternal summer, and of joy,
Far from the cares of this world,

With happiness and with youth anew.

There is a pause for a few moments. The priestess shall place the three boughs of evergreen atop the coffin, saying:

> *As the evergreen does grow and prosper*
> *Both in summer and in winter, year after year,*
> *So also does the soul continue*
> *From life to life to life . . .*
> *Growing ever stronger, wiser, and richer.*

The priest then places flowers upon the casket, saying:

> *May the servants of the gods*
> *Escort you with honor*
> *To their own land*
> *Of light, of beauty, and of joy.*
> *Blessed Be!*

All: Blessed Be!

Flowers should be strewn on and about the coffin by all present. All those who are present should retire to relax, and have a memorial dinner. All should endeavor to by degrees turn sorrow into light-heartedness and joy, for with death only the physical body is lost . . . and nothing more.

The four torches should be stuck in the ground about the grave and left there to burn out.[4]

Both the aforementioned rites assume a burial involving enclosure in the earth, but they could, no doubt, also be adapted for cremation. There probably are rites which accommodate the dispersal of the ashes or burial at sea, but these would need to include prayers to the elementary forces or tutelary deities involved, especially if they were carried out at the express wish of the deceased.

In contrast, here is an old Aztec Funerary Rite:

[*The Aztec Funerary Ritual*]

When among the Aztecs a mortal died the 'straw death', before the corpse the priest uttered these words:

Our son, thou art finished with the sufferings and fatigues of this life. It hath pleased our Lord to take thee hence, for thou hast not eternal life in this world; our existence is as a ray of the sun. He hath given thee the grace of knowing us and of associating in our common life. Now the god Mictlantecutli and the goddess Mictecaciuatl (Lord and Lady of Hell) have made thee to share their abode. We shall all follow thee, for it is our destiny, and the abode is broad enough to receive the whole world. Thou wilt be heard of no longer among us. Behold, thou art gone to the domain of darkness, where there is neither light nor window. Neither shalt thou come hither again, nor needst thou concern thyself for thy return, for thine absence is eternal. Thou dost leave thy children poor and orphaned, not knowing what will be their end nor how they will support the fatigues of this life. As for us, we shall not delay to go to join thee there where thou wilt be.

Then upon the head of the body, like another baptism, the priest let fall a few drops of water and beside it placed a bowl of water:

Lo, the water of which in this life thou hast made use; this for thy journey.

And like another Book of the Dead, in due order certain papers were laid upon the mummy-form corpse:

Lo, with this thou shalt pass the two clashing mountains . . .
With this thou shalt pass the road where the serpent awaiteth thee . . .
With this thou shalt pass the lair of the green lizard . . .
Lo, wherewith thou shalt cross the eight deserts . . .
And the eight hills . . .
And behold with what thou canst traverse the place of the winds that drive with obsidian knives.

Thus the perils of the Underworld Way were to be passed, and the soul to arrive before Mictlantecutli, whence after four years he should fare onward until, by the aid of his dog, sacrificed at his grave, he should pass over the Ninefold Stream, and thence, hound with master, enter into the eternal house of the dead, Chicomemictlan, the Ninth Hell.[5]

It is interesting to note the inclusion of the dog as the companion of the nether world. This theme is to be found in ancient religions worldwide. The Egyptian Anubis, for example, the Greek Cerberus, Merlin's Black Dog and the Eskimo tale of the goddess who married a dog and who now dwells peacefully with her husband in the subterranean regions over which they both rule. Also Sirius, which has ever exerted an influence on the development and evolution of this planet, is known as the 'Dog Star' so there could well be a secondary significance there. The psychology behind this theme would appear to be an inner acknowledgement of the fact that no one knows for sure what lies beyond the gates of death, and this has prompted the creation of a protective archetype capable of guiding one's steps safely through the vast unknown. Dogs, after all, are renowned for their skills at leading the blind in everyday life, so why not even more so in the shadowy regions beyond the grave?

There are countless other Funerary Rites and Rites of Departure from various cultures throughout the world, both past and present. However, they all appear to add up to the same thing: a preparation for transformation.

In other words, as much as the more logically orientated among us may protest at the irrational approach towards the death syndrome adopted by so many of our fellow humans, we have to admit that there must be some unconscious mechanism which automatically comes into play at or near to our time of demise. I once discussed this subject with a doctor who was an atheist and dialectical materialist. He admitted to me in confidence that on one occasion, while out sailing, he had run into a patch of fog and his craft had capsized. A particularly large wave had thrown him well clear of it and, believing himself to be alone in the waters with no one around to help, he was convinced that his end had come. He related to me quite seriously how he had 'hallucinated' to the extent that he actually looked into 'another world' in which he saw his late father, grandmother and old college professor waiting to greet him! As he reached out to them, however, he was conveniently rescued by a nearby launch which appeared out of the mist and when he came to rationalize his experience later, he 'felt quite stupid'!

Now what we have to ask ourselves is, which of the two personalities displayed by Dr X was the real one; the former — the rational materialist, or the latter — the instinctive and intuitive? The former is obviously influenced by the left hemisphere of the brain, while the latter would most certainly be a product of right cerebral activity. From stories of death and near-death related and well-documented by such scientific stalwarts as Dr Lyall Watson (*The Romeo Error, Supernature*, et al.), one is inclined to conclude that we are all subconsciously programmed to the fact that sooner or later we have to die or 'transform', there being no possible way of escape. During those times when the over-programming we have received from certain educational channels is bypassed, we perceive the truth, that which we have been unconsciously aware of all the time. As the approaching years or some terminal illness alerts us to the proximity of death, so we adjust our programming to meet the oncoming requirements. The part played by the Rite is therefore an important one in that it aids this adjustment prior to the transition, and assists the soul to adapt to the next dimension upon its arrival there.

Endnotes:

1. *Practical Egyptian Magic* Murry Hope, pp. 134–138.
2. *From Primitives to Zen* Mircea Eliade, p. 337.
3. *The Tree – the Complete Book of Saxon Witchcraft* Raymond Buckland, pp. 88–90.
4. *A Book of Pagan Rituals* (ed. Herman Slater), pp. 50–52.
5. *Ibid.* Eliade, pp. 344–345.

Part 2
Psychological Breakdown

Chapter 10

PSYCHOLOGICAL AND SOMATIC SIDE-EFFECTS

As we have already established, some rites can effect certain psychological and somatic changes. In order to understand what actually takes place, we must first examine the mechanisms involved, these being:

1. The Autonomic Nervous System
2. The Brain
3. The Mental System
4. The Endocrine System

The Autonomic Nervous System. So named because it acts autonomously and consists of two parts, the sympathetic and the parasympathetic systems, which assume opposing roles in monitoring the internal states of the body. These two systems, which are controlled from centres in the midbrain beneath the hypothalamus, regulate several bodily functions and influence much of the activity of our internal organs. Although subject to endocrine and emotional influences, they are outside the reach of direct voluntary control.

The Sympathetic Nervous System operates through two chains of ganglia which run one on each side of the vertebral column. The incoming nerves to the chain come from the twelve thoracic segments of the spinal cord. The outgoing nerves leave the chain to run in a complex network to the heart, lungs, skin, blood vessels and internal organs. When stimulated, this system releases adrenaline at its nerve endings, a portion of which enters the bloodstream to prepare the body for 'fight or flight'.

Stimulation of the sympathetic system produces the following effects: (a) increases the speed and force of the heartbeat and its output of blood; (b) raises the blood pressure; (c) constricts some blood vessels and dilates others — this results in an increased blood supply to the muscles at the cost of a reduced supply to the abdominal organs and the skin, thereby redistributing the body's blood flow as appropriate for strenuous physical activity; (d) dilates the bronchioles, making for easier access of air to the lungs; (e) dilates the pupils of the eyes; (f) causes the skin to become cold due to the reduced blood flow; (g) makes hair stand 'on end'; (h) activates sweat glands; and (i) tightens up bladder and bowel sphincters (although extremes of fear may overrule the latter and cause incontinence).

Sympathetic nervous stimulation is a costly affair in terms of energy and although well-justified in times of emergency, it is potentially damaging to the body if the system is repeatedly activated in response to emotion that is not allied to physical action. As many of the somatic phenomena of fear are the result of sympathetic nervous activity, the beta blocking drugs — which selectively block sympathetic nerve action — have become widely used to help protect the heart and blood vessels from over-stimulation, reduce high blood pressure and lessen the effects of nervous apprehension.

The Parasympathetic System issues from the brain stem and spinal cord in two sections, both of which are controlled from the centre of the midbrain. The nerve fibres of the upper section affect the cranial nerves to the eye, face and head, and most important of all (as far as the subject matter of this book is concerned) to the vagus nerve, which is sometimes called the 'nerve of fear'. The vagus is the tenth cranial nerve and its old name, the 'pneumogastric' nerve reminds us of its supply to the lungs, stomach and intestines as well as to the heart. The nerves of the lower section run from the lowest segments of the spinal cord to the pelvic organs, particularly the lower bowel, bladder, sphincter and genital organs.

Parasympathetic nerve action produces the exact opposite of sympathetic action, in that it: (a) constricts the pupils of the eyes;

(b) stimulates salivary gland secretions; (c) slows down the heart, reducing its output, and although it does not directly reduce blood pressure, it achieves this effect indirectly by inhibiting the sympathetic system (and vice versa); (d) constricts the bronchioles; (e) gently stimulates stomach and bowel activity, while activating their gland secretions; and (f) controls contraction in the rectum and bladder by relaxing the sphincters. Sexual activity involves parasympathetic stimulation to the genital organs, although orgasm and ejaculation are the result of sympathetic activity.

The autonomic nervous system, being vulnerable to emotion and immune to reason, is highly susceptible to the kind of external stimuli that can result from psychic activity, altered states of consciousness, astral projection, hypnosis, the performance of certain rites, or some of the more questionable pseudo-psychological practices which pass as alternative therapies.

The Brain. Anatomists divide the brain into three main parts: the hindbrain, the midbrain and the forebrain or cerebrum — the midbrain being the small part of the brain stem that joins the hindbrain to the forebrain. Body areas can be identified in the motor and sensory cortex of each hemisphere, the left cortex controlling the movement of the right half of the body, and vice versa. Some fundamentally important muscles, such as those which handle respiration, are under bilateral cerebral control. Stimulus of the motor cortex induces co-ordinated movement of limb or trunk (the organization of muscular activity takes place in a different area and involves the cerebellum). The role of the sensory cortex is to access, judge and compare sensory stimuli, which it achieves through co-ordination with memory. It is interesting to note that scientists have observed a connection between memory and dreams, and the limbic system which is located in the middle of the brain and governs basic activities such as self-preservation, reproduction and the expression of fear and rage.

The two hemispheres of the brain, which are joined by the *corpus callosum*, have become associated with different kinds of mental activity, such as memory, speech, writing and abstract thought. The left hemisphere, which functions in what I refer to as linear or 'inner' time, is generally concerned with logic, analytical abilities, and day to day factual matters. The right hemisphere, which governs creativity, spatial perception, abstract thought, and musical and visual appreciation, tends to function in 'outer time', or a state of timelessness; hence its strong connection with the supraphysical. (Further details of the various areas of the brain, especially as related to paranormal functions are supplied in the Glossary.)

Messages are transmitted from the brain to the body via the nervous system as fast as 328 feet (100 m) per second. The sensory nerves signal physical conditions such as pain, touch, heat and cold; the motor nerves then instruct the body to react in an appropriate manner, that is, by sweating when it is hot and shivering when it is cold. Changes in the motor nerves which control the muscles can cause many of the disorders that affect the nervous system generally.

The Mental System. This system involves those states of mind which control the personality, behaviour and feelings rather than the physical functions of the human body. These can, in turn, affect the physical system, causing what are commonly referred to as psychosomatic illnesses. (See also 'Mind' in the Glossary.)

The Endocrine System. This consists of the pituitary, adrenals, thyroid, parathyroid, ovaries and testes, plus the insulin-producing portion of the pancreas. These glands produce substances called 'hormones' which are secreted into the blood and which act to regulate, integrate and co-ordinate a wide variety of chemical processes carried out by the other tissues and organs of the body.

The pituitary gland, slightly larger than a pea and located in a small depression at the base of the skull, is composed of an anterior lobe and a posterior lobe. The hormones produced in the anterior lobe act to control the secretions of the other endocrine glands — the adrenals, thyroid, ovaries and testes — as well as the insulin-producing portion of the pancreas. The posterior lobe secretes hormones which affect the heart and circulation, the kidneys and the uterus. Because of this wide range of actions and effects, the pituitary has been termed the 'master gland'.

The adrenals are two small, triangular structures located above each kidney. They are divided into a central medulla, where the hormone adrenalin is made, and an outer zone, the cortex, where several vital hormones controlling salt and carbohydrate metabolism are produced.

The thyroid gland is located in front of and around the sides of the trachea, at the base of the neck. The hormones produced by

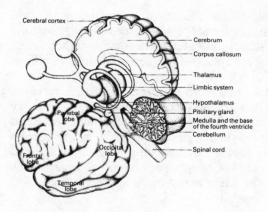

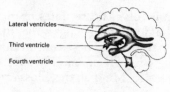

The Brain

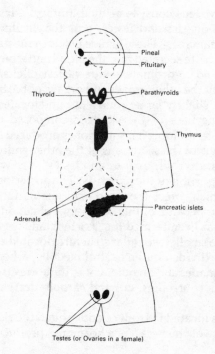

The Endocrine System

the thyroid affect the general level of activity of all the cells of the body, acting as a kind of chemical thermostat.

There are four parathyroid glands, each about the size of a split-pea, located in pairs behind the thyroid gland. Parathormone, the hormone produced by these glands, exercises control over the calcium and phosphorus of the body, maintaining the proper level of these minerals in the blood and bones.

Widely distributed through the substance of the pancreas are small groups of cells known as the Islets of Langerhans, where the hormone insulin is produced. Insulin is one of the main hormones which regulates the metabolism of sugar in the body and controls the amount of sugar in the blood.

The ovaries in the female and the testes in the male are also endocrine glands, producing hormones which control sexual development and reproduction.

Also mentioned in terms of the endocrine or ductless glands, are the thymus and pineal glands. The thymus is a ductless gland-like structure situated just behind the top of the breast bone, but unlike the other endocrines it does not act by secreting hormones. Its main role is performed in the latter part of foetal life and in early infancy when it processes lymphocytes, which it endows with the power to distinguish between 'self' and 'not self' cells and proteins. Processed lymphocytes (T lymphocytes) circulate in the lymphatic system and settle in lymphoid tissue (mainly in the lymph nodes). Their successors subsequently alert the body's immune defences against foreign proteins, tissues, and micro-organisms, and activate B lymphocytes which generate anti-bodies against foreign protein and toxins (antigens). Some lymphocytes are killer cells, a fact which I find intriguing as it would appear to indicate that the thymus programmes our future health from a very early age. In metaphysical terms it could be said to effect a blueprint or karmic pattern of our life ahead, and having done its duty it then withdraws!

The pineal gland, is a small, reddish vascular body in the posterior part of the third ventricle of the brain. Until recently, its function in Homo sapiens was uncertain, although in other animal species it is known to secrete a substance called melatonin. Recent research, however, has come to link it with the effect of light and seasonal variations on the bodily functions. Seasonal depressions are now believed to have pineal origins, while the pigment melatonin appears to be connected with skin colour. One cannot help thinking that the originators of the Seasonal

Rite, long ago, might have been aware of all this, the Rite being evocative of energies designed to effect the seasonal pineal adjustment.

The Chakras. Let us step aside from orthodox medicine for a moment and examine another, less obvious system, which is closely allied to the endocrine glands: the chakras.

The word chakra is said by some authorities to mean 'wheel', while others assure me that the correct translation is 'spinning knife'. According to Eastern arcane tradition, the chakras are small vortices or force fields which act as interconnectors between, or transformers for, those energies that pass from the subtle frequencies to the physical body. The number of these chakras is debatable — I have heard talk of eight or even nine, but the most popular figure would appear to be seven. Each chakra equates with an area in the human anatomy and with one of the endocrine glands. When the energy flow between the chakras becomes out of balance, the related endocrines will also be affected and symptoms of physical illness associated with that part of the body will start to manifest.

There is some variance of opinion as regards the chakras and their corresponding endocrines, the upper two and lower three being the most controversial. Some authorities allocate the Sahasrara chakra to the pineal gland and the Ajna to the pituitary gland — beliefs also differ concerning the relationship between the reproductive organs and the Svadisthana/Muladhara complex. (In radionics, these occupy reversed positions from those I will outline.) Although the Manipura chakra is frequently allotted to the adrenals due to the energizing qualities of adrenalin, it is also associated with the insulin-producing pancreas. The adrenal cortex and medulla behave like two separate glands — the adrenal cortex, which is essential for life, producing hydrocortisone in addition to a certain type of sex hormone. Destruction of the adrenals can result in Addison's disease, loss of salt, fall in blood pressure, the inability to react to stress, and eventually death. The following list is therefore a general one, and not related to any particular doctrine or therapeutic practice. For the benefit of those working in ritual, I have also included the colour correspondences as given by chromotherapist Mary Anderson.[1]

Closely tied in with the chakric system is the *Kundalini* concept (see also Chapter 6). The Kundalini, or Serpent Fire, which plays such an important role in Eastern mysticism, is conceived of as a

Chakra	Endocrine Gland	Area of the body	Colour
Muladhara	reproductory organs	base of spine	red
Svadisthana	pancreas (or kidneys — adrenals)	sacral or spleen	orange
Manipura	adrenals (or pancreas)	solar plexus	yellow
Anahata	thymus	breasts/heart	green
Visuddhu	thyroid/parathyroid	throat	blue
Ajna	pineal	between the eyes	indigo
Sahasrara	pituitary	top of head	violet

spiral force which is believed to lie dormant at the base of the spine in the region of the lowest chakra, until it is awakened by the process of spiritual evolution. It then begins to uncoil in serpent fashion and ascend the spinal column, sparking off each of the other chakras as it goes. The male and female energy channels of the Ida and Pingala are also believed to coil and cross each other up the spine, and some schools of belief are of the opinion that any efforts made to activate the chakras by unnatural means can upset the balance of these energies, which will, in turn, effect serious anima/animus imbalances. With the awakening of each chakra, subtle changes are believed to take place in the personality and transcendental perception. Unless this development is carefully balanced, somatic and psychological problems can result.

The rising Kundalini is considered by some schools of thought in terms of an ascending level of consciousness which can be effected and controlled by physical and mental disciplines such as meditation and yoga, while others see its ascent in terms of spiritual growth and evolution as related to one's soul age. In my own healing days I observed a close connection between the chakras, general health, and the mental state. For example, people suffering from sexual hang-ups, or physical problems involving the reproductive organs, nearly always seemed to have blockages in the lower chakras. Whether it is the blockage that causes the mental frustration or the mental attitude that causes the blockage is open to debate, but I rather suspect the latter.

Any variation in the patterns of experience normally encountered in the daily routines of everyday life can, in fact, have an effect on either the endocrine or autonomic nervous systems. Let us take an example.

Suppose you are a young mother in the habit of collecting your seven-year-old son from school. The journey to and from the school is uncomplicated, and you usually stroll easily along the road, passing the time of day with neighbours and popping into the odd shop for provisions. But one day, as you approach the school, you see a crowd of people gathered outside, two fire engines are parked there and clouds of smoke issue from the building. You race forward, the adrenalin starting to flow. Where is your child? Is he safe? What has happened? Your heart rate increases and you start to sweat with fear. For a moment all your social programming is thrown to the wind; manners are forgotten and you push your way to the front of the crowd and shout to the policeman who is standing there to tell you what has happened to your son. He calmly tells you that the children are all safe in the hall across the street, and that the fire didn't start to spread until they were well clear. Your body chemistry then undergoes its first reversal, and when you are reunited with your son in the village hall it finally returns to neutral, but not without leaving a lot of somatic debris to be dealt with later. This debris we call 'shock'.

When recovering from shock the body is required to rebalance its chemistry and until this is satisfactorily effected, the sufferer will feel ill or 'off-colour'. Should the occasion arise when we are required to act promptly in an emergency situation which might involve perhaps stepping beyond the normal limits of valour to save the life of another, the psyche may override the normal autonomic responses to the extent that, quite out of character, we act calmly and with a logical precision. Afterwards, however, the body chemistry catches up with us and we suffer what is referred to as 'delayed shock', which then has to be dealt with in the same way as an initial state of shock.

When faced with a frightening situation, the effect on the autonomic nervous system may be so pronounced that one loses temporary control of the personal functions, while women confronted with rape have been known to commence immediate menstruation, thus confirming the strong endocrine reaction to the initial mental stimulus.

Emotional reactions are not the same in everyone, however, as consultant neurophysiologist Dr Peter Nathan comments:

> People have different constitutions. Some react to different situations by increasing the activity of the parasympathetic nerves to their stomachs and bowels; others cause changes in the blood vessels of the coverings of their brains, and get migraines; others induce spasms in muscles and get headaches, backaches, pains in their chests. Others do not express states of emotion or stressful psychological conditions physically, their bodies are not used to play out the dramas of their lives. They deal with them in the outside world. They create emotional situations, they quarrel with their friends, they become involved in traffic accidents; or they get depressed or neurotic in many ways. Sometimes shocks of a psychological kind can affect the endocrine balance of the body. Some disorders result from the continual use, perhaps in an unbalanced or pathological way, of the parts of the autonomic nervous system.[2]

What then, has all this to do with the Rite? A considerable amount, in fact. Excitatory rites, for example, which are conducive to the build-up of adrenaline, are extremely dangerous, and regular participation in these can eventually activate symptoms of severe stress which, if not professionally treated, can result in mental or physical breakdown. The kind of overbreathing which accompanies hysterical outbursts, or which is sometimes deliberately induced (as in the practice of 'Rebirthing', which is popular amongst certain groups today), has the effect of washing out carbon dioxide from the blood and tissue fluid to an abnormal degree. This induces a state of alkalosis, which diminishes the level of calcium ions in the blood and therefore causes tetany — spasms of hand and leg muscles, tingling, and light-headedness. Some rituals may intentionally employ overbreathing, while in others it is an individual response to a different psychological perspective (altered state of consciousness) that may arise during the period of physiological disturbance which the overbreathing has induced. This will produce the same effect as certain hallucinogenic drugs, glue-sniffing or laughing gas.

Those participating in a rite may also find themselves exposed to situations which they are mentally unable to compute, or psychic frequencies to which their physical systems are intolerant. These will, in turn, effect changes in either the endocrine or autonomic nervous systems, depending on the nature and quality of the energies invoked or evoked. Such effects may not manifest immediately; in fact, the recipients may well feel uplifted and very happy at the time, but upon arriving home later the troubles will commence, the delayed shock having set in. I witnessed this particular phenomenon in connection with an Egyptian ritual (which I shall be dicussing in Chapter 12) and in the case of a young girl who, after attending a psychic ceremony, was subsequently found wandering around Earls Court in a daze and brought to my healing group by the local police!

Exposure to energies which are incompatible with one's own personal resonances, or to which one is unaccustomed, can result in all kinds of psychological side-effects. This is why, in olden times, there were Public or Outer Rites, in which everyone could join without fear of discomfort of any kind, and Inner Rites which were for the initiated or those who had by practice and experience accustomed themselves to faster or more elevated frequencies. This is, of course, what the Path is all about.

I have heard certain 'magical' energies described as being 'radioactive', especially those emitted from the Elemental Kingdoms. Even a minimum dose of this or any form of radioactivity can give some people headaches or nausea while others are unaffected by it. In the case of the Elemental Kingdoms, it would appear to depend on how close one is to these Essences, and whether one has earned their respect by mastering the qualities which they represent, although I am also given to understand that there is a dietary factor involved.[3] It should also be borne in mind that because a frequency, or the particular quality of an energy, does not accord with one's own personal 'vibes', that does not necessarily make it wrong or evil. It simply cautions one to become more aware of oneself and one's personal limitations, and like it or not, we all have those. Many occultists advise against mixing systems, and I hope that by the end of this book it will become obvious to the reader as to why.

Rituals can effect a subliminal programming which may or may not be correct for the recipient. While on this subject it is as well to pay heed to the question of ethics. On these I am not prepared to moralize, as they must be a question for the individual conscience. I can only repeat what has already been said: *like attracts like.* So, if your intentions are selfless, caring, kind and loving when you perform your Rite, be that of a solitary or group nature, you will attract energies of similar resonances to your own.

The Rite can uplift, instruct, discipline, illumine, and generally aid the transcendental quest. But it can also cause a whole range of imbalances, some of which will manifest as phobias, complexes, delusions, neuroses or psychoses, and others as physical problems, depending upon which chakras have been affected and the nature of the energies that have been generated or liberated. Repetitive chants and sounds, for example, can produce hypnotic effects which tend to switch the brain from left to right hemisphere activity. This automatically cuts out the reasoning mechanism, and logic gives way to feelings. Sympathetic or parasympathetic responses in the autonomic nervous system will be effected according to the qualities of the Rite: paraphronesic activities (dervish dancing, bacchic rites, ritual war dances and so on) tend to activate the former; quiet, well-disciplined practices such as Raja yoga, the latter. The hypnotic state of ecstatic frenzy effects a temporary bypassing of the function of the sensory nerves, so that sensitivity to pain is either decreased or suspended completely. Should the motor nerves also be affected, loss of physical sensation or total unconsciousness may result. Phenomena such as fire-walking, piercing the flesh with skewers, and other forms of physical abuse, are frequently inflicted during a state of trance, those concerned having no recollection of the proceedings on the following day.

Insensitivity to pain can also be caused by the secretion of endorphins within the nervous system. These chemicals attach to, and block receptors for pain in a similar way to morphine. This phenomenon does not last long, however, and usually only accommodates the duration of an emergency or crisis; during battle, when soldiers have been known to rescue comrades while they themselves are severely wounded, in a fire rescue situation, or in momentary desperation.

These are just a few of the physical manifestations of the effects of the Rite. At the mental level there are many, many more — some helpful, others not so.

Now a rite may be well-organized as far as the Leader or Celebrant is concerned, but there could be one person present whose intentions are less than generous and that one person will constitute a danger to the whole group, as they will act as a magnet for disruptive energies akin to their own thought patterns. This will tend to give rise to unconscious tensions which will immediately affect the autonomic nervous systems of those present who are of a more sensitive nature. I have experienced this personally. One suddenly becomes aware that something is wrong and yet, on the surface, all seems calm. The pulse begins to race, one starts to perspire, respiration becomes accentuated, and the adrenaline flows as it would in a typical fear situation. Here we have a perfect example of the imperceptible effecting a perceptible, somatic reaction.

One very interesting phenomenon which would appear to be experienced regularly in psychic or occult work is heat. I am the chilliest of mortals, my normal blood temperature being around 97 degrees, but when I am engaged in any form of paranormal activity my body heat rises considerably — and I am not alone in this. In fact, many people I know are obliged to extinguish fires or turn off the central heating prior to a sitting or a working. When the activity is completed the body temperature returns to normal. The clinical implication here would appear to be an increased supply of blood from the heart effected by the autonomic nervous system. Whether we are personally responsible for these phenomena in that we subconsciously create the conditions for their manifestation, or whether they are effected by external agencies present during such sessions is open to conjecture.

I have talked to both men and women who have experienced pronounced endocrinal activity following participation in a magical rite. To be fair, I have also encountered the same reaction resulting from traumatic or stress situations in everyday life — hence my earlier example of the mother and the school fire. It must be agreed, however, that while the shock which the mother underwent was not the direct result of her own actions, traumas which result from ritual participation *will* be the responsibility of the individual concerned. In other words, one does not *have* to take part in a rite if one does not wish to.

Although special effects in ritual practice, such as flashing lights, stimulatory music, drumbeats, or other psychedelia have not as yet come up for discussion, these should be seriously considered as constituting a danger area in ritual practice. A regular beat that is maintained at a pace fractionally faster than the human heartbeat has a hypnotic effect, while flashing lights are known to affect cerebral functioning. The Romans used to sit their slaves in front of a moving wheel which was placed facing the direct sunlight to see whether or not they were epileptic, the flashing of the beams between the spokes being known to induce fits. Likewise, flashing lights on police cars, fire engines or ambulances, and the intermittent light of the sun between rows of trees can produce alpha rhythms. Now these may be all very fine if one is sitting down to meditate, but when one is behind a steering wheel in fast-moving traffic they can affect one's speed of response, which could cause a serious accident. Epilepsy, like migraine, is caused by an electrical disturbance in the brain, which emphasizes the vulnerability of that organ to external stimuli. As the aforementioned obviously constitute danger factors in everyday life, without the added complication of heightened states of awareness and possible occult phenomena, they should, like any other artificial stimuli, be avoided in *all* magical workings. Migraine-type headaches may also result from some psychic practices — clairvoyance in particular — and those who suffer this side-effect are advised to leave well alone.

It must appear to my readers that I have spent too much time commenting on the negative effects of the Rite and not enough extolling its positive virtues. The repeated rhythms of gentle poetry, uplifting music, meditation and dedicated prayer can indeed do wonders, both for the physical health and the spiritual upliftment of the participant. Rites which accentuate: the functioning of the parasympathetic nervous system; diaphragmatic rather than thoracic breathing; right brain hemisphere functioning which is gentle and creative; altered states of consciousness which are controlled; alpha rhythm tranquillity which generates equilibrium — all are highly beneficial. So too are those rituals which serve to bring us in closer communion with nature, the animal and plant kingdoms and the spirit of the planet Herself.

Endnotes:

1. *Colour Healing* Mary Anderson, p. 25.
2. *The Nervous System* Peter Nathan, MD, FRCP, p. 133.
3. *Practical Celtic Magic* Murry Hope, Chapters 19 and 22.

Chapter 11

A QABALISTIC PATHWORKING

In this and each of the following five chapters we shall be examining a complete Rite and looking into the discipline or system from which it originated. The nature of the energies associated with each ritual will be analysed, and consideration given to possible psychological or somatic effects, beneficial or otherwise.

The Qabalah is usually one of the first studies to be encountered by those who enter the occult field via the 'Western Mystery Tradition', most magical practitioners of note having contributed some comment regarding its efficacy, subtlety or veiled symbolism. It therefore constitutes a basis for much of what is practised in Western magic. There is ample literature available which explains the intricacies of the system, and students of the occult have debated its origins with a scholarly zeal worthy of some senior research prize! In fact, its history is as colourful as the characters who have utilized it. A E Waite wrote of it:

> The Qabalah is responsible for, broadly speaking, all that strange tissue of symbolism and ceremonial that has made up the magic of the Middle Ages and at a later period sought to transform alchemy.[1]

The Qabalistic system itself is classified under four headings:

1. The Practical Qabalah, which covers talismanic and ceremonial magic.

2. The Dogmatic Qabalah, which consists of Qabalistic literature.

3. The Literal Qabalah, which deals with the use of letters and numbers (gematria).

4. The Unwritten Qabalah, which embodies a correct knowledge of the manner in which the symbolic systems are arranged on the Tree of Life.

The system is conveyed to the mind by means of a glyph referred to as 'The Tree of Life', or 'Otz Chiim', which consists of ten points known as 'Holy Sephiroth'. These are arranged in a particular pattern and connected by lines called the thirty-two paths of the Zepher Yetzirah or Divine Emanations. There are actually only twenty-two and not thirty-two, but the Rabbis treated the ten Sephiroth themselves as paths — which tended to confuse the student.

The twenty-two letters of the Hebrew alphabet are associated with these paths as are also the twenty-two tarot trumps sometimes referred to as the twenty-two abodes of Thoth. Also placed on the glyph are the signs of the zodiac, seven of the planets, and the four elements.

The Qabalistic Tree has four 'octaves' or 'worlds' as they are called, which are named as follows:

1. Atziluth: the archetypal world or world of emanations.

2. Briah: the world of creation, also called 'Khorsia' or the world of thrones.

3. Yetzirah: the world of formation and of angels.

4. Assiah: the world of action and of matter.

The ten Holy Sephiroth are said to have their points of contact with each of the four worlds as described.

Atziluth manifests through the ten holy names of God in Hebrew scripture; Briah through the ten mighty archangels, or the Ray of Ceremonial Magic; Yetzirah through the angelic choirs or intermediaries in spirit; and Assiah through the lower astral or etheric planes which form the background of matter.

Qabalists recognize four planes of manifestation and three of un-manifestation, or Negative Existence. The first of these is called *Ain*, Negativity; the second *Ain Soph*, the Limitless; and the third *Ain Soph Aur*, the Limitless Light.[2] These would appear

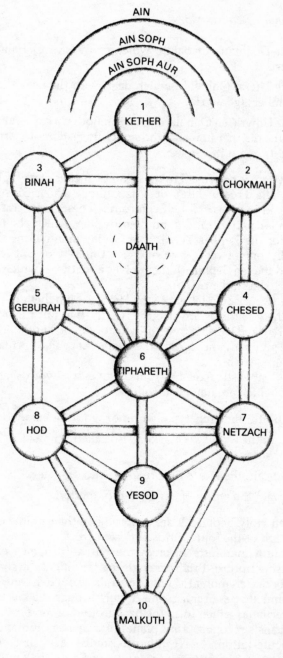

The Qabalistic Tree of Life

to be nothing more than paradigms, or algebraic-type symbols for abstract states for which there are no adequate terms of reference in our present vocabulary.

A diagram of the Tree is given opposite, and an illustration of the Three Pillars on page 114 — the left hand or Pillar of Severity is considered to be negative or feminine, the right hand or Pillar of Mercy is regarded as positive and masculine, while the Middle Pillar represents Mildness and Equilibrium. These pillars, we are told, may also be equated with the Shushumna, Ida and Pingala in the Yoga system.

I do not intend to embark on further detail concerning the nature and function of the Tree other than in the context of the Rite, as it would take several books to do it justice. However, some years ago when I was carrying out a study of the nature of the double helix or DNA (deoxyribonucleic acid) molecule which carries the hereditary factor, something which caught my eye was the similarity between the shape and structure of the molecule and the Tree. This may be evidenced in the now famous X-ray photograph of the molecule in its *B* form in Professor James D Watson's book *The Double Helix* (see page 115). The design in the molecule is, however, symmetrical — nature not having effected the adjustment to what Qabalists refer to as 'The Fall', which is said to account for the lack of symmetry in the Tree glyph. The DNA glyph is also shown lying sideways and not with the point to the top.

While on the subject of the double helix, another interesting factor comes to light which would confirm Jung's concept of the universal language of symbology. The schematic view of the molecule as shown in *The Double Helix* presents us with a perfect outline of a caduceus. Can it be pure coincidence that one aspect of the genetic life molecule resembles the Tree of Life and the other the Wand of Balance? I was so fascinated by this whole study that I wrote a long article about it which was published in a popular magazine in the early seventies.

Watson and his team were awarded the Nobel Prize for their contribution to science in the analysis of the DNA structure in 1962, and his book telling the story of the incidents leading to the discovery was published in 1968. Since then new discoveries in the field of subatomic and quantum physics have lent even more credence to the concept of a constant universal plan, the existence and language of which was known to the ancients long before the dawn of history as we know it.

SEVERITY   MILDNESS   MERCY

The Three Pillars

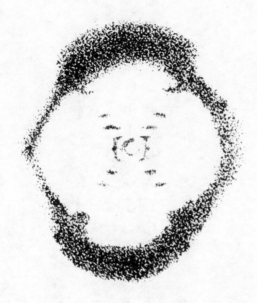

An artist's impression of the DNA molecule

One of the most popular approaches to Qabalistic magic is undoubtedly the Pathworking. Dolores Ashcroft-Nowicki, who has come to specialize in this aspect of the Rite says of it:

Pathworkings are an ancient and valid form of occult training, but it is only in recent times that they have been made available to those outside the magical fraternities. Even within the schools and Orders of the Western Tradition they have been neglected and their full value in the mental and spiritual training of students has been and still is very underrated. Nor is this entirely the fault of their teachers, for many who eagerly apprentice themselves to The Path of High Magic prefer to press on to the more glamorous ritual work until they gain a little wisdom and begin to see the value of such training.

Later in the same chapter she makes another point that is worthy of mention:

We have seen that pathworking is a term used to describe the trained use of the creative imagination and that such journeys within the mind can inform, calm, heal, relax and train the mind and its tool, the brain. We also know that it can cause events to happen in accordance

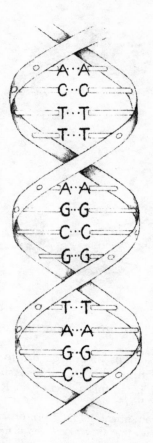

The Double Helix

with the will, not always as precisely as we could perhaps wish but, given training, time and the all-important mental discipline, an occultist can expect a reasonable amount of success. A few people can do it with no training at all and absolutely no idea of what it is or how it works. They are the success phenomena. Men and women who seem to do everything right first time off. They are in the right places at the right times with the right contacts and they have the ability to grasp the situations and make them work. Why? Because they have subconsciously caused those events and have already prepared themselves to deal with them beforehand.[3]

This statement leads me right back to the work of Professor

Caduceus

Stephen Braude, who has an unusual explanation for this type of phenomenom which is based on empirical research:

> . . . one would not expect typical PK effects to be flagrantly obvious. But once we entertain the possibility that small- or large-scale PK might insinuate itself into everyday affairs, we can see how an appeal to PK might explain phenomena or regularities that would otherwise be considered mysterious or fortuitous. Pervasive and refined PK (and ESP) could explain why some people are healthier than others, or remarkably luckier or unluckier than others. For example, it could explain why some soldiers escape serious injury, despite taking repeated heroic risks on the battlefield. It might explain why incompetent or reckless drivers continue to avoid the automotive catastrophes that befall others, and emerge unscathed from those which they initiate. It might even explain why some always seem to find parking spaces. And however distasteful the thought might be, consistent bad luck or misfortune could be an external PK analogue to psychosomatic illness. We should perhaps explore the relationship between a person's misfortune and his self-image (e.g. his degree of self-hatred), and be prepared to see him as disposing events to reinforce his image as a victimized, cursed, or unworthy individual. Of course, an even more sinister possibility is that others are the cause

of the misfortune. We should perhaps investigate the deep relationships between unlucky persons and their acquaintances and relatives
— possibly even connections with strangers whose interests conflict
with theirs. But on the brighter side, again, refined unconscious psi
might undergird the careers of those who are successful in business
and finance, and who seem to have a knack for speculation. It might
even play a role in athletics.[4]

It is interesting that Braude should single out the parking place
finders. I have firsthand experience of this myself. In fact, I taught
my husband to use this particular facility to advantage, although
we adopt the occult approach rather than the psychological one
that Braude suggests. They both boil down to exactly the same
thing, however. In other words, the human mind, working via its
own personal computer (the brain) can effect all kinds of phenomena through any of several channels of expression — religious,
humanistic or magical. In the final analysis labels are of little
consequence, the ultimate power residing within the determi-
nation and will of the individual. One is tempted to speculate that
one's karmic blueprint might well carry a PK programme which
determines its ratio in proportion to the avenues of expression
through which it is destined to manifest, in accordance with the
chosen lessons of the particular life.

To reproduce a complete set of pathworkings on the Qabalistic
Tree would take more space than this present work allows. I
therefore asked Mrs Ashcroft-Nowicki if she would kindly
recommend one in particular for inclusion and analysis. She
suggested the twentieth Path, Tiphareth to Chesed, from her
book *The Shining Paths*. This Pathworking is reproduced in full
in Appendix I.

When studying this rite the first thing that struck me was the
structured programming of the pathworking, which, if carried
out in the disciplined manner suggested, would certainly implant
a definite set of codes. This can either be viewed in the psychological context as an inurement for 'that which is expected of one',
or as a primary occult discipline which is essential to positive
mystical growth. Both approaches are harmless enough providing they do not impose further limitations on the student to the
extent that thought-patterns become stereotyped and creative
imagination stifled.

The twentieth Path, we are told, is that of the Hermit (or Wayshower) which leads from the sphere of the Sun (Tiphareth) to

that of the Master Teachers (Chesed). The eclectic nature of the true Quest is well emphasized, which allows the student some degree of inter-cosmic manoeuvrability. The main theme of the mental exercise would appear to be the rebirth or regenerative principle, the opportunity to *become* a new person, as Mrs Ashcroft-Nowicki puts it. The archetypal Hermit is essentially the loner: he or she who no longer feels the need to lean on others for mental support, but prefers to make his or her own way through the labyrinths of the mind. This would appear to be synonymous with the psychological concept of individuation which unites the anima and animus in perfect balance, thus alleviating the need for recourse to a set of preselected dogmas. The true acceptance of the state of continual change is ever symbolic of maturity, in both the material and spiritual contexts. The person who accepts the winds of change without hankering after some mythical past, or yearning for some imaginary future, is not afflicted in the same way as one who resists these conditions. 'The reed that bends in the wind . . . '

The abstract concepts of Zen Buddhism, which are frequently summed up in the phrase 'There is no logic but illogic', would also appear to be in place here. In other words, the psyche is issuing instructions to its economies (or the higher self/superconscious reprogramming the lower or conscious self) to dispense with earlier conditioning and transpose its resonances up an octave and into another key.

The visualizations are highly graphic and could possibly benefit from the artist's touch. One wonders if anyone has thought of an illustrated book of pathworkings? The figure of Gabriel is archetypally lunar, and once again the 'Malachim' referred to colour the scene in Hebrew tones. Mrs Ashcroft-Nowicki uses Raphael, whom I always believed to be the Angel of Healing and therefore aligned with Hod. There is an explanation for this, however, which will be covered in Chapter 15. The colours, robes and so on, are purely a matter of personal taste and poetic graphics.

The ensuing symbolism presents us with a castle, with classic drawbridge and courtyard. To the psychoanalyst, the castle would be the self; the crossing of the moat, as representative of the collective unconscious or watery primordial state, being symbolic of a conscious move to overcome the pull of the emotions and enter a more transcendental level of awareness — the chapel. The sign of Virgo over the door is suggestive of the anima, or receptive nature, as manifest through its triple aspects — the Instinctive, Rational and Intuitive — seen by some faiths in terms of the Triple Goddess or Maiden, Mother and Crone. The descriptions of the vigil are reminiscent of the experience undergone by Jung during a period of illness which followed a heart attack:

> Everything around me seemed enchanted. At this hour of the night the nurse brought me some food she had warmed — for only then was I able to take any, and I ate with appetite. For a time it seemed to me that she was an old Jewish woman, much older than she actually was, and that she was preparing ritual kosher dishes for me. When I looked at her, she seemed to have a blue halo around her head. I myself was, so it seemed, in the Pardes Rimmonim, the garden of pomegranates, and the wedding of Tifereth with Malchuth was taking place. Or else I was Rabbi Simon ben Jochai, whose wedding in the afterlife was being celebrated. It was the mystic marriage as it appears in the Cabbalistic tradition. I cannot tell you how wonderful it was.

> Footnote: *Pardes Rimmonim* is the title of an old Cabbalistic tract by Moses Cordovero (sixteenth century). In Cabbalistic doctrine Malchuth and Tifereth are two of the ten spheres of divine manifestation in which God emerges from his hidden state. They represent the female and male principles within the Godhead.[5]

It is interesting to observe that Jung underwent this experience during what he described as a 'period of deliriums and visions'. In other words, unlike the pathworking under consideration, it was not devised or pre-ordered, and could be described in terms of drifting into the collective unconscious and ending up on the Hebraic Ray!

To return to our pathworking. The allusion to the coldness of the pyramid is suggestive of ancient Initiation Rites, the words of Maat to the facing of the true self, and the Grail Quest to the search for the transpersonal. The King and his retinue can either be viewed in the archetypal context as aspects of the psyche or as pre-programmed symbols exclusively related to the collective unconscious of mankind, which would probably not apply as distinctly in other worlds. The parting from the place of the path, and the re-earthing, serves to anchor the psyche to the one sphere in which it can perceive a degree of logical reality, that which we refer to as the 'Now'.

The next question must be: what effect, if any, will this particular pathworking have upon those who carry it through?

The answer to this must, of course, vary with each individual. If one follows the recommended method of ascent through the Paths of the Tree, one would not commence at Tiphareth, but seek a lower rung on the ladder from which to proceed — Malkuth, for example. However, as we are dealing with Tiphareth and Chesed, one must bear in mind that these two spheres are represented astrologically as the Sun and Jupiter. Tiphareth is traditionally associated with those saviours or sacrificed gods who appear with inevitable regularity in the mythology of many of the world's religions — redemption and propitiation being an ever-recurring theme in man's transcendental quest.

Chesed as represented by Jupiter, being the first Sephira of Microprosopus or the manifested universe, is both the Instructor and Expander, and therein lies danger number one: the possibility of 'blowing a fuse'. While many may romp happily through this pathworking, absorbing its virtues and learning from its imagery, there will be some who cannot handle its radiant and expansive energies, which also imply the concretion of the abstract. While their own subconscious minds might well be capable of activating the necessary safety mechanisms, in cases where the ego over-rides the natural protective barriers of the psyche, there could be a danger of delusion or fragmentation. An electric circuit which is only wired to take so many amps will blow a fuse if overloaded; and so it is with the human mind. The brain itself is no more than a complex computer, and computers have a strange logic as anyone who works with them will know. Stay within that logical framework if you wish to avoid a 'loop'; in other words, don't take on more than you are able to compute. New concepts need new programs, and new input must be fed in the correct sequence or it will not be accepted.

The effects of a Pathworking Rite of this nature are more likely to be psychological than physiological although, as has already been emphasized, 'As above, so below!' So if you, the reader, have been indulging in a pathworking programme and your health seems to have deteriorated, ask yourself whether you are breaking mental ground for which you are not psychologically equipped. Also if you are suffering from, for example, an affliction of the thyroid gland, check your Chesed or Binah connections.

Qabalistic rites are probably among the safest to use, being Earth-orientated, although in my own experience I would say that they do not carry the same intensity of energy as some of the

Egyptian or Sothic/Siriun rituals. But then the latter can also constitute a greater source of danger, as we shall shortly see. A pathworking under the direction of an experienced occultist like Mrs Ashcroft-Nowicki can be highly instructive to the student, especially in the recognition of the archetypes and the effect these may have on the psyche, and as such it would appear to constitute an effective method for stepping out into uncharted areas of consciousness.

Closely allied to the Qabalistic Rite is the sacred science of gematria, described as:

> The science by which the letters of a word are converted into their numerical equivalent. Once one knows the numerical value of the word one may then find a correspondence between the original word and another with the same numerical value. In this way, a number can become representative of several ideas, all of which are thought of as being interpretative of each other.[6]

Gematria, however, would appear to embody several early magical systems having Greek, Gnostic and Eastern connotations. Those wishing to employ it in Qabalistic rites are referred to *Gematria* by Frederick Bligh Bond, ARIBA, and Thomas Simcox Leigh, Vicar of St Austell. (*Gematria* is published by the Research into Lost Knowledge Organisation and distributed by Thorsons Publishing Group.)

As a final comment, I would like to refer to the three pillars of Severity, Mildness and Mercy. It is interesting to note that Severity is considered as feminine and Mercy as masculine, which on the surface would appear to deny the real-life condition. The message must surely be that until we can temper Severity with the intuition and gentleness of the anima and Mercy with the strength and purpose of the animus we are not likely to manage the ascent up the central path of Mildness — which, interestingly enough, requires a command of the material level (Malkuth), an understanding of the principle of fluidity or constant state of flux (Yesod), the sacrifice of the self (Tiphareth), and the descent through the Abyss of Daath before the Crown of Kether can be achieved (Samadhi).

Endnotes:

1. *The Occult Sciences* A E Waite. pp. 181–187.

2. *The Mystical Qabalah* Dion Fortune, p. 32.
3. *Highways of the Mind* Dolores Ashcroft-Nowicki, pp. 17 and 21.
4. *The Limits of Influence* Stephen E Braude, pp. 278-279.
5. *Memories, Dreams and Reflections* C G Jung, p. 274.
6. *Kabbalah* Charles Poncé, p. 170.

Chapter 12

AN ANCIENT EGYPTIAN RITE

History readily attests to the antiquity of Egyptian religious and magical rites, while certain arcane schools of belief see these as reaching back even further into the pre-Flood days of Atlantis and Mu.

Much of the information regarding the beliefs and rites of the ancient Egyptians has filtered down to us through the oral mystery traditions rather than those somewhat impressive sets of hieroglyphics which appear on stelae and tombs. However, the *Book of the Dead* does supply us with some idea of the Egyptian concept of the hereafter and, of course, the god-forms or archetypal energies which were venerated in those times.

The *Book of the Dead* was to the ancient Egyptians rather like the Bible is to the Evangelical religions of today, the inference being that it was taken rather too literally in later times. The very title itself is a misnomer, its literal translation being 'Chapters of the Coming Forth by Day'. The sole reason for referring to it as the *Book of the Dead* would appear to be the preoccupation of its contents with death and the life thereafter.

Only fragments of this work, in the form that it has come down to us, are actually concerned with magical ritual, whereas whole portions of it do refer to the state of the soul that has passed over and its trials and existences in other dimensions. Several scholars, notably A E Wallis Budge, are of the opinion that the work is *not* of Egyptian origin. The Heliopolitan or First Recension, which was in use during the fourth and fifth dynasties, can be dated back to before 3500 BC, and there is evidence from the copying that the scribes of the time were dealing with texts which were so remote as to make their job extremely difficult, if not impossible. Thus many original meanings were lost and inaccuracies inevitably crept in.

The ancient Egyptians were, however, an eminently practical people who were sensible enough not to leave details of their most sacred religious rites and truths scattered around for the profane to abuse. This is no doubt why the inner secrets of Egyptian magic are seldom, if ever, to be found amongst the generous supply of hieroglyphics which have been discovered on the walls of tombs and sarcophagi, coffins and funeral stelae, papyri and amulets.

The majority of the texts of the *Book of the Dead* are translations of hieroglyphics found at Thebes, and taken together they are generally termed the Theban Recension of the *Book of the Dead* — the Theban dating, which was roughly 1600 to 900 BC, being by no means the earliest. Much of what we are presented with must therefore be questioned, as I doubt that it bears much resemblance to the beliefs and rites of the earlier dynasties. As this aspect of Egyptology is a study in itself, I would recommend those seeking greater detail to the works of scholars such as Budge, Flinders Petrie or Maspero, although in my *Practical Egyptian Magic* I have covered it briefly in relation to the religious and magical beliefs of the ancient Egyptians.

The ritual I have chosen for analysis in this chapter (which is given in full in Appendix II), combines passages from the *Book of the Dead* with knowledge of the Egyptian system obtained from other sources, both historical and esoteric. Together these form a distinctive Rite, the theme of which is 'Twinning', or 'Polarizing' or 'Balancing'. The ancient Egyptians conceived of the twin soul, or two halves of the one spirit, although their allusions to the Ra/Osiris and Osiris/Horus relationships are also thought by some to relate to reincarnations or aspects of the same Essence appearing in different periods of time. I do not see how this could be applied in some of the cases, however: the Twin Lion Gods, for example.

My own impression is that the Priesthood carried an oral arcane tradition which had been handed down to them since the days of Atlantis or earlier, and that this indicated a knowledge of the dual nature of the soul. To refer to this in the modern psychological terms of anima and animus would be too simplistic, as I rather tend to feel that the real explanation is somewhat deeper.

There is a school of thought which designates the soul or psyche as consisting of two halves, each of which spends the learning process of its evolutionary struggle searching for the other. When both have finally absorbed their lessons they then reunite, at which point they are in a state of development and understanding far beyond our present comprehension. Either way, from both an occult and psychological standpoint, the balancing of the two aspects within the self is a good thing, as it aids spiritual growth, makes for a well-integrated personality and opens wide the door to individuation.

Each of the *dramatis personae* featured in the Rite represents a clear-cut archetype which is doubly accentuated in: (a) the initial roles: Celebrant, Scribe, Protector, Scryer and Keeper; and (b) the god-forms themselves. If, however, a number in excess of the basic five is used the additional roles will stand on the god-form alone. As this is a Twinning Rite, the deities must be paired, which requires an even number of participants.

The Rite is dedicated to Bast, whom Herodotus informs us was the daughter of Isis and Osiris and twin sister of Horus, which secret information was imparted to him by the Egyptian priests themselves. Bast is traditionally represented with a cat's head and a woman's body, and her sacred instrument is the sistrum.

The sistrum is a very important instrument in the Egyptian Rite. Shaped like an ankh, it has four bars suspended across the loop head (later representations often appear with only three but these are incorrect). The bars fits loosely in their sockets so that when the instrument is shaken, using the lower part as a handle, the four loose bars act as a sort of rattle. Small bells or cymbals are often strung across the bars in tambourine style. Plutarch mentions it as a magical instrument of great importance to the Egyptians:

1. The sistrum . . . also shows that existent things must be shaken up . . . and never have cessation from impulse, but as it were be awakened up and agitated when they fall asleep and die away.

2. For they say they turn aside and beat off Typhon (Set) with sistra — signifying that when corruption binds nature fast and brings her to a stand, [then] generation frees her and raises her from death by means of motion.

3. Now the sistrum has a curved top, and its arch contains the four [things] that are shaken. For the part of the cosmos which is subject to generation and corruption, is circumscribed by the sphere of the

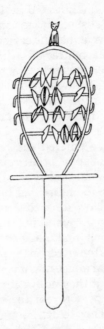

Sistrum

moon, and all [things] in it are moved and changed by the four elements — fire and earth and water and air.

4. And on the arch of the sistrum, at the top, they put the metal figure of a cat with a human face, and at the bottom, below the shaken things, the face sometimes of Isis and sometimes of Nephthys, — symbolizing by the faces generation and consummation (for these are the change and motions of the elements), and by the cat the moon, on account of the variable nature, night habits and fecundity of the beast.[1]

The sistrum has connections with three goddesses: Isis, Hathor and Bast. However, as it is more often than not depicted with the figure of a cat, its closest association is with the Cat Goddess. One legend has it that it was a gift to Bast from her divine mother Isis, its allocation to Hathor only occurring in much later times. Full explanations of this, and other Egyptian ceremonial paraphernalia are given with illustrations in my aforementioned book on Egyptian Magic, together with the rules for laying out an Egyptian Rite, the colours and ritual impedimenta associated with each god-form.

The predominant colour for a Bast ritual is always turquoise. A quick reference to the list of chakras and related endocrines given in Chapter 10 will reveal that the essence of this colour focuses on the heart and throat centres — while the subsidiary colour, orange, relates to the pancreas or sacral area of the body, which helps to keep the Rite well-earthed. The pyramid shape arrangement, being made up of two triangles, is connected with the concept of time on the one hand, and protection and conservation on the other.

Now that we have entered the realms of ceremonial High Magic, the question of appropriate robes and special names needs to be dealt with. Colour and symbols are highly important, so care should be taken to ensure that both the temple and participants are decorated or adorned according to the nature and deities appropriate to the working. This book is not, however, an instruction manual in ritual magic, and the point is only raised insofar as it concerns the effect on the psyche. Those participating in a Rite of ceremonial magic might well feel psychically safer and more mentally alert if they adopt a mode of dress and a special identity or magical persona for the occasion. The only danger here might be a tendency to depersonalize, but providing the Rite is correctly observed and the Celebrant or Lodge Leader knows what he or she is doing, there should be no problem. After all, ceremonial robes and titles have been employed in worship as far back as history takes us and no doubt further, and they are used in churches, cathedrals, mosques, synagogues and temples throughout the world to this day.

The first conjuration is to the spirits of the four elements, using the Egyptian references associated with the canopic jars in the ancient funerary rites.* The hymn of praise to Ra is from the

---

*According to some authorities, Duamutef was assigned the eastern point of the compass, Quesnuf the west, Imseti the south, and Hapi the north. However, as I see no occult connection between these elementary assignments and the pictorial representations, I have chosen to disregard them, and based by allocations on graphic appearance and generally accepted magical tradition. Quebsnuf, for example, being hawk-headed and therefore associated with the bird kingdoms, naturally resonates with the element of air rather than that of water. Using the traditional correspondences, I have therefore allocated the four sons of Horus as follows:

Earth	North	(Ape-headed Hapi)
Fire	South	(Jackal-headed Duamutef)
Air	East	(Hawk-headed Quebsnuf)
Water	West	(Human-headed Imseti)

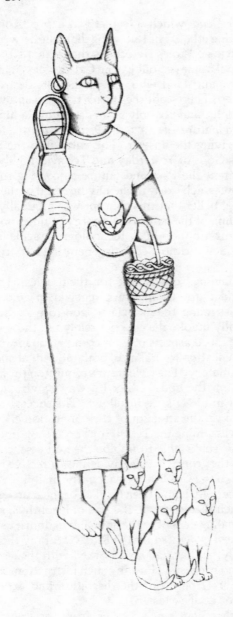

The Cat Goddess, Bast

Book of the Dead, which, I feel, effects a direct connection with the originating ethos. The following dialogue between the participants in their god-roles, re-echoes the eternal struggle between good and evil as played out by the Cat Goddess in her role as the agent of the Sun God who, on his behalf, destroyed the evil serpent Apep. This establishes Bast's position as a vehicle for the Forces of Light, and possibly as an aspect of Ra himself.

The twin nature of Ra and Osiris is then questioned, the Celebrant giving the answer. The entry into the drama of the Twin Lions Gods of Yesterday and Today is highly meaningful. They represent the Past and Future as coming together in the Eternal Now which exists in the Divine Mind of the Creator. It is my personal belief that this concept was originally based on an understanding of the nature and energy of time, possessed by an earlier civilization of high technological achievement which became extinct, its knowledge degenerating into tribal myth and folklore.

The remaining roles speak for themselves. They represent Wisdom and Truth; Change and Renewal; Harmony and Movement. In assuming the associated god-forms, the participants automatically invoke the energies related to those virtues, while stimulating allied aspects of their own personalities.

Bast's invocation for balance, both individual and worldwide, is self-explanatory. The Celebrant's request to the Scryer for any message from the gods, either by way of visualization, clairvoyance or in direct speech follows. The success of this request will depend on the strength of the connection effected between whoever is assuming the Tefnut (or Scryer) role and the extent to which he or she is able to imbibe the god essence and relay its message to the group. If a clearly defined directive is given, it will then be up to the Celebrant to act accordingly.

As an example, I have been the Celebrant at an Egyptian Lodge Rite in which the Scryer, in the role of Nephthys, suggested that help and healing be sent to the animal kingdoms, using the power that had been generated by the Rite. Naturally this was effected immediately, and as I always worked with the sistrum anyway there was no problem. How any such instructions are carried out will, of course, be up to the discretion and experience of the Celebrant or Lodge Master.

The final prayer is again taken from the *Book of the Dead*. Personally, I would have preferred not to include these old prayers as they are somewhat cumbersome, but I know that there are many to whom they afford great comfort and security.

The Protector's final prayer and closing is, of course, by way of a mini-banishing Rite, which ensures that nothing untoward is left around and that the ritually-invoked/evoked energies are restored to their correct level in the cosmic scheme of things.

That is the Rite as seen through the eyes of the occultist, although in reality it is not quite so simple. For one thing, the assumption is that those participating are in harmony with themselves, the ancient Egyptian Ray, and the other members of the group — but true life seldom runs so smoothly. Mrs Ashcroft-Nowicki reminds her pupils of the dangers of stepping into what she refers to as the 'High Magic' of ancient Egypt, and warns of the risks it carries for the unwary and the profane. She also tells us that too hasty a withdrawal from the energies of the Egyptian Rite can cause migraine.[2]

This is highly confirmatory of my own experiences and one reason why I ceased to practise it with any form of group or Lodge. On one occasion in the past when I did so, two of those who participated were adversely affected, both physically and mentally. One young man claimed to be afflicted with severe headaches; while the other, a woman in her thirties, became illogically frightened and uncomfortable. Both exhibited temporary symptoms of paranoia. As any psychiatrist will confirm, paranoiac fears are usually totally irrational, and although other members of the Lodge tried hard to reason with the two concerned they had both managed to convince themselves that the forces of ancient Egypt were conspiring with another Lodge member and me to make their lives uncomfortable. This was entirely delusory, which the young man later admitted. I have never seen the woman since, however. None of the other members suffered even the slightest upset or discomfort, either psychological or somatic.

One additional point. Prior to forming this Lodge I expressed great doubts concerning the mental suitablity of the two people in question, but was persuaded by a male member of the group that I was being unreasonable. One just has an instinct about these things, however.

What actually happened in this instance? As I see it now (the aforementioned incident took place twelve years ago and I hope I have learned something since then), the two people concerned were obviously incompatible with the Egyptian Ray, and I should have effected some simple Egyptian working with them before-hand which would have had roughly the same effect that the Roman wheel had on epileptics. Those who wish to employ the rites of Egyptiana should first ensure that they are completely at home with its frequencies or they will only hurt themselves, as well as causing a lot of unnecessary unpleasantness to those with whom they work.

The magical energies of ancient Egypt are not entirely of this planet, being a hybrid of Atlantean, indigenous African, and inter-cosmic resonances. Those who find they are not comfortable with this mixture are advised to stay with the more Earth-orientated systems such as the Christian or Qabalistic in the Western tradition, or those remnants of the old Mu-an faiths that are still to be encountered in parts of Asia and the Indian subcontinent.

We are back to the problem of energies generated by a Rite which are incompatible with the personal frequency or karmic background of the participant. In the aforementioned cases within my own group, the mental balance was affected and also the Ajna chakra, while both people concerned, it seems, found themselves frightened for no logical reason. This tells us that their autonomic nervous systems were adversely stimulated by the resonances to the extent that they were unable to over-programme the side-effects with left hemisphere logic. Fortunately, at the time, I was on friendly terms with more than one occultist of experience and repute so I was able to have my own role thoroughly checked for defects, and fortunately emerged with a clean bill of health!

What effects will the Twinning Ritual have upon those who use it? Provided that the participants are in harmony with the Egyptian tradition, the Rite is carried out in sincerity and the intentions of those present are orientated towards selflessness and the Light of Truth, then they should only benefit from it spiritually, psychologically and somatically. If on the other hand there is disharmony, then discordant energies will be attracted by the Rite. Jealousy, petty annoyances, greed, self-interest: all of these thought-patterns will attract essences and energies of like nature which will manifest through the Egyptian Ray in an intensity commensurate with the personal powers of those present. This will come rather hard on the genuinely sincere, and the Celebrant in particular, unless he or she is fortunate enough to have a more powerful Protector who can prevent them from entering the space of the Rite in the first place. This is difficult, however, when the 'enemy has contacts within the castle'!

Egyptian Magic strongly effects the Visuddhu and Ajna chakras, those who are suited to it being well endowed with 'the sight' plus the ability to talk about or teach what is disclosed to them from the inner planes. Conversely, if its energies are incompatible with those of the recipient, he or she is likely to become self-deluded and illogically talkative about it. Anyone who experiences the slightest discomfort with Egyptian god-forms is advised to stay clear of them. Sekhmet, in particular, like all the archetypes of elimination and regeneration, is a difficult energy to handle, especially for those people who are not naturally adaptable or who have few or no planets in mutable signs in their birth charts. A thorough study of the nature of these archetypes should therefore be effected before one indulges in the Rite.

Personally, I am thoroughly at home in Egyptiana, but in all fairness there are other systems in which I am not comfortable. We are what we are, and there is no shame in admitting to our limitations. Better to do that than end up with the magical, psychological and somatic side-effects of an overblown ego, and I think that by now we all have a fair idea as to what those are likely to be.

Endnotes:

1. *Thrice Greatest Hermes* G R S Mead, Vol. I, p. 344.
2. *First Steps in Ritual* Dolores Ashcroft-Nowicki, pp. 31–32.

Chapter 13

A TRIPLE GODDESS RITE AND AN OLD CELTIC HEALING RITE

Celestial phenomena were featured in most of the early rites, moon worship in particular being essentially part of what the Greeks referred to as the 'Silver Age', or time when the social and religious codes were built around a matrist system. Remnants of these creeds and their associated rituals are to be found in modern Wicca, albeit modified somewhat by cultural overlays and adapted to the psychological needs of the age. The phases of the moon appeared to the early peoples as a three-aspected goddess, and rites and prayers to this triple divinity were abundant in those times. The one I have chosen to feature in the Appendix is by Wiccans Janet and Stewart Farrar, who have employed the god-forms and symbology from the Irish Celtic mythological cycle.[1]

A Triple Goddess Rite (see Appendix III):

The three aspects of the Goddess — Maiden, Mother and Crone — were deeply entrenched in many of the older religions that flourished throughout Europe prior to the advent of Christianity. The Farrars designate them as representing enchantment, inception, expansion — ripeness, fulfilment, stability — wisdom, retrenchment and repose. When it comes to relating this tripleaspected archetype to the human psychological economy, how-ever, I find this categorization too simplistic, and prefer to think of it in terms of the instinctive, practical and intuitive aspects as expressed through the anima. I appreciate, however, that this classification is too broad to merit serious consideration and obviously demands a more detailed analysis. The maternal aspect, for example, is seen by many in either the libidinous or emotional context, whereas the age period it encompasses is frequently the most practical or down to earth part of our life. In youth we tend to follow our natural instincts, while the fullness of maturity inclines us to the kind of deeper thought and introspec-tion which allow the unconscious better facility for the sub-mission of its esoteric message.

The moon, however, is not representative of the feminine principle in all beliefs. Among the Germanic peoples the sun and solar power were distinctly feminine, as represented by the goddesses Sol and Sunna, and the Rune ⚡ , while the moon was masculine. Dominant sun goddesses were also to be found in Egypt, while among the deities of the Eskimos, Japanese and Khasis of India the solar goddesses were accompanied by subor-dinate brothers who symbolized the moon.[2]

The Greeks were also careful to emphasize through their archetypes that the anima or animus can dominate in either male or female, as may be evidenced in the warrior qualities of Athene or the feminine appearance of Dionysus. (See *Practical Greek Magic*).

This particular rite is in the Wiccan tradition, so how it is likely to react on the participants will depend on the skill and know-ledge of the High Priestess and High Priest who are leading it. If there is genuine devotion to the Principle and a harmony of purpose among those taking part, the effects will be nothing if not beneficial. Third Degree Wiccans are usually very careful about whom they allow into their covens, so any words of caution would tend to apply to those who are less qualified or outside the Craft who might be tempted to make use of this rite.

An Old Celtic Healing Rite (See Appendix IV):

Here we have a classic example of a hindbrain rite in which the instinctive awareness patterns and the connection with the collec-tive unconscious are accentuated. Rites of this nature are probably among the safest to execute unless, of course, one has become so religiously indoctrinated against the order of nature that one has a phobia about all things natural and creates one's own demons as a result. For those who are eco-conscious, who love animals, flowers, streams, stones and all natural phenomena, this is the sort of rite to go for as it moves gracefully with the cosmic stream, acknowledging the life force in all things and entering into that flow on an equal footing, without the inflated egotism which has become so much a part of the thinking patterns of Homo sapiens.

The Rite, which has animistic undertones, is a fine example of sympathetic magic. It is also watery and lunar by nature, and therefore closely associated with the emotional nature of man. Even the Bible acknowledged the allocation of the elemental qualities. They appear in Ezekiel's vision, and are later seen as representing the four mystic beings of Christian tradition as portrayed by the Evangelists: The Ox — Earth (Luke), the Eagle —Air (John), the Lion — Fire (Mark) and The Man — Water (Matthew).

This is not, therefore, an Intellectual Rite, but rather one which can be handled comfortably by those preferring the more simple approach to the transcendental. Yet, in its own way it is just as powerful as some of the more complicated rituals which many people feel to be somewhat beyond them, and although they may not qualify as High Magic in the esoteric sense, rites of this kind can often prove more effective at the practical level than those which deal in more exalted frequencies.

The reason for the suggested time of 7 p.m. for working is the third, or hidden aspect of the Goddess, while the number seven is always sacred. The effigies or figurines need not necessarily be carved from oak; other woods will do if there is nothing else, but plastics of any kind or man-made fibres should be avoided at all cost. It is also advisable to select a spot where one is not likely to be disturbed by passers-by who might mistake the intentions of the Rite. The semi-circle is, of course, lunar and the water edge is not open as many might suppose, as the motion of the watery element itself constitutes the protective closing.

The washing away of guilt (sin) appears in many religions, in some of the older faiths the inference being a karmic one. I have also included in the invocation a request for world healing as it is my belief, and that of many others, that we all share in the malaise from which this planet is suffering as a result of centuries of mishandling and abuse on the part of mankind.

Both Tree Magic and Water Magic were greatly favoured by the Celtic peoples. Irish writer Frank Delaney, appearing in a recent BBC television series entitled *The Celts*, based on his book of the same name, showed some samples of little figurines which had been cast into the water by our ancestors, but had become caught up in some side pool or reeds and consequently never made their way down to the mighty ocean.

The psychological or somatic effects of this rite are likely to be minimal, if indeed there are any at all. The invocation to the gods of healing at the primitive level could have the effect of drawing those very energies into the participants themselves, so that any sickness from which they might be suffering could well be alleviated. Close contacts with nature are usually beneficial to mankind, provided illogical superstitions have not been adopted, either during childhood or subsequently, which could include false fears of such things as 'ghoulies', 'ghosties', the darkness itself or things that are supposed to go 'bump' in the night! If you are of a nervous disposition, the advice would therefore be to keep the performance of this Rite to the lighter evenings.

Primitive peoples were, of course, afraid of the supernatural to the extent that they endeavoured to placate it (or the energies it represented) as far as possible. If, therefore, you are working from the hindbrain, you may well revert to the primitive instinct and experience a sense of foreboding should the wind suddenly whip up. But remember, our ancestors sustained a healthy relationship with these forces by working through and *with* them. So when in doubt, simply unite with the essences of nature and become as one with them. After all, no one in their right mind ever harms their own!

A tasty repast and a warm drink never goes amiss after a ritual of this kind. The Rites of Sympathetic Magic are nothing if not practical and earthy, and if you can raise a song between you all, then so much the better. The old Celtic gods were ever impressed by the sound of the human voice.

Endnotes:

1. *The Witches' Way* Janet and Stewart Farrar, pp. 72–76.
2. *Practical Celtic Magic* Murry Hope, p. 83.

Chapter 14

TWO PROTECTION RITES

As protection would appear to be one of the most important issues in both solitary and group rituals, I have chosen two completely contrasting rites, both of which can be used either in the solitary or group context. The first of these is a short Catholic ritual which I acquired under rather unusual circumstances.

Some years ago an acquaintance of mine, who was reading medicine at London University with a view to specializing in psychiatry, professed an interest in the psychic and allied subjects, anticipating that he might encounter these in his future career. Although he was not a practising Catholic, his grandparents had been of that persuasion and he was anxious to ascertain the Catholic attitude towards the occult. To this end, he had made an appointment with a Jesuit priest, and knowing my interest in these matters, he asked if I would kindly accompany him for moral support.

Upon our arrival we were graciously received by an elderly Jesuit in a threadbare cassock, who took us to a small, dark anteroom for the interview. I can recall quite distinctly that there was an enormous chair in the corner and for one moment I almost thought I saw the ghost of some grim-faced cleric eyeing me suspiciously. Our approach to the subject was strictly clinical and related purely to the effects of metaphysical studies and practices on mental health. Our host's response, however, was quite the opposite; in fact, he got quite carried away. Realizing he had a captive audience, he embarked on a series of tales, which I can recall to this day, about his supernatural adventures, as a missionary in India and Africa.

At least an hour and a half elapsed before he ended his saga with the strong admonition that we, as 'vulnerable young people', should be careful to protect ourselves against 'the forces of evil', because in the world of the mentally sick we were likely to encounter devils galore! As we were about to take our leave he went over to a large, dusty, old cabinet which stood in one corner, opened one of its many drawers and withdrew a crumpled piece of paper, yellow with age, which he pressed into my hand. It had been given to him he claimed, by a saintly old monsignor who had 'specialized in that kind of thing' and it had never failed him, devils come what may. As he knew it by heart and had no further use for it, he begged me to take it. This all took place some thirty years ago and the paper has long since disintegrated, but I did manage to type it out for my files and it is reproduced in Appendix V.

This is a typical Protection Rite in the Emotional Code, wherein the supplicant invokes the angelic forces and sacred figures of Roman Catholicism to aid his or her quest for safety. It does, however, assume an acceptance of personalized evil forces counterbalanced by the angelic forces of Light. In other words, a dualism is implied. This tells us a little about the psychology of those who are likely to employ it, in that they are probably subconsciously aware of their own personal vulnerabilities, or those of their id. Now this is fair enough as few of us, if any, are without some quirk or imbalance in our lower nature, and as long as the fear of personalized evil forces does not become an obsession, there is no inherent danger.

Most writers who specialize in these subjects receive a regular bombardment of letters and pleas from people who feel they are being 'occultly attacked'. A large proportion of these poor sufferers would be better served by the psychiatric profession, for while one acknowledges the power of thought and the effects it can have, adverse resonances can only afflict one if they are accepted and absorbed. In other words, people who feel they are being 'attacked' tend to fantasize and magnify the situation until it assumes the aura of a magical assault. Few allegations of occult assault are ever what is claimed of them, and simply consist of one or two personality clashes which have been blown out of all proportion and conveniently hung on the magical peg. Of course, there is always the exception to the rule, and my advice to those who have no desire to tangle with their fellow practitioners of the art is to stay clear of them in the first place.

To return to our Rite: this is quite a legitimate form of protection for those who adhere to the Catholic faith or who follow the path of Christian Angelology. After all, several of the great sages of the past had recourse to this kind of working, and the Society of Jesus is known to specialize in exorcism.

Our next Protection Rite stands in stark contrast to the former. This is a Severity Code banishment ritual in the Norse/Teutonic Tradition known as the Hammer Rite which is reproduced in Appendix VI.[1]

The runic system is one in which I have always felt very comfortable in spite of its coding, but then we all take on lives at some point in our evolutionary journey in which either the anima or animus predominate. A lot of ladies I know do not feel happy in Severity Code Rites, and I cannot say that I blame them. However, we must each find our own way along the transcendental path, and there are bound to be times when we allot ourselves tasks which may appear unnecessarily harsh in the light of the gentler or more intuitive modes.

Rune Magic carries a strong discipline, and because it is animus-orientated it can provide an excellent balancing factor for those women who are a little too timid for their own good. The converse applies, of course, with men who are too 'macho', who would be best advised to look to Celtica or Wicca for ritual expression.

How to construct your Rune Wand, and which Runes to use, is all laid out in Edred Thorsson's book *Futhark*. There are also several other Rune books available for those who would like to work Rune Magic, while avoiding its more severe applications.

The equilateral cross is always a safe symbol of protection, although I would advise the use of an alternative colour to red at number 4. This would depend on the ritual intention, as Thorsson points out, but when in doubt amethyst shades are always acceptable to the Norse or Teutonic deities, Odin in particular.

Apart from the likelihood of over-energizing the solar plexus centre (the colour red could have this effect on some people), this simple rite is fairly straightforward, and as long as the psychological possibilities which I have already mentioned are borne in mind, it should not constitute a danger to those who use it. Rune Magic is very close to the Earth Plane, and therefore extremely effective in practical, everyday life. Provided one observes its disciplines, the chances of becoming psychologically fragmented or neurotic are less, perhaps, than with certain other systems, although Severity Codes can err on the side of the obsessive.

Endnotes:

1. *Futhark* Edred Thorsson, pp. 90–93.

Chapter 15

AN ENOCHIAN ANGELIC RITE

As the Angelic Kingdoms would appear to play an important role in both religious and magical practices, it is befitting that its associated rites should come under scrutiny in this work. There is a wide diversity of opinion, both religious and secular, regarding the nature and function of angels, or whether in fact they exist at all. The psychologist would no doubt view them either as aspects of the psyche, the products of an over-active imagination, or archetypal vestiges of earlier beliefs which have assumed a reality in the collective unconscious. These criteria would, of course, apply to all preternatural personae.

My own knowledge of the Angelic Kingdoms goes back to my days at boarding school when I was taught to recite the names of the nine Choirs of Angels during compulsory religious studies. Different angels, we children were told, performed different functions in the universal scheme of things, and to complicate matters even further not all angels were nice, there were also the 'baddies' to contend with.

It is not difficult to conceive of the existence of intermediaries — the idea of there being nothing else in the universe except God and man, with some sort of space or void in between, tending to strain the credulity. I was later to discover that the angelic list of my childhood was the pseudo-Dionysian, as given in *Celestial Hierarchy*, and in St Thomas Aquinas' *Summa Theologica*. The early Christian fathers and doctors were generous with their sprinklings of angelic nomenclatures, many of which found their

way into the labyrinths of medieval magic. Those seemingly
never-ending lists of the emissaries of light and darkness, which
the Hermetic or Qabalistic Initiate was required to learn in days
past, are also reminiscent of the many names and passwords
chanted by the Egyptian Priests for the benefit of the departed.

There are angels for each day of the week, each month of the
year, even each hour of the day, and the efficacy of angelic magic,
we are told, is reliant to a degree upon the right name being
spoken or written at the right time and in the correct order.

The existence of a celestial hierarchy is by no means limited to
the Jewish and Christian faiths. Islam also has its angels — Israfel,
the 'burning one' of Arab folklore, for example, was companion
to Mohammed for the period of three years, during which he
initiated him into the role of prophet. Once this task was
completed, Gabriel then took over to guide Mohammed through
his ministry.

The nine Orders or Choirs of Angels, according to Dionysius
the Areopagite, are: Seraphim, Cherubim, Thrones, Dominations, Principalities, Powers, Virtues, Archangels and Angels.
The Seraphim, Virtues and Powers are designated as of a fiery
nature; the Cherubim are terrestrial; the Thrones and Archangels
are aquatic; and the Principalities and Dominations are aerial.

Another group of angels, the Archons (rulers), are identified
with the Aeons of Gnosticism, although there is more than one
opinion regarding their function. Gershom Scolem's definition of
an Archon is simply 'great angel', while they are also seen as
ruling over nations.[1] In occultism they are often viewed as
primordial planetary spirits, while the Manicheans saw them as
'Sons of Dark who swallowed the bright elements of Primal
Man'. The *Papyri Graecae Magicae* name five Archons: Uriel,
Michael, Raphael, Gabriel and Shamuil. Gnosticism designates
seven: Jaldabaoth, Jao, Sabaoth, Adonaios, Astanphaios,
Ailoaios and Oraios.[2] Many of today's metaphysicians believe
them to be associated with the creation of universes through the
fusion and fission of atoms, in which capacity the ancient
Egyptians would no doubt have referred to them as the Servants
of Ptah, the Master Builder.

Another angelic group which often makes its appearance in
magical workings is the Watchers, also known as the Grigori.
According to the *Book of Jubilees*, the Watchers are the sons of
God (Genesis 6) sent from heaven to instruct the children of men.
They 'fell' after they descended to earth and cohabited with the

daughters of men, for which act they were condemned (according to the legend) and became the 'fallen angels'. Not all of them took the wrong path, however. The good ones who remained reside in the Fifth Heaven, while the evil Watchers dwell either in the Third Heaven or in Hell![3]

Damaskios enumerates six Orders in the Chaldean Categories as follows:

1. Gods that are purely mind.
2. The Gods subsisting before all subordinate dominion.
3. Rulers.
4. Archangels.
5. Divinities that are confined to no specific space or service.
6. Divinities or geniuses with specific duties.

Scutellius lists nine classes of Spiritual Beings:

1. Invisible Gods.
2. Visible Gods of the Sky.
3. Archangels.
4. Angels.
5. Demons.
6. Leaders.
7. Princes.
8. Heroes or demi-Gods.
9. Souls.

(The term 'demon' is used in this context to indicate a 'genie' or 'deva' spirit, and not a denizen of the realms of darkness.)

St Paul, in his Epistle to the Ephesians, offers the following list:

1. Princes.
2. Authorities.
3. Kosmokrators or Princes of the Cosmos.
4. Spiritual essences in the super-celestial spheres.[4]

Much confusion has occurred, however, as a result of the many variations in the lists of duties or rulerships assigned to different angels by earlier authorities. For example, Al-Barceloni gives Raphael as the angel of the Sun and Michael as ruler of Mercury, whereas according to Barrett these are reversed, Michael being the solar ruler and Raphael, traditionally a Healing Angel, the genius of Mercury. For the days of the week, Michael is listed for Sunday, Gabriel for Monday, Camael for Tuesday, Raphael for Wednesday, Sachiel for Thursday, Anael for Friday and Caffiel for Saturday. Gabriel alone, as the Angel of the Moon, appears consistent in all listings.[5]

Works such as *The Heptarchia Mystica* of John Dee, and the Denning and Phillips *Enochian Texts* with their complex system of names, gematria and diagrams, are guaranteed to daunt all but the keenest pursuant of the Path — which was probably what they were designed to do anyway. On the subject of conjurations (and with the aforegoing in mind, no doubt), Denning and Phillips tell us:

> There is frequently perceptible a certain idiom of address to inhabitants of the non-material spheres: a lyricism rather than any fixed system or metre of Rhyme, a tradition persistent because effective in circumstances and surroundings widely differing; from the medieval Exorcism of Benedictbeuern —
>
> *Omnes genus demoniorum*
> *Cecorum, claudorum, sive confusorum,*
> *Attendite iussum meorum*
> *Et vocationem verborum* —
>
> to extant invocations such as, 'Come in a form intelligible to us and not terrible to us: and in speech that is known to us and manifest to us, be your true answers addressed to us'. Many series of 'barbarous names', too, show similarly broken rhythms and assonances, which thereby, even apart from their other associations, build up a strangely compelling atmosphere when vibrated with power.[6]

In view of the immense amount of literature available on Angelic Rites, much of which forms part of the liturgy or theurgia of several established systems of magical belief, the selection of a suitable Rite for analysis proved to be something of a problem. After much deliberation, however, I selected one which I felt to be fairly representative of Angelic Rites generally: 'How to Invoke the Angels and Archangels', an Invocatory Rite in the Intellectual Code. Due to the complexity of the Enochian Magical System I am only able to give a broad outline of this Rite in

Appendix VII, as the provision of the full lists of angelic nomenclatures and the numerous tables required would fill several chapters.

However, let us analyse its likely effects on those who might see fit to employ it. In the first instance, the memorization and the attention to the diagrams calls for a degree of left hemisphere activity which would not be conducive to alpha patterns. In other words, the Rite itself has an intellectual rather than mystical content as far as the participants are concerned, and is not of a relaxing nature. In a working of this kind, which is not of the role-playing variety, close attention to detail is absolutely essential. Considered in terms of a mental discipline it could prove beneficial in that few of us these days really know how to focus our minds on any one thing for very long. The question is, what is one likely to conjure up? The object of the exercise would appear to be to attract the attention, presence or good offices of an Angelic Essence, who is obliged by the nature of the Rite to attend upon the demands of the caller!

This strains my credulity somewhat. I do not doubt that many who invoke, let us say, the Archangel Michael, will find themselves tuned into *something*, but Michael himself? Well, that would surely depend on the power and effectiveness of the magus. No doubt if there is an angelic being somewhere in the universe who answers to that name, and he is the great archangel we are led to believe, he will have an army of lesser angels and devas who carry out his every command. Since like attracts like, it would seem logical to assume that the invoker will get exactly what or whom he or she deserves, no more and no less.

Of course, this principle could be said to apply with any ritual. We may call upon Isis in an Egyptian Rite and not attract the energies of the Goddess herself. Likewise we may invoke Gabriel or Raphael and, if we are of an unkind, cruel or nasty disposition, we will most certainly end up with an essence of equal undesirability rather than a Being of Light. Now that may simply be our own id, or some chthonic aspect of ourselves that chooses to utilize the energy of the Rite as a convenience through which to surface, but either way it is not calculated to do us any good.

One of the dangers in a Rite of this kind, especially if it is carried out in the name of one of the orthodox religions, such as Christianity or Judaism, is the assumption that the collective power of that body is (a) an 'open sesame' to any magical command that might take one's fancy, and (b) because one adheres to that particular faith, one is automatically immune from any undesirable side-effects. The sad truth is that in the final analysis we are each responsible for our own actions. So, if our ethics leave something to be desired, and we elect to invoke Gabriel in the name of the Roman Catholic Church, we will still only get what we deserve. Whereas, although we are not perfect (who is?), if our intentions are pure and selfless and we strive to do the best we can with our lives, we will attract kindly, helpful essences no matter which banner we fly when we make our ritual request.

Endnotes:

1. *A Dictionary of Angels* Gustav Davidson, p. 347.
2. *Ibid.* p. 52.
3. *Ibid.* p. 349.
4. *The Egyptian Mysteries* Iamblichos, p. 81.
5. *Op. cit.* Davidson, p. 343.
6. *The Magical Philosophy, Book V, Mysteria Magica* Melita Denning and Osborne Phillips, p. 165.

Chapter 16

RITUAL WORLD TOUR

Attitudes and approaches to the Rite worldwide would appear to differ considerably, although if one looks deeper there is undoubtedly an underlying thread that connects them all. I have, therefore, selected some samples from across the globe which I feel will serve to highlight mankind's psychological need for ritual enactment. Some of these are Public Rites; others are of a Solitary nature. As there has so far been a tendency towards a preponderance of rituals from the Western Tradition, the Eastern schools are well represented in the following examples.

A SHINTO HARVEST FESTIVAL ('Norito')

The Praying for Harvest, or Toshigohi no Matsuri, was celebrated on the 4th day of the 2nd month of each year, at the capital in the Zhingikuwan or Office for the Worship of the Shinto Gods, and in the provinces by the chiefs of the local administration. At the Zhingikuwan there were assembled the Ministers of State, the functionaries of that office, the priests and priestesses of 573 temples, containing 737 shrines, which were kept up at the expense of the Mikado's treasury, while the governors of the provinces superintended in the districts under their administration the performance of rites in honour of 2,395 other shrines.

The service began at twenty minutes to seven, The officials of the Zhingikuwan arranged the offering on the tables and below them, according to the rank of the shrines for which they were intended. The final preparations being now complete, the ministers of state, the virgin priestesses and the priests of the temples to which the offerings were sent by the Mikado entered in succession, and took the places severally assigned to them. The horses which formed part of the offerings were next brought in from the Mikado's stable, and all the congregation drew near, while the reader recited or read the *norito*. This reader was a member of the priestly family or tribe of Nakatomi, who traced their descent back to Amenokoyane, one of the principal advisers attached to the sun-goddess' grandchild when he first descended on earth.

The earliest account of the proceedings on these occasions is contained in the Record of the year 871. The harvest ritual translated by Satow contains thirteen prayers and invocations. The text reproduced below is the third in that series:

He says: 'I declare in the present of the sovran gods of the HARVEST. If the sovran gods will bestow in many-bundled ears and in luxuriant ears the late-ripening harvest which they will bestow, the late-ripening harvest which will be produced by the dripping of foam from the arms and by drawing the mud together between the opposing thighs, then I will fulfil their praises by setting-up the first fruits in a thousand ears and many hundred ears, raising high the beer jars, filling and ranging-in-rows the bellies of the beer jars, *I will present them* (i.e. *the first fruits*) in juice and in ear. As to things which grow in the great-field-plain — sweet herbs and bitter herbs; as to things which dwell in the blue-sea plain — things wide of fin and things narrow of fin, down to the weeds of the offing and weeds of the shore: and as to CLOTHES — with bright cloth, glittering cloth, soft cloth and coarse cloth will I fulfil praises. And having furnished a white horse, a white boar and a white cock, and the various kinds of things in the presence of the sovran god of the HARVEST, I fulfil his praises by *setting up* the great OFFERINGS of the sovran GRANDCHILD'S augustness.[1]

It is interesting to note the similarity between this Rite and its Western equivalents. Harvest festivals are celebrated in Christian churches throughout the world to this day, as well as in many other creeds. This Rite comes under the Seasonal category, with Instinctive undertones. As with the Eleusinia it may only be executed by certain priestly families, and yet it is Public in that the general populace are invited to the ceremony. The solar nature of the Goddess is worth noting, for, as mentioned earlier, not all feminine aspects of the deity are lunar.

We move to the Americas for our next Rite, an old Aztec ceremony, which would appear to have much in common with modern baptism.

THE AZTEC CEREMONIAL BATHING OF THE NEWBORN

The Priest addresses the Goddess of the flowing Waters:

'Merciful lady Chalchiuhtlicue, thy servant here present is come
unto this world, sent by our father and mother, Ometecutli and
Omeciuatl, who reside at the ninth heaven. We know not what gifts
he bringeth; we know not what hath been assigned to him from the
beginning of the world, nor with what lot he cometh enveloped. We
know not if this lot be good or bad, or to what end he will be followed
by ill fortune. We know not what faults or defects he may inherit from
his father or mother. Behold him between thy hands! Wash him and
deliver him from impurities as thou knowest should be, for he is
confided to thy power. Cleanse him of the contamination he hath
received from his parents; let the water take away the soil and the
stain, and let him be freed from all taint. May it please thee, O
Goddess, that his heart and his life be purified, that he may dwell in
this world in peace and wisdom. May this water take away all ills, for
which this babe is put into thy hands, thou who are mother and sister
of the gods, and who alone art worthy to possess it and to give it, to
wash from him the evils which he beareth from before the beginning
of the world. Deign to do this that we ask, now that the child is in thy
presence.'[2]

Birth Rites can usually be classified as Social/Instinctive in that
they have existed since the earliest of times and have always
formed part of the social structure of society. The allusion to
some kind of original or inherited guilt will no doubt catch the
attention of many.

From Hinduism we are reminded of the necessity for the
purification and dedication of the body.

PERSONAL WORSHIP: PŪJĀ

The Purification and Dedication of the Body:

The dedication of the body of the worshipper to the deity is a
necessary prelude to ceremonial worship. In this rite the worshipper
purifies and consecrates each part of his person that he may become fit
to appear before a god.

No man should worship a deity so long as he himself has not
become a deity. If the repetition of sacred utterances is performed
without previous dedication of the parts of the body to the different
deities, this repetition of *mantras* is demoniacal and without useful
effect. To worship a deity, a man must become the Self of that deity
through dedication, breath control, and concentration until his body
becomes the deity's abode. (*Gāndharva Tantra.*)

1. The first step is the purification of the worshipper and of the accessories of worship.

The purification of the person of the worshipper consists in bathing. The purification-of-the-subtle-elements (*bhuta shuddhi*) of the body is done through breath control and through the dedication of the six main parts of the body to the six deities to which they correspond. After this the other forms of dedication are performed.

2. The purification of the place of worship is done by cleaning it carefully, adorning it with an auspicious ornamentation made of powders of five colours, placing a seat and a canopy, using incense, light, flowers, garlands, etc. All this must be done by the worshipper himself.

3. Purification of the ritual utterances, the *mantras*, is done by repeating the syllables which compose them in the regular order and then in the reverse order.

4. Purification of the accessories is done by sprinkling water consecrated with the basic *mantra* and the weapon-*mantra* (*astra-mantra*, i.e., the sound *phat*) and then displaying the cow-gesture (*dhenu-mudrā*).

5. Purification of the deity is done by placing the image on an altar invoking the presence of the deity through its secret *mantra* and the life-giving breathing-*mantra* (*prāna-mantra*), bathing the image three times while reciting the basic *mantra*, then adorning it with garments and jewels. After this an offering of incense and light should be made. (*Kulārnava Tantra.*)

Removing Obstacles:

The worshiper should bow with respect to the deities of the doors, first at the eastern door of the house of worship, then, successively at the southern door, the western door, and the northern door. After this he should bow to his chosen deity present in the form of its *yantra*. (*Nigama-kalpalatā 14.*)

If the sanctuary has only one door, the worship of the deities of the three other directions should be done mentally. The sacrificial house should be entered with the right foot. (*Shivārcana Candrikā*); with the left foot if it is a left-hand sacrifice.

The worshipper should remove obstacles of celestial origin by the godly look (looking with wide-open, unblinking eyes). Obstacles of the intermediary world are removed with the help of water consecrated with the *astra-mantra*. Terrestrial obstacles are avoided by doing three taps with the heel of the right foot. (*Shāmbavī Tantra.*)

The Praise of the Deity:

Just as gold is freed from its dross only by fire and acquires its shining appearance from heat, so the mind of a living being, cleansed from the filfth of his actions and his desires through his love for me, is transformed into my transcendent likeness. The mind is purified through the hearing and uttering of sacred hymns in my praise. (*Bhāgavata Purāna 11, 14, 25.*)

The glorification of a deity is something different from meaningless praise. The *Brhad-devatā* (1, 6) says: 'The praise of something consists in the utterance of its name, the description of its shape, the proclaiming of its deeds, the mention of its family.

We cannot know a thing without knowing its merits, its qualities. All knowledge or science is based on a form of praise. A dictionary is but the praise of words. The works of science are filled with glorification. Everything which is an object of knowledge is as such a deity and is glorified in the Scripture that deals with it. (Vijayānanda Tripāthī, Devatā tattva, *Sanmārga, III,* 1942.)

Meditation:

Meditation is of two kinds, gross and subtle. In the subtle form meditation is done on the 'body of sounds', that is, the *mantra* of the deity. In the gross form meditation is on one image with hands and feet . . . The suprasensory can seldom be reached by the mind; hence one should concentrate on the gross form. (*Yāmala Tantra.*)

The worshipper should engage in meditation, gradually concentrating his mind on all the parts of the body of his chosen deity, one after another, from the feet to the head. He can thus acquire such an intense state of concentration that during his undisturbed meditation the whole body of the chosen deity will appear to his mind's eye as an indivisible form. In the way the meditation on the deity in its formal aspect will gradually become profound and steady. (Siva Candra Vidyārnava Bhattāchārya, *Principles of Tantra.*)

Japa, the Repetition of Mantras:

Japa, as the repetition of a mantra, has been compared to the action of a man shaking a sleeper to wake him up.

Once the image of the chosen deity has been formed in the mind by concentration, the seed-mantra should be repeated, withdrawing the mind from all other thoughts . . . Japa is of three kinds, audible, articulate but inaudible, and mental . . . Japa concentration by this means is perfected, the consciousness of the worshipper is transferred to the deity represented by the utterance and he ceases to have an individuality distinct from that of the deity. (Baradā Kantha Majumdar, *Principles of Tantra.*)[3]

This rite is really self-explanatory in that its aim to purify the body and banish unwanted energies from the scene is made quite clear. There would also appear to be a combination of codes in the strict discipline observed on the one hand and the contemplative nature of the yogic practices on the other, while the eventual unification with the deity is suggestive of the ecstatic state.

The Solitary Rite, although originally more favoured in the East, is slowly gaining popularity in the West. The necessity for sitting in silence, without deliberately *seeking* enlightenment, is emphasized in the following Buddhic observation from the Japanese tradition.

SITTING AND THE KŌAN

In the pursuit of the Way (Buddhism) the prime essential is sitting (*zazen*) . . . By reflecting upon various public cases (*Kōan*) and dialogues of the patriarchs, one may perhaps get the sense of them but it will only result in one's being led astray from the way of the Buddha, our founder. Just to pass the time in sitting straight, without any thought of acquisition, without any sense of achieving enlightenment — that is the way of the Founder. It is true that our predecessors recommended both the *kōan* and sitting, but it was the sitting that they particularly insisted upon. There have been some who attained their enlightenment through the test of the *kōan*, but the true cause of their enlightenment was the merit and effectiveness of sitting. Truly the merit lies in the sitting.[4]

Silence is a state which some of us are well able to handle but others are not, in the same way that a still mind comes hard to the busy Westerner. I am a 'silence' person myself, in that I can happily live without the noisy accompaniment of television, radio and the general background roar of modern urban life. However, I do find it stressful if I am subjected to the latter for any period of time. Conversely, many people I know are totally unable to handle silence and the lack of background sound causes them to feel insecure or cut off from the rest of the world. Sensory deprivation experiences would therefore cause considerable stress to such people, whereas the Zen Buddhist — or those among us who can think more clearly when our auditory senses are not under continual bombardment — would probably find it highly beneficial. The pros and cons of this kind of meditative rite would therefore depend on the personality type, although it could no doubt prove therapeutic to the highly nervous or hyperactive.

The Australian Aborigines can certainly be counted among the modern custodians of the Primitive Rite and their ceremonies, which incorporate both Recollective and Instinctive Rites, represent genuine survivals from prehistoric times. As these are unlikely to effect the modern reader, in that they are essentially part of a closely knit tribal system, a psychological comment is unnecessary. They obviously work well for the aborigines who seem able to employ them for both practical and spiritual/ ancestral contacts.

RAIN-MAKING

It is universally believed by the tribes of the Karamundi nation, of the Darling River, that rain can be brought down by the following ceremony. A vein in the arm of one of the men is opened and the blood allowed to drop onto a piece of hollow bark until there is a little pool. Into this is put a quantity of gypsum, ground fine, and stirred until it has the consistency of a thick paste. A number of hairs are pulled out of the man's beard and mixed up with this paste, which is then placed between two pieces of bark and put under the surface of the water in some river or lagoon, and kept there by means of pointed stakes driven into the ground. When the mixture is all dissolved away, the blackfellows say that a great cloud will come, bringing rain. From the time that this ceremony takes place until the rain comes, the men are tabooed from their wives, or the charm will be spoiled, and the old men say that if this prohibition were properly respected, rain would come every time that it is done. In a time of drought, when rain is badly wanted, the whole tribe meets and performs this ceremony.[5]

THE CORROBOREE

The corroboree, or ceremonial gathering and dance of the Australian Aborigine, is employed for a variety of ceremonial purposes. As the Aborigines endowed every major topographical feature with mystical or mythological significance, it is little wonder that Ayers Rock, for example, came to feature so strongly in their rites. The fact that they were not given to erecting monuments for religious purposes emphasizes their use of natural landmarks for magical ritual occasions. The Aborigine concern for the dead is expressed through a series of complex rites which may go on for weeks. These rituals are designed to safeguard the living from the anger of the spirit of the deceased, and to ensure the safe return of the dead person's spirit by way of the sky, a waterhole, or an offshore island to the spirit home or totemic centre. Aborigine expert Dr Josephine Flood tells us:

Totemism is the religious system in which people are identified with a particular animal, plant, or natural feature, which, like themselves, in the Dreamtime was endowed with life essence by creation ancestors. These totems are used to distinguish groupings in society and can be influenced by ceremonies conducted by their human 'kinsmen', such as ceremonies to maintain the natural species. Some totemic increase sights [sic] are marked by arrangements, not of stones, but of bones. Thus, in the Northern Territory a striking star-shaped pile of crocodile bones was found on the floor of Sleisbeck rock shelter, and a group of emu skulls was found at Ingaladdi. These are rare examples of evidence of ceremonial life surviving in the archaeological record.

Elaborate drawings in the sand or earth were part of the ritual in many ceremonies. On the ceremonial or bora grounds of New South Wales large, elaborate mythological figures as much as 10 metres long were often moulded in earth or clay in the centre of the bora ring. Such sand or earth sculptures were not meant to last. The most usual form of bora ground was two circles surrounded by low earth banks, linked by a connecting path, which was also marked by earth banks. One of the bora signs was a 'public place', where women and children participated in the corroborees and preliminary ceremonies. At the climax of ceremonies like these, the young men to be initiated would be led away by tribal elders to the second, secret ring for the further rituals of initiation, which might involve tooth avulsion or circumcision.

The trunks of trees surrounding the ritual site were often carved, and ceremonial grounds are on record as being surrounded by from between six and a hundred and twenty trees carved with massive geometric designs. Carved trees, also called dendroglyphs, have designs carved into the wood, whereas a tree from which bark has simply been removed to make a container, shield, canoe, or other artefact is known as a scarred tree. Carved trees were associated particularly with burial or initiation sites; initiation trees tend to have carvings only in the bark, whereas the engravings on the burial trees are in the inner sapwood or heartwood.[6]

The similarity between these ritual tree associations and later tree cults which surfaced in Europe is worth noting. It would appear that the tree has always held shamanic connotations that have continually surfaced over the period of man's development on this planet, being coloured and ritualized by each respective culture or ethos.

THE GREAT HA KAHUNA PRAYER RITE

Personally I find this one of the most interesting rites to come through to us from the past, as there would appear to be very little difference, if any, between its self-programming concept and those advocated by certain modern schools of psychology and self-help. The correct use of the *Ha* prayer Rite enabled the ancient Kahunas to contact some indefinable personal force or energy field to answer prayers and perform miracles.

Max Freedom Long, who made an in-depth study of Huna, tells us that the secret lay in the Kahunas, ability to enlist the aid of their own higher selves. This rite can therefore be used by anyone who is sincerely seeking self-mastery, and who follows the format prescribed by the Kahunas.

According to Huna, man has three 'bodies': the Low Self, the Middle Self and the High Self. Each of these bodies has its own supply of *mana*, or vital force. The Hawaiians saw the Low Self as operating with simple *mana*, the Middle Self using *mana-mana*, which was of a faster or more powerful frequency, and the High Self employing *mana-loa*, a form of supercharged energy that could effect truly miraculous changes. *Mana* could probably be equated with PK, physical magnetism or left brain hemisphere activity; *mana-mana* with mental energies, right brain workings and the subconscious mind; and *mana-loa* with the supercon- scious, or those unseen frequencies that are of a metaphysical or preternatural nature — or alternatively one's mature soul frag- ments in some other, more exalted time zone. The Low Self *mana*, which is created from the intake of food, comes under the domain of will; *mana-mana* is the substance of thought with all that this implies; while *mana-loa* is of such force that it can effect imme- diate results such as instantaneous healing.

According to Huna psychology, the conscious or Low Self is unable to approach the High Self directly — this can only be achieved by way of the subconscious (Middle Self) and this procedure involves the use of the Rite. Here then are the four steps in their correct ritual order, but before proceeding with Step 1, the prayer or request should be carefully chosen and the image firmly set in the mind:

Step 1: The Middle Self must instruct the Low Self to make some extra *mana*. In other words, sit quietly and concentrate on a build-up of energy (which suggests that this is not a ritual to be undertaken when one is physically tired). Four deep breaths should then be inhaled and exhaled very slowly. Each of these four breaths has a number and name. The first is called *kahi*, which means 'to cut or split'. Although this is sometimes seen as referring to an actual cutting, such as a circumcision, I see it more as a severance from the Low Self or material world. The second breath, *elua*, means 'to combine', 'to give assistance', 'to adhere' — also 'to call or invite attention', in this case that of the High Self. *Kolu* is the third breath, 'to accomplish', 'to fulfil', 'to bring to pass'; and *kauna* or *ha*, the fourth, means 'to breathe strongly' and 'a trough for running water'. Once the vital *mana* has been aroused it must then be held in readiness for the next step.

Step 2: This step in the rite is executed by the Low Self under orders from the Middle Self. With the accumulated *mana* that has been built up by the Low Self, the Middle Self reaches up through the *aka* cord until it makes a successful contact with the High Self.

Step 3: When this contact has been established, the Low Self releases its store of *mana* as a kind of sacrificial gift to the High Self, and this vital force can then be utilized by the High Self to answer the prayer.

Step 4: As the *mana* is sent up the *aka* cord, it must be accompanied by a mental image of whatever is being prayed for. It is essential that the High Self be given an absolutely clear picture of the request; constantly fluctuating images will not work, nor will the Rite be effective if it is simply used as an occasional convenience without discipline or pattern of execution. Consistency is therefore a *must*.

Some authorities suggest that repetition be adopted as a fifth step, as this also constitutes an essential ingredient to the effective working of the Rite.

As the Low Self *mana* would appear to play such an important role in this Rite in that the High Self does not appear to be able to effect much without it, numerous methods have been devised, both by the Kahunas themselves and subsequent students of their art, to built it up. Brad Steiger tells us that the late Baron Eugene Ferson — who was well known for his lectures on magnetism and its effects — advocated his pupils to stand in the 'star position', feet wide apart, arms extended at the sides level with shoulders and repeat the affirmation: 'The universal life force is flowing through me now . . . I feel it!'[7]

However, as it would appear that the *mana* simply acts as an earthing agent for the superior energies of the superconscious, the more logical approach would be to ensure that a healthy state of balance is maintained between the three selves. Of course, the sacrificial idea could contain a grain of truth in that we may well need to give of our lower selves, or transmute our baser energies, in order to achieve some modicum of transcendental control or achievement.

My interest in Huna was first aroused some three years ago, but I left it to one side with the intention of indulging in a more in-depth study when time permitted. The fires of curiosity have recently been rekindled and I have practised this Rite with some success, although the inherent dangers in its practice did surface. The first of these lies in undertaking the Rite when one is physically low, because if the offering of the Low Self *mana* is of insufficient quantity or quality to enable the High Self to execute the request, the vital energies become so depleted as to produce temporary symptoms of complete exhaustion. If, on the other hand, the Low Self *mana* is plentiful but the substance of the request is not beneficial for the person concerned, the request will be granted, but it will backfire in some way.

The third problem with this Rite lies in the visualization process, which evokes an analogy between the reception of the message by the High Self and literal computer logic. For example, if one visualizes oneself opening a letter containing, let us say, some good news regarding the health of a member of the family, unless the picture is absolutely specific the result will not be as desired. During one transmission, prior to projecting the proposed image, I found myself thinking about a certain dear friend whom I had not heard from recently. The next post brought me a very welcome, long and serious letter from her, but not the content of the request I had actually sent to my High or Transpersonal Self.

I have encountered the problem of visualization techniques misfiring in the past, and there is a classic true story which was told to me many years ago to illustrate this point. It concerned a lady who continually visualized a pink cheque for two hundred and fifty pounds — a giant sum in those days — and who finally received it just as she had envisioned, but as compensation for an accident in which she sustained a broken leg, among other injuries. So it would seem that no matter how we approach the *I want* syndrome, in the final analysis there is some karmic 'ring-pass-not', as the late Dion Fortune would say, which is the deciding factor as to what we may or may not acquire for ourself by means ritualistic or otherwise!

Our final Rite comes from the Eskimo or Iglulik people, and takes the form of a shamanic experience in which those making the request are also allowed to participate. The descent to the abode of Takánakapsâluk is undertaken by the shaman on special request. Sometimes this concerns an illness and sometimes bad hunting luck, but only in the latter case does the shaman receive any practical compensation. It sometimes happens, however, that no game is to be found and the village is threatened with famine, in which case all the villagers gather together at a pre-selected spot to indulge in the shamanic seance, the ecstatic experience of the shaman or shamaness being undertaken in the name of the whole community.

DESCENT TO THE BOTTOM OF THE OCEAN

Those present must unfasten their belts and laces, and remain silent, their eyes closed. For a time the shaman breathes deeply, in silence, before summoning his helping spirits. When they come the shaman begins to murmur, 'The way is made ready for me; the way opens before me!' and the audience answer in chorus: 'Let it be so.' And now the earth opens, and the shaman struggles for a long time with unknown forces before he finally cries: 'Now the way is open.' And the audience exclaim in chorus: 'Let the way be open before him; let there be way for him.' Now, first under the bed, then farther away, under the passage, is heard the cry, 'Halala-he-he-he, Halala-he-he-he'; this is the sign that the shaman has set off. The cry grows more and more distant until it is no longer heard.

During this time the audience sing in chorus, their eyes closed, and sometimes the shaman's clothes — which he had taken off before the seance — come to life and start flying about the house, over the heads of the audience. The signs and deep breathing of people long dead are also heard; they are dead shamans come to help their colleague on his dangerous journey. And their signs and their breathing seem to come from very far under water, as if they were sea beasts.

Reaching the bottom of the ocean, the shaman finds himself facing three great stones in constant motion barring his road; he must pass between them at the risk of being crushed. (This is another image of the 'strait gate' that forbids access to the plane of higher being to anyone but an 'initiate', that is, one who can act like a 'spirit'.) Successfully passing this obstacle, the shaman follows a path and comes to a sort of bay; on a hill stands Takánakapsâluk's house, made of stone and with a narrow entrance. The shaman hears sea beasts blowing and panting, but does not see them. A dog with bared teeth defends the entrance; the dog is dangerous to anyone who is afraid of it, but the shaman passes over it, and it understands that he is a very powerful magician. (All these obstacles oppose the ordinary shaman, but the really powerful shamans reach the bottom of the sea and the presence of Takánakapsâluk directly, by diving beneath their tent or snow hut, as if slipping through a tube.)

If the goddess is angry with men, a great wall rises before her house. And the shaman has to knock it down with his shoulder. Others say that Takánakapsâluk's house has no roof, so that the goddess can better see men's acts from her place by the fire. All kinds of marine animals are gathered in a pool to the right of the fire, and their cries and breathings are heard. The goddess's hair hangs down over her face and she is dirty and slovenly; this is the effect of men's sins, which have almost made her ill. The shaman must approach her, take her by the shoulder, and comb her hair (for the goddess has no fingers with which to comb herself). Before he can do this, there is another obstacle to be overcome; Takánakapsâluk's father, taking him for a dead man on the way to the land of shades, tries to seize him, but the shaman cries, 'I am flesh and blood!' and succeeds in passing.

As he combs Takánakapsâluk's hair, the shaman tells her that men have no more seal. And the goddess answers in the spirit language: 'The secret miscarriages of the women and breaches of taboo in eating boiled meat bar the way for the animals.' The shaman now has to summon all his powers to appease her anger; finally she opens the pool and sets the animals free. The audience hears their movements at the bottom of the sea, and soon afterward the shaman's gasping breathing, as if he were emerging from the surface of the water. A long silence follows. Finally the shaman speaks: 'I have something to say.' All answer. 'Let us hear, let us hear.' And the shaman in the spirit language, demands the confession of sins. One after another, all confess their miscarriages or their breaches of taboos and repent.[8]

There are several aspects of this shamanic ritual which contain psychological connotations. The necessity for public confession, for example, the open expression of guilt appearing to supply a form of energy which enabled the shaman to appease the goddess; while the fact that the actions of the people affected the ecobalance appears to support the interrelatedness of all life forms.

The descent to the bottom of the ocean is suggestive of a journey into the primordial waters of the collective unconscious, through which the shaman is able to effect contact with the group consciousness of the tribe as a whole, or the subconscious minds of those present. The goddess's lack of fingers also implies a dependency upon others — ourselves — the inference being that when people do not co-operate with nature (as represented by the goddess or the Earth Mother) she suffers, the shaman seeing our neglect in terms of her personal care. An interesting corollary to this may be seen in the recent observation that when abused children receiving psychiatric treatment are asked, as part of their therapy, to draw those who had assaulted them, they frequently depicted their assailants without hands or fingers, as though subconsciously severing the weapons of pain!

Shamanism and strong PK seem to go hand in hand. Professor Braude would, no doubt, have loved to see the clothing flying around the room, and might conceivably have arrived at the same conclusion reached by myself and others — that psycho-kinetic energies and Huna Low Self *mana* have something in common.

There are many other fascinating rites about which one could offer comment and analysis. Voodoo Macumba, for example, which combines the magical elements of pagan Africa with Catholic practices, and the Tarantella Healing Rite from Italy, with its strong sexual overtones. But one has to stop somewhere, and this point is as good as any.

Endnotes:

1. *From Primitives to Zen* Mircea Eliade, pp. 237–238.
2. *Ibid*. p. 239.
3. *Ibid*. pp. 252–255.
4. *Ibid*. p. 511.
5. *Ibid*. p. 229.
6. *Archaeology of the Dreamtime* Josephine Flood, pp. 241–242.
7. *Kahuna Magic* Brad Steiger, p. 33.
8. *Op. cit.* Eliade, pp. 441–442.

Chapter 17

INITIATION RITES

Initiation was ever an important feature in primitive society, and in those cultures in which it did not play a prominent role, knowledge of somatic and spiritual transitions was inevitably supplied from sacerdotal sources, priestly or shamanic. The attitude towards Initiatory Rites has naturally changed as civilizing influences have made their presence felt over the centuries, the physical tortures of old now being symbolically enacted either at a mental level or in the arena of everyday life. As I write this, the media is busy reporting cases of cruelty and torture which have been carried out in certain military establishments with disastrous results under the guise of initiation.

Rites of transition which help the psyche to adjust to the next stage in its development are inevitably seen as trials of extreme endurance. The psychology of this is quite simple if viewed in the light of those painful learning processes which appear as natural advents preceding new cycles of experience. The word 'initiation' in itself implies the commencement of something which is new or not hitherto experienced.

The popular concept of initiation held by many beginners in the occult field is that it consists of a series of memorizations and ritual practices, after which someone of purported higher rank puts one to some kind of test and, assuming one has come up with all the right answers, pronounces one ready to be upgraded. In fact, it is nothing so simple, the old concepts which tested character and endurance being far nearer to the truth. In occult initiation there is, in fact, a clear parallel with the stages of development through which we pass in our everyday lives. There is also evidence to suggest that these stages are not limited to times of birth, puberty, fertility and death — but rather that they occur in cycles which vary with the individual, the most widespread being a seven-year cycle.

As we move from one set of circumstances to another in life, the initial period following the move is inevitably one of adjustment. Depending upon our psychological make-up, we may either take that adjustment in our stride, or it may cause us considerable mental and physical (psychosomatic) pain. My own theory is that these tests, which have been pre-programmed prior to entry into incarnation, are self-imposed, and therefore constitute valid channels for the pursuit of both self-improvement and transcendental realization.

Following a similar pattern, occult initiation is not governed by a series of magical A-Levels, but works roughly in this way: the neophyte (or noviciate) seeks to expand his or her level of cosmic comprehension and gain mastery of the mind either through solitary, group or public rites, or by employing mental techniques designed to encourage the manifestation of heightened states of consciousness. Thus a new level of awareness is attained and the initiation lies in the handling of that state.

However, at this stage, the neophyte may possibly find him or herself mentally bombarded by alien energies, confusing archetypes and abstract concepts which he or she is unable to compute. In this case one of three things is likely to happen:

1. The neophyte will realize his/her limitations and drop back gracefully to the preceding stage.

2. He/she will step down, but carry an enormous resentment against those who have managed to handle the initiation successfully. This frequently manifests in a totally illogical condemnation of any information or experience of a metaphysical nature which he/she is incapable of assimilating.

3. A nervous breakdown may be suffered.

In the psychic and occult world one frequently encounters groups whose members proclaim that they accept only so much, and any hint of a state of beingness or preternatural experience which is not encompassed by their dogmatic limitations produces a fear reaction and is therefore condemned out of hand. Equally there are those who shelter comfortably beneath the umbrella of orthodoxy, believing that some higher force, usually in the form of the founder of the chosen religion, is always there to bail them out of any really troublesome situation. True initiation, however, is a solitary matter. One is completely and utterly on one's own. If one can come to terms with the next level to which one ascends as a result of one's efforts to attain self-mastery and enlightenment, then that particular initiation has been passed. But, in truth, for the aspiring occultist there is no last or final test as these trials never cease; they follow one after another right through life, each stage becoming progressively more difficult than the previous. If, on the other hand, one is fortunate enough to overcome them, then one is proportionately strengthened so that the ensuing episodes are never more than can be handled — if only just!

There is a belief that those who aspire to the Path, but are unable to negotiate it in practice, are not ready for it in the first place, or it may not be part of their programming for this life. There is no disgrace in failing an initiation, most of us do it all the time in our everyday lives, no one's Achilles heel being spared. On the other hand, there is no reason why we should not each find our own level and feel free to function there in spiritual and mental comfort, without fear of persecution or interference from those who do not find our ways compatible with theirs. Young souls are ever missionaries, finding strength and comfort in the fact that they can persuade others to embrace their views. Whereas mature souls, being individualized from the collective or group soul, are usually more aware of the essential need for the freedom to explore a broader transcendental horizon.

Let us now embark on a journey into the past and view the initiatory practices of earlier cultures. Generally speaking, the history of religion distinguishes three categories of initiations which are classified by Eliade as follows:

> . . . collective rituals whose function is to effect the transition from childhood or adolescence to adulthood, and which are obligatory for all members of a particular society. Ethnological literature terms these rituals 'puberty rites', 'tribal initiation', or 'initiation into an age-group'.
>
> The other two categories of initiations differ from puberty initiations in that they are not obligatory for all members of the community

and that most of them are performed individually for comparatively small groups. The second category includes all types of rites for entering a secret society, a *Bund*, or a confraternity. These secret societies are limited to one sex and are extremely jealous of their respective secrets. Most of them are male and constitute secret fraternities (*Männerbünde*); but there are also some female secret societies. On the level of primitive cultures, societies open to both sexes are extremely rare; where they exist, they usually represent a phenomenon of degeneration. But in the ancient Mediterranean and Near Eastern world, the mysteries were open to both sexes; and although they are a little different in type, we can put the Greco-Oriental mysteries in the category of secret confraternities.

Finally, there is a third category of initiation — the type that occurs in connection with a mystical vocation; that is, on the level of primitive religions, the vocation of the medicine man or the shaman. A specific characteristic of this third category is the importance that personal experience assumes in it. Broadly speaking, we can say that those who submit themselves to the ordeals typical of this third kind of initiation are — whether voluntarily or involuntarily — destined to participate in a more intense religious experience than is accessible to the rest of the community. I said 'voluntarily or involuntarily', because a member of a community can become a medicine man or a shaman not only in consequence of a personal decision to acquire religious powers (the process called 'the quest') but also through vocation ('the call'), that is, because he is *forced* by Superhuman Beings to become a medicine man or shaman.

I may add that these last two categories — initiation imposed upon entrance to a secret society, and initiation requisite for obtaining a higher religious status — have a good deal in common. They might even be regarded as two varieties of a single class. What principally tends to distinguish them is the element of ecstasy, which is of great importance in shamanic initiations. I may add too that there is a sort of structural common denominator among all these categories of initation, with the result that, from a certain point of view, all initiations are much alike. But it seemed best to begin by drawing a few guiding lines in this extremely wide field, for without them we might easily get lost.

Initiation represents one of the most significant spiritual phenomena in the history of humanity. It is an act that involves not only the religious life of the individual, in the modern meaning of the word 'religion'; it involves his *entire* life. It is through initiation that, in primitive and archaic societies, man becomes what he is and what he should be — a being open to the life of the spirit, hence one who participates in the culture into which he was born. For as we shall soon see, *the puberty initiation represents above all the revelation of the sacred — and, for the primitive world, the sacred means not only everything that we now understand by religion, but also the whole body of the tribe's mythological and cultural traditions.*[1]

I was particularly interested in Professor Eliade's allusion to 'the quest' and 'the call', having met people who fall into both categories. Quest neophytes or initiates have usually struck me as being more outgoing, fearless and courageous than their 'called' colleagues, who have (as in my own case), oft times tried to dodge the issue and sneak away to some quiet backwater — only to be catapulted back to the front line of fire by one of Eliade's 'Superhuman Beings', in the guise of a series of practical circumstances — a situation to which many of my readers will, I am sure, have no difficulty in relating.

Another aspect of initiation which features strongly in primitive rites is a sense of timelessness. This applies particularly to the Australian Aborigines, who would appear to view the past, present and future as aspects of their pre-life (or the pre-world) state which exists within their dreamtime concept. Eliade says of this:

> Since the initiation ceremonies were founded by the Divine Beings or the mythical Ancestors, the primordial Time is reintegrated whenever they are performed. This is true not only for the Australians, but for the entire primitive world. For what is involved here is a fundamental conception in archaic religions — the repetition of a ritual founded by Divine Beings implies the re-actualization of the original Time when the rite was first performed. This is why a rite has efficacy — it participates in the completeness of the sacred primordial Time. The rite makes the myth present. Everything that the myth tells of the Time of beginning, the *'bugari* times', the rite reactualizes, shows it as happening, *here and now.*[2]

This statement surely adds force to the occult concept of role-playing, the implication being that a state of timelessness can be attained as long as the archetypal structures are correctly adhered to and handled with a balanced perspective.

Many primitive male initiation rites involved the practices of circumcision and subincision. The latter, which involved the infliction of a genital wound to give the appearance of a female organ, having been suggested to them as offering a counterpart of the female menses. Just as the woman is able to discharge 'bad blood' during menstruation so, in critical times, the subincised male could open his wound and release a certain quantity of blood. It would seem that sanguinary mutilations of this kind afforded the novice radical regeneration. This mystical connection between food, blood and sexuality apparently constituted a strong initiatory pattern in Melanesian and Indonesian rites.[3]

One interesting phenomenon of ancient rites which is still practised to this day is the ceremonial renaming of the novice. This is both widespread and archaic. A person's name was believed to resonate to the note or wavelength of his or her essence or soul. The initiation being representative of a rebirth, it was only natural that a new name would follow. In today's world Wiccans usually have private coven names, while the pseudonyms of some occult and mystical personalities loudly proclaim their traditions and preferences: the appellation 'Gareth Knight', for example.

The primitive concept of initiatory death and rebirth is clearly outlined in the following commentary:

[Scenarios of Initiatory Death]
The rites of initiatory death grow longer and more complex, sometimes becoming real dramatic scenarios. In the Congo and on the Loango coast, the boys between ten and twelve years old drink a potion that makes them unconscious. They are then carried into the jungle and circumcised. Bastian reports that they are buried in the fetish house, and that when they wake they seem to have forgotten their past life. During their seclusion in the jungle they are painted white (certainly a sign that they have become ghosts), they are allowed to steal, are taught the tribal traditions, and learn a new language.

   Characteristic here are death symbolized by a loss of consciousness, by circumcision and by burial; forgetting the past; assimilation of the novices to ghosts; learning a new language. Each of these motifs recurs in numerous puberty rites of Africa, Oceania, and North America. As it is impossible to cite them all, I shall confine myself for the moment to a few examples of forgetting the past after initiation. In Liberia, when the novices — who are supposed to have been killed by the Forest Spirit — are resuscitated to a new life, tattooed, and given a new name, they seem to have entirely forgotten their past existence. They recognize neither their families nor their friends, they do not even remember their own names, and they behave as if they had forgotten how to perform even the most elementary acts — washing themselves, for example. Similarly, initiates into some Sudanese secret societies forget their language. Among the Makua the novices spend several months in a hut far from the village and are given new names; when they return to the village they have forgotten their family relationships. As Karl Weule puts it: by his stay in the bush, the son is dead in his mother's eyes. Forgetting is a symbol of death, but it can also be interpreted as betokening earliest infancy. Among the Patasiva of western Ceram, for example, the women are shown the bloody lances with which the spirit is supposed to have killed the novices. When the novices come back to the village, they behave like infants — they do not speak, and pick things up by the wrong end.[4]

There is something here which suggests the forgetting of former lives prior to rebirth or reincarnation, a vestige of a far deeper knowledge perhaps, passed down from antiquity, the real meaning of which had been long since forgotten. The 'born again' statement, based on the biblical passage 'Unless a man be born again . . . ' (John 3:3), is currently popular among certain Evangelical collectives, where it has assumed an almost initiatory relevancy.

Being swallowed by monsters is frequently featured in primitive Initiatory Rites. Modern analysis would probably view this as a return to the primordial womb from which the novice is then reborn as his or her own self, as distinct from the childhood manifestation of the psyche which was essentially a unit of the maternal/paternal scene. Initiation monsters come in all shapes and sizes and include crocodiles, snakes, bears, whales, fishes, and a variety of mythical creatures. It would also be easy to read this tussle between the novice and the monster as relating to the battle between the High Self, and the id or lower nature. The animals, however, are not necessarily of malign intent and frequently fall into their respective roles purely to help the initiate overcome some character weakness. In fact in most primitive religions there is not the distinction between animals and man which became such a strong element in later religions. To the shaman, for example, the Creator could assume the shape of either, or even appear as an elemental force — stone, tree, river, mound of earth and so on.

The mysteries of gestation and childbirth are expressed by a series of homologous images such as entrance into the womb of Mother Earth or the Great Mother, or into the body of a sea creature, wild beast or domestic animal. The Eskimo shamans believe that we each have an 'animal person' as part of our psychological economy. Eskimo artist and sculptor Lawrence Ahvakana explains: 'For a lot of people their second person is an animal. I have a second person. I think it is a seal or an owl. And I use these animals a lot within my sculpture pieces, and I try to make it realistic. It's not a fairy tale that I'm going through. It's real, because I've felt it many times.'[5]

In the shamanic trance state this aspect is frequently contacted to act as a bridge between the somewhat limited thinking patterns of Homo sapiens and the 'broadcasting' frequencies of other intelligent forces in the universe.

Heroic initiations are often of a strictly secret nature, and involve a descent into the depths of some murky and hostile chthonian underworld. Eliade tells us:

> . . . There is a Polynesian myth which admirably illustrates this type of initiatory return to the womb. After a life full of adventures, Maui, the great Maori Hero, returned to his native country and the house of his ancestress Hine-mi-te-po, the Great Lady (of Night). He found her asleep and, throwing off his clothes, entered the giantess' body. He made his way through it without being stopped, but when he was about to emerge — that is, when half his body was still inside her mouth — the birds that were accompanying him burst out laughing. Waking suddenly, the Great Lady (of Night) clenched her teeth and cut the Hero in two, killing him. It is because of this, the Maoris say, that man is mortal. If Maui had been able to get out of his ancestress' body safe and sound, men would have become immortal.[6]

In other words, until we are able to individuate, or effect a successful balance between anima and animus, we are chained to a series of often painful mortal existences.

This Rite is by no means limited to the Maoris, however. It may be evidenced in Celtic mythology in the Keridwen/Gwion/Taliesin saga, and the Finnish myth of the blacksmith Ilmarinen, to take but two examples — there are dozens more.

Escape from the primordial womb is only one initiatory image with which the novice is likely to be faced. Others may include the Symplegades (the two rocks at the entrance of the Black Sea that clashed together intermittently, but ceased their activity for long enough to allow Jason and the Argonauts to pass through safely), dancing reeds, gates shaped like jaws, razor-edged restless mountains, clashing icebergs, and much more phantasmagoria which serve to illustrate the insurmountable difficulties of passage to other dimensions.

Going berserk is also a feature of Initiatory Rites, especially those relating to heroes, shamans and godlings. Hercules underwent a period of madness, as did Dionysus, the temporary loss of control and regaining of sanity through personal effort apparently being an essential part of the initiatory process. Many of the horrendous tales of shamanic and heroic initiation would appear to be no more than the hallucinations and confused states of mind with which the novice is inevitably confronted to this very day.

A fine example of the Berserk State is to be found in the *Volsunga Saga*, Chapters 7–8:

'They went without shields, and were mad as dogs or wolves, and bit on their shields, and were as strong as bears or bulls; men they slew, and neither fire nor steel would deal with them; and this is what is called the fury of the berserker'. This mythological picture has been rightly identified as a description of real men's societies — the famous *Männerbünde* of the ancient Germanic civilization. The berserkers were, literally, the 'warriors in shirts (*serkr*) of bear'. This is as much as to say that they were magically identified with the bear. In addition they could sometimes change themselves into wolves and bears. A man became a berserker as the result of an initiation that included specifically martial ordeals. So, for example, Tacitus tells us that among the Chatti the candidate cut neither his hair nor his beard until he had killed an enemy. Among the Taifali, the youth had to bring down a boar or a wolf; among the Heruli, he had to fight unarmed. Through these ordeals, the candidate took to himself a wild-animal mode of being; he became a dreaded warrior in the measure in which he behaved like a beast of prey. He metamorphosed himself into a superman because he succeeded in assimilating the magicoreligious force proper to the carnivora.

The *Volsunga Saga* has preserved the memory of certain ordeals typical of the initiations of berserkers. By treachery, King Siggeir obtains possession of his nine brothers-in-law, the Volsungs. Chained to a beam, they are all eaten by a she-wolf, except Sigmund, who is saved by a ruse of his sister Signy. Hidden in a hut in the depths of the forest, where Signy brings him food, he awaits the hour of revenge.

When her first two sons have reached the age of ten, Signy sends them to Sigmund to be tested. Sigmund finds that they are cowards, and by his advice Signy kills them. As the result of her incestuous relations with her brother, Signy has a third son, Sinfjotli. When he is nearly ten, his mother submits him to a first ordeal: she sews his shirt to his arms through the skin. Siggeir's sons, submitted to the same ordeal, had howled with pain, but Sinfjotli remains imperturbable. His mother then pulls off his shirt, tearing away the skin, and asks him if he feels anything. The boy answers that a Volsung is not troubled by such a trifle. His mother then sends him to Sigmund, who submits him to the same ordeal that Siggeir's two sons has failed to sustain: he orders him to make bread from a sack of flour in which there is a snake. When Sigmund comes home that night, he finds the bread baked and asks Sinfjotli if he did not find anything in the flour. The boy answers that he remembers having seen something, but he paid no attention to it and kneaded everything up together. After this proof of courage Sigmund takes the boy into the forest with him. One day they find two wolfskins hanging from the wall of a hut. The two sons of a king [have] been transformed into wolves and could only come out of the skins every tenth day. Sigmund and Sinfjotli put on the skins, but cannot get them off. They howl like wolves and understand the wolves' language. They then separate, agreeing that they will not call on each other for help unless they have to deal with more than seven men. One day Sinfjotli is summoned to help and kills all the men who had attacked Sigmund. Another time Sinfjotli himself is attacked by eleven men, and kills them without summoning Sigmund to help him. Then Sigmund rushes at him and bites him in the throat, but not long afterward finds a way to cure the wound. Finally they return to their cabin to await the moment when they can put off their wolfskins. When the time comes, they throw the skins into the fire. With this episode, Sinfjotli's initiation is completed, and he can avenge the slaying of the Volsungs.[7]

One wonders how much of this was actually experienced and how much was pure hallucination resulting from an artificially produced (or otherwise) state of frenzy. Severity code rites of this nature are inevitably warrior-orientated, another example which has come down to us being Cuchulainn's famous initiation:

According to the old Irish *Tain Bo Cualnge*, Cuchulainn, nephew of Conchobar, king of Ulster, one day overheard his master, the druid Cathba, saying: 'The little boy that takes arms this day shall be splendid and renowned for deeds of arms . . . but he shall be short-lived and fleeting.' Cuchulainn sprang up and, asking his uncle for arms and a chariot, set off for the castle of the three sons of Necht, the worst enemies of the kingdom of Ulster. Although these heroes were supposed to be invincible, the little boy conquered them and cut off their heads. But the exploit heated him to such a degree that a witch warned the king that if precautions were not taken, the boy would kill all the warriors in Ulster. The king decided to send a troop of naked women to meet Cuchulainn. And the text continues: 'Thereupon the young women all arose and marched out . . . and they discovered their nakedness and all their shame to him. The lad hid his face from them and turned his gaze on the chariot, that he might not see the nakedness or the shame of the women. Then the lad was lifted out of the chariot. He was placed in three vats of cold water to extinguish his wrath; and the first vat into which he was put burst its staves and its hoops like the cracking of nuts around him. The next vat into which he went boiled with bubbles as big as fists therein. The third vat into which he went, some men might endure it and others might not. Then the boy's wrath (*ferg*) went down . . . and his festive garments were put on him.'[8]

In Chapter 10, I commented on the feeling of heat or excessive warmth which often manifests during psychic or occult work. So important, in fact, was this experience to the shamans of old that they actually instituted rites to encourage it. The heat phenomenon was seen in the magicoreligious context, and experts are of the opinion that the mystique which grew up around it is extremely archaic. On the symbolism of magical heat Eliade comments:

> Many primitives think of the magicoreligious power as 'burning', and express it by terms meaning heat, burn, very hot. It is for the same reason that shamans and medicine men drink salt or highly spiced water and eat aromatic plants — they expect thus to increase their inner heat. That this magical heat corresponds to a real experience is proved by the great resistance to cold displayed both by shamans of the Arctic and Siberia and by Himalayan ascetics. In addition, shamans are held to be 'masters over fire', — for example, they swallow burning coals, touch red-hot iron, walk on fire. Similar experiences and conceptions are also documented among more civilized people. The Sanskrit term *tapas* finally developed the sense of ascetic effort in general, but its original meaning was extreme heat. It was by becoming heated through asceticism that Prajapati created the universe; he created it by a magic sweat, as in some North American cosmogonies. The *Dhammapada* says that the Buddha is 'burning' and Tantric texts assert that the awakening of the kundalini is manifested by a burning. In modern India, the Mohammedans believe that a man in communication with God becomes 'burning hot'. Anyone who performs miracles is called 'boiling'. By extension, all kinds of people or acts involving any magicoreligious power are regarded as burning. This sacred power, which causes both the shaman's heat and the heating of the warrior, can be transformed, differentiated, given various colorings, by subsequent efforts.[9]

Shamanic initiation is a study in itself and demands more space and attention than I can afford it in a general work of this nature. There are a few facts concerning its nature that can be discussed, however, the most important being how one comes to be a shaman in the first place.

The path of shamanism may be assumed by vocation, hereditary transmission or personal quest. Occasionally, the will of the tribe may also be brought to bear on the chosen man or woman.

However, the shaman is only recognized fully after he or she has received instruction by way of dreams, visions, trances and traditional techniques, such as learning the names and functions of the various orders of spirits, mythology, ancestral genealogy and the secret language of magic. These instructions are received from old master shamans at the earthly level, and those spirits who guide him or her on the inner planes. Some shamanic Initiation Rites are public, but whether or not they are performed individually, for the few, or in sight of the many is of little consequence, as the process can just as easily take place in the candidate's dreams or ecstatic experiences. In other words, it can be negotiated in altered states of consciousness.

Strange behaviour has ever been part of the shamanic role and pronounced hysteria is a common phenomenon amongst them. Most shamans seek a great deal of personal solitude when they are not performing their works of healing or spiritual ministrations.

A man or woman could sometimes become a shaman following a deeply traumatic experience, accident or highly unusual event. This, among other things, has frequently promoted scholars to associate shamanic manifestations with conditions suggestive of mental illness or cerebral irregularities such as epilepsy. Crises involving states of temporary insanity have to be resolved by the candidate before he or she can assume the full and well-earned title of shaman. Some do not make it, however, but then this applies to many avenues of expression, both transcendental and otherwise. The old tales I was told when I first ventured onto the Path — like being shut up in a pyramid or barrow for three days and three nights at the end of which, if one came out mentally intact, one had passed the initiation (otherwise it was a local asylum or the undertaker) — may have contained a grain of truth.

There are well-documented cases of people who have developed psychic gifts or PK following a severe accident or electric shock, while a form of rebirth effecting a personality change has been known to succeed temporary amnesia. It would appear that people have changed little, if at all, over the ages.

Shamans tell us that during their period of initiation they 'die', and lie inanimate in their *yurt* in a solitary place for three to seven days. During this period they are cut up by demons or strange beasts, and their bodies reassembled so that they contain magical properties, knowledge and great psychic gifts. Death, burial and resurrection have ever been the lot of those sacrificed divinities who have concerned themselves with the welfare of mankind — the alchemical inferences of transformation and sublimation being obvious.

Trees appear to feature strongly in shamanic out-of-the-body initiatory experiences — the birch in particular — while the number nine would also seem to hold some special significance. The birch is called *udeshi burkhan*, 'the guardian of the door', for it is said to open the door of heaven to the shaman.[10]

In Celtic lore the birch is *Beth*, the first letter of the Tree Alphabet, whose magical attribute is *inception*. In the thirteen Celtic Stations *Beth* represents Absolute Deity. The initiating spirit descends to the state of 'Chaos' from which it emerges triumphant in its reborn form. In the Tree Alphabet Chaos is represented by the hawthorn, whose attribute is *cleansing* and whose power lies in the realms of dreams. That this tree language is an archaic remnant of some past era in the evolution of this planet when all lands were interconnected, may also be evidenced in the rites of the Australian Aborigines as outlined in the preceding chapter.

Trees have ever been associated with god-forms and the denizens of other worlds. The oak tree was sacred to the Druids, the ash to the Scandinavian peoples, the lime tree in Germany, the fig tree in India. The pine was sacred to Attis, the cedar or tamarisk to Osiris, the persea to Isis, the sycamore to Aphrodite, the elm to Hephaestus, the oak to Zeus, the laurel to Apollo, the olive to Athene, and so forth. In Christian iconography there is the Cross of Redemption and in the Hebrew tradition the Qabalistic Tree of Life.

Jung saw the tree as an archetypal transformation image of great significance and antiquity, and devoted a substantial part of his work *Alchemical Studies* (pp. 272–349) to its considerations. He tells us:

> . . . where suffering and sadness play so great a role, it is not surprising that the tree was brought into connection with the cross of Christ. This analogy was supported by the old legend that the wood of the cross came from the tree of paradise. Another thing that contributed to it was the quaternity, whose symbol is the cross; for the tree possesses a quaternary quality by reason of the fact that it represents the process by which the four elements are united. The quaternity of the tree goes back beyond the Christian era. It is found in Zarathus-

tra's vision of the tree with four branches made of gold, silver, steel
and 'mixed iron' . . .

The tree also appears as a symbol of transformation in a passage in
Dorn's *Speculativa philosophia*, which is very interesting from the
point of view of the psychology of religion: '[God] hath determined to
snatch the sword of his wrath from the hands of the angel, substituting
in place thereof a three pronged hook of gold, hanging the sword on a
tree: and so God's wrath is turned into love'.[11]

The emphasis so far in this chapter has tended to fall upon
primitive rather than more recent Initiation Rites, as many of the
latter are well-documented historically, while the ceremonies and
practices of the major world religions are still in common use.
The faiths of the classical cultures also engaged in initiatory
ceremonies, however, not the least of which were the Rites of Isis
as enumerated by Apuleius of Madaura, a well-known lawyer,
novelist and orator of his day who lived in the second century AD.
Apuleius is probably best-known for his famous *Metamorphoses*
in which his hero, Lucius, being over-curious about magic, is
accidentally changed into an ass (confronted by his lower self?).
He is finally restored to human form by the good offices of the
goddess Isis, after which he undergoes a full ritual initiation into
her mysteries. The relevant texts are believed to contain some of
the most inspiring passages in classical literature as well as
acquainting the reader with the nature and details of the Isian
rites.[12]

The Buddhist sage Kūkai (774–835) studied in China and
introduced to Japan the Buddhism known as the 'True Words'
(Mantrayāna in Sanskrit, *Shingon* in Japanese). The following
passages, which concern his initiation, were written by Kūkai
himself and are extracted from reports he wrote to the Emperor
on his return:

One day, in the course of my calls on eminent Buddhist teachers of the
capital, I happened by chance to meet the abbot of the East Pagoda
Hall of the Green Dragon Temple. This great priest, whose Buddhist
name was Hui-kuo, was the chosen disciple of the Indian master
Amoghavajra. His virtue aroused the reverence of his age; his
teachings were lofty enough to guide emperors. Three sovereigns
revered him as their master and were ordained by him. The four
classes of believers looked up to him for instruction in the esoteric
teachings.

I called on the abbot in the company of five or six monks from the

Hsi-ming Temple. As soon as he saw me he smiled with pleasure, and he joyfully said, 'I knew that you would come! I have been waiting for such a long time. What pleasure it gives me to look on you today at last! My life is drawing to an end, and until you came there was no one to whom I could transmit the teachings. Go without delay to the ordination altar with incense and a flower.' I returned to the temple where I had been staying and got the things which were necessary for the ceremony. It was early in the sixth moon, then, that I entered the ordination chamber. I stood in front of the Womb Mandala (*Garbha mandala*) and cast my flower in the prescribed manner. By chance it fell on the body of the Buddha Vairochana in the centre. The master exclaimed in delight, 'How amazing! How perfectly amazing!' He repeated this three or four times in joy and wonder. I was then given the fivefold baptism and received the instruction in the Three Mysteries that bring divine intercession. Next I was taught the Sanskrit formulas for the Womb Mandala, and learned the yoga contemplation on all the Honoured Ones.

Early in the seventh moon I entered the ordination chamber of the Diamond (*Vajra*) Mandala for a second baptism. When I cast my flower it fell on Vairochana again, and the abbot marvelled as he had before. I also received ordination as an *āchārya* early in the following month. On the day of my ordination I provided a feast for five hundred of the monks. The dignitaries of the Green Dragon Temple all attended the feast, and everyone enjoyed himself.[13]

Initiation into the Mysteries teaches many lessons and opens doors to many secrets — material, mental and spiritual: the hidden laws of matter; the nature of the soul's sojourn in the dark realms of ignorance and suffering; the dormant powers that lie imprisoned within the mind. Its culmination or crowning experience is the mystical vision in which the gods appear in resplendent light, or a state of gnosis is achieved according to the order and nature of the Rite.

I should like to conclude this chapter with two short commentaries on initiation, the first of which concerns Plato's teaching on the subject:

It looks as if those also who established rites of initiation for us were no fools, but that there is a hidden meaning in their teaching when it says that whoever arrives uninitiated in Hades will lie in mud, but the purified and initiated when he arrives there will dwell with the gods. For there are in truth, as those who understand the mysteries say, 'Many who bear the wand, but few who become *Bakchoi*.' Now these latter are in my own opinion no others than those who have given their lives to true philosophy.[14]

One is reminded of the quote from the biblical parable about many being called, but few being chosen! (Matthew 22:14)
Finally, the words of Plutarch:

> The soul (at the point of death) has the same experience as those who are being initiated into great mysteries . . . At first one wanders and wearily hurries to and fro, and journeys with suspicion through the dark as one uninitiated: and then come all the terrors before the final initiation, shuddering, trembling, sweating, amazement: then one is struck with a marvellous light, one is received into pure regions and meadows, with voices and dances and the majesty of holy sounds and shapes: among these he who has fulfilled initiation wanders free, and released and bearing his crown joins in the divine communion, and consorts with pure and holy men, beholding those who live here uninitiated, an uncleansed horde, trodden under foot of him and huddled together in mud and fog, abiding in their miseries through fear of death and mistrust of the blessings there.[15]

Endnotes:

1. *Rites and Symbols of Initiation* Mircea Eliade, pp. 2–3.
2. *Ibid.* p. 6.
3. *Ibid.* p. 27.
4. *Ibid.* pp. 30–31.
5. *Shaman* Joan Halifax, p. 78.
6. *Op. Cit.* Mircea Eliade, p. 61.
7. *From Primitives to Zen* Mircea Eliade, pp. 294–295.
8. *Ibid.* p. 296.
9. *Rites and Symbols of Initiation* Mircea Eliade, pp. 85–86.
10. *Ibid.* p. 93.
11. *Alchemical Studies* C G Jung, p. 332.
12. *From Primitives to Zen* Mircea Eliade, pp. 305–311.
13. *Ibid.* pp. 314–315.
14. *Ibid.* p. 305.
15. *Ibid.* p. 302.

Chapter 18

WOMEN'S RITES

In presenting a separate chapter exclusively for Women's Rites I am implying neither the superiority nor inferiority of that sex, but rather emphasizing the fact that in a male-orientated society the role of women, in the deeper or more transcendental sense, tends to be either neglected or conveniently swept under the proverbial carpet. This is mainly due to a combination of erroneous teachings of certain major religions on the one hand, and the general tendency among many women to assume the sacrificial mode on the other. To this day Hebrew males are still taught to offer the daily prayer: 'Blessed Art Thou O Lord our God, King of the Universe, who has not made me a woman'![1]; while according to Buddhist tradition it is not possible for a female to attain the 'thousand petalled Lotus', or control of the Crown Centre, which is believed to be indicative of supreme enlightenment. She has to move further forward along the evolutionary path to return or incarnate as a male before she can carry that power!

In a so-called civilized society I find such thinking extraordinary, but then it only serves to fortify my previous remarks concerning collective programming, the shackles of which are extremely hard for many to throw off. In fact, one could view the situation in terms of a weakness on the part of those men who are still encapsulated in archaic dogmas which the light of reason and the recent strides in technology and social awareness have failed to illumine.

Unfortunately there are still many women who support the view that they are destined for the subordinate role, but thankfully such emotionally based Piscean Age phenomena are doomed to fade away as the fishes effect their laborious return to the maternal sea of the great unconscious, and make way for the more logical and enquiring Aquarian approach.

The doctrines of Freud, about which Jung comments as follows, did little to help the female cause:

The motif of the Gnostic Yahweh and Creator-God reappeared in the Freudian myth of the primal father and the gloomy superego deriving from that father. In Freud's myth he became a daimon, who created a world of disappointments, illusions, and suffering. But the materialistic trend which had already come to light in the alchemists' preoccupation with the secrets of matter had the effect of obscuring for Freud that other essential aspect of Gnosticism: the primordial image of the spirit as another, higher god who gave to mankind the *krater* (mixing vessel), the vessel of spiritual transformation. The *krater* is a feminine principle which could find no place in Freud's patriarchal world. Incidentally, he is by no means alone in this prejudice. In the realm of Catholic thought the Mother of God and Bride of Christ have been received into the divine thalamus (bridal chamber) only recently, after centuries of hesitancy, and thus at least been accorded partial recognition. But in the Protestant and Jewish spheres the father continues to dominate as much as ever. In philosophical alchemy, on the other hand, the feminine principle plays a role equal to that of the masculine.[2]

Feminist writers like Merlin Stone have worked hard to break the bonds of ignorance concerning the role of women in both the transpersonal and temporal contexts, but it is no easy task. The old brainwashers certainly knew their trade, and it will probably take many more years, even centuries perhaps, to finally undo the dreadful, psychological and spiritual harm that their efforts effected.

All of the older civilizations did not fall into such erroneous ways, however. The ancient Greeks accorded the role of Wisdom to a Goddess, Athene, who interestingly enough was portrayed as a Warrior Archetype, thus succesfully uniting the anima and the animus. Athene was not by nature aggressive, but the fact that in a showdown of arms she, and she alone could defeat the surly Ares, God of War, at his own game must surely contain a message of hope and perhaps a hint of strategy for the ladies of the present and future!

Rites which are exclusive to the female sex have tended to receive less historical coverage than those which are purely male-orientated, although most of the early rites of priesthood and shamanism were open to both sexes, so these do not need to be repeated. Some of the more secret female puberty rites have been less accessible to ethnologists, mainly because they were often individual, but the principles involved would appear to be the same. The young girl is removed from her familiar world and isolated from the community while the initiation begins with a break or rupture. The main difference between male and female puberty rites lies in the fact that the segregation takes place in each case immediately after the first menstruation, and is therefore individual, whereas the experience undergone by the boys is collective. The length of this segregation varies from culture to culture, from three days (in Australia and India) to twenty months (in New Zealand) and several years in some cases (for example Cambodia).

As the individuals come together the girls do eventually form a group, after which their initiation is formed collectively, usually under the direction of an older female relative (as in India), or an old woman of the tribe (as in Africa). The girls are fully instructed in the secrets of sexuality and fertility, taught the customs of the tribe and those of its religious traditions that are relevant to their future role within it. Certain tribal secrets are not made available to women, just as the secret knowledge relayed from woman to woman is not readily imparted to the men of the tribe. The education given covers both religious and secular duties to the society in question, while also emphasizing the sacrality of women. Each girl is then ritually prepared for her specific role as a creatress, and her responsibilities as an adult female.

Female Initiatory Rites would appear to be considerably less dramatic than those endured by the males, although there is still much that is not known regarding their specific content. The important element is segregation or the detachment from the parental home. This usually takes place in a forest (as with the Swahili) or in a special cabin as among the North American Indian Tribes (the Shushwap and Wintun, for example), in Brazil (Coroado), the New Hebrides, the Marshall Islands, and among the Veddahs and also some of the African peoples.[3]

The symbolism of darkness also appears in the ritual segregation of the girls, as they are inevitably held in a dark house, hut or place in the forest, and in some cases forbidden to see the sun. The last mentioned taboo is connected with the mystical association between the phases of the moon and the physiology of the female body. In certain South American societies, girl novices are forbidden to touch the ground and are obliged to spend their period of isolation suspended in hammocks! There are also strong dietary restrictions and special clothing to be worn during this phase.

The period of segregation is then followed by the Rite itself, which varies from tribe to tribe. In northern Australia, the girl undergoing her first menstruation is isolated in a cabin for three days, during which time she is subjected to various dietary taboos. She is then painted with ochre and richly decorated by the older women, who escort her at dawn to a fresh water stream or lagoon. Following this ritual bath, she is then led in procession to the main camp to be socially accepted as a fully matured woman.

In earlier times it appears that the Rite was a far more complicated one involving songs, dances, and so forth. However, as in so many of these cases, by the time the ethnologist is able to make the necessary contact and become accepted by the tribe, the old institutions are on the verge of disappearing and only vague vestiges of the originals are left to observe.

In some places the segregation was terminated by a collective ritual dance — this was particularly characteristic of the early cultivators (*Pflanzervölker*) — after which the girls were then exhibited, made a great fuss of and showered with gifts. There were also external signs to mark the fulfilment of the initiation, such as tatooing and blackening of the teeth, which were influenced by the respective totemic culture.[4]

The essence of the Rite is, therefore, the solemn exhibition of the girl to the entire community as a ceremonial announcement that the mystery has been accomplished and she is *shown* to be an adult, which means assuming the modal expression and full responsibilities of womanhood. Eliade tells us that:

To show something ceremonially — a sign, an object, an animal, a man — is to declare a sacred presence, to acclaim the miracle of a hierophany. This rite, which is so simple in itself, denotes a religious behaviour that is archaic. Perhaps even before articulate language, solemnly showing an object signified that it was regarded as exceptional, singular, mysterious, sacred. Very probably this ceremonial presentation of the initiated girl represents the earliest stage of the ceremony. The collective dances . . . express the same primordial experience in a way that is at once more plastic and more dramatic.[5]

Among some peoples there were several degrees of female initiation. For the Yao, for example, it commenced with the first menstruation, was then repeated during the first pregnancy, and concluded with the birth of the first child. The essential revelation for the woman in many of these rites would appear to be her role as a creatrix, which in itself constitutes a religious experience that is exclusive to her gender. The three degrees of Yao initiation emphasized the continuity of the female role, while the belief in the power of the female over the creation of life often gave rise to secret women's fraternities.[6]

Traces of strange mystical scenarios have also surfaced in Europe. In Schleswig, as recently as the last century, when it was heard that a child had been born, all the women of the village would dance to the house of the new mother, and any unfortunate man whom they chanced to encounter on their way suffered the indignity of having his hat knocked off and filled with dung! If a cart chanced to bar their way it would be broken to pieces and the horse turned loose. Following the meeting at the house of the new mother, they would run frantically through the village, shouting, cheering, entering houses and helping themselves to whatever they wanted in the way of food and drink. No doubt in earlier times certain rituals were performed in the house of the new mother. It is known, for example, that in Denmark in the thirteenth century women gathered at the new mother's house where they made a straw dummy which they called an 'Ox'. They then each would take a turn at dancing with this figure to the accompaniment of much singing, shouting and lascivious gestures.[7]

One of the functions of the Puberty Rite for girls was to teach them certain ritual songs, dances and practical skills — spinning and weaving, for example. The goddesses of destiny were inevitably associated with the craft of spinning, for it was believed that the moon, as representing women generally, was seen to 'spin' time and 'weave' human lives.

Spinning has ever held occult connotations. Athene, Greek goddess of wisdom was considered to be adept at it, while mid-European and Germanic folklore abounds with tales of fairies and denizens of the Middle Kingdoms to whom this skill is sacred.

Eliade sees a mystical connection between female initiations, spinning and sexuality. He comments:

> Even in developed societies, girls enjoy a certain prenuptial freedom, and their meetings with boys take place in a house where they gather to spin. The custom was still alive in Russia at the beginning of the twentieth century. It is surprising that in cultures where virginity is highly prized, meetings between young men and girls are not only tolerated but encouraged by their parents. We have here not a case of dissolute manners but a great secret — the revelation of female sacrality; the experience touches the springs of life and fertility. Prenuptial freedoms for girls are not erotic in nature, but ritual; they constitute fragments of a forgotten mystery, not profane festivities. In the Ukraine during certain holy periods, and especially on the occasion of marriages, girls and women behave in a manner that is almost orgiastic. This complete reversal of behaviour — from modesty to exhibitionism — indicates a ritual goal, which concerns the entire community. It is a case of the religious need for periodical abolition of the norms that govern profane life — in other words, of the need to suspend the law that lies like a dead weight on customs, and to re-create the state of absolute spontaneity. The fact that cases of such ritual behaviour have been preserved down to the twentieth century among peoples long since Christianized proves, I believe, that we are here dealing with an extremely archaic religious experience, a basic experience of woman's soul.[8]

These views accord perfectly with those expressed by priests and scholars of other historical cultures and civilizations which have received mention in earlier chapters of this book.

There has always been a close connection between women's rites and the totemic horse, particularly among the early Celts, who accorded great reverence to the Horse Goddess, Epona. Eliade sees the horse as essentially a symbol of male militarism, and its intrusion into the world of women's rites as something of a misplacement. He cites details of a secret women's society among the Mordvins, whose emblem is a hobby horse and whose members are called horses: 'Around their necks they wear a purse full of millet, representing the horse's belly.'[9] The Celts were, however, like the Amazons, female-orientated and their women frequently fought side by side with their men, the details of which history has generously supplied us.

During the research I undertook for this book I was kindly

loaned two small volumes about the North American Indians —
their ways, customs and later wrangles with the American
government over the allocation of lands and the reservation
system. One of these, entitled *Daughter of Copper Woman*, I
found particularly moving. It concerns a few dedicated women
belonging to an Indian matriarchal, matrilineal society in
Western Canada, who made a special request that their identities,
rituals and details of their originial tribe be kept secret. In due
deference to their feelings, the author Anne Cameron, popular
Canadian writer and poetess, complied.

It would be impossible to convey in a few clinical comments the
depth of feminine wisdom contained in this book, and the
sufferings endured by a gentle people who were close to nature
and the Old Ones. However, I should like to quote a few poignant
paragraphs which will, I hope, serve to illustrate the psychological suffering endured by a female society deprived of their natural
rites and dignity:

> And then new men arrived. Men who never talked to women, never
> ate with women, never slept with women, never laughed with
> women. Men who frowned on singing and dancing, on laughter and
> love. Men who claimed the Society of Women was a society of
> witches.
>
> 'Thou shalt not suffer a witch to live,' they insisted, but the people
> would not allow them to kill the women of the society.
>
> Instead, the priests had to be content to take the girl children.
> Instead of being raised and educated by women who told them the
> truth about their bodies, the girls were taken from their villages and
> put in schools where they were taught to keep their breasts bound, to
> hide their arms and legs, to never look a brother openly in the eye but
> to look down at the ground as if ashamed of something. Instead of
> learning that once a month their bodies would become sacred, they
> were taught they would become filthy. Instead of going to the waiting
> house to meditate, pray and celebrate the fullness of the moon and
> their own bodies, they were taught they were sick, and must bandage
> themselves and act as if they were sick. They were taught the waves
> and surgings of their bodies were sinful and must never be indulged or
> enjoyed.
>
> By the time the girls were allowed home to their villages, their
> minds were so poisoned, their spirits so damaged, their souls so
> contaminated they were not eligible for candidacy in the Society of
> Women.
>
> The boys were taken away, too, and taught that women were
> filthy, sinful creatures who would tempt a man away from his true

path. They were taught women had no opinion that counted, no mind
to be honoured, no purpose other than to serve man.[10]

The only comment I feel I want to add here is a metaphysical
rather than a socio-psychological one. Somewhere along the line
there must be an inordinate amount of karma to be paid, both
personal and groupwise.

Chiparopai, an old Yuma Indian, adds her voice to those of her
sisters from the north:

> Sickness comes with you (the white man) and hundreds of us die.
> Where is our strength? . . . In the old times we were strong. We used
> to hunt and fish. We raised our little crop of corn and melons and ate
> the mesquite beans. Now all is changed. We eat the white man's food,
> and it makes us soft; we wear the white man's heavy clothing and it
> makes us weak. Each day in the old times in summer and winter we
> came down to the river banks to bathe. This strengthened and
> toughened our firm skin. But white settlers were shocked to see the
> naked Indians, so now we keep away. In the old days we wore the
> breechcloth, and aprons made of bark and reeds. We worked all
> winter in the wind — bare arms, bare legs, and never felt the cold. But
> now, when the wind blows down from the mountains it makes us
> cough. Yes — we know that when you come, *we die*. [11]

The book from which the latter extract was taken simply bristles
with Amerindian rituals, including the Sacred Circle and Sun
Dance Rites. I do not feel, however, that justice could be done to
the Indians and their ceremonies by citing a few, incidental
details, as these Rites are so much an integral part of their culture
as a whole, and therefore need to be viewed in that context in
order to be fully understood and appreciated. The book is called
Touch the Earth — A Self-Portrait of Indian Existence, compiled
by T C McLuhan, and for those who would like to pursue this
study further, full details are given in the Bibliography.

Most of the Women's Rites from earlier cultures were connected with goddess worship, and as it was the custom for the
temples of the various goddesses to be served by priestesses the
concept of the 'sacred prostitute' arose. Merlin Stone tends to see
many of the early Women's Rites as being either flagrantly sexual
or containing sexual overtones, but this was not always the case.
There were other priesthoods which demanded absolute chastity
of both the men and the women in their service. One very
informative and fruitful essay written by Plutarch and addressed
to a lady by the name of Klea who, it would appear, held a

distinguished position among the priestesses of Delphi and had also been initiated into the Osiriac Mysteries, mentions disciplines of diet, personal hygiene and chastity which were nothing if not exacting!

In many archaeological texts, female religions are frequently referred to in fertility cult terms, as though they contained no depth or sublimity and were simply vessels for fecundity and conveniences for pleasure. Ms Stone observes the word 'cult' to have implicit connotations of something less fine or civilized than religion, which is nearly always implied to mean the worship of female deities. The 'fertility cult' tag, she suggests, may be a gross over-simplification of a complex theological structure. This is certainly borne out by Dr R E Witt in his absorbing and scholarly book *Isis in the Graeco-Roman World*, which renders a deep insight into the profundity of the Isian religion.

Although the fertility role is frequently ascribed to women, it has far wider connotations than the human reproductory process, being also concerned with husbandry, agriculture, hunting, and the necessities of life in general, including the medium of exchange. Fertility, in fact, implies the multiplication principle, wherever and to whatever this might apply.

Jungian analyst Bani Shorter has made a special study of Women's Rites and their effect on the female psyche. She argues that Western women may live lives without ritual or ceremonial Rites of Passage, but such rituals can constitute a route to spiritual freedom, and because their element is missing in modern society there are many women who suffer as a result. From her involvement with anthropology, she is aware of those rites which have in different times and places marked the initiations in women's lives — the awareness of the creatrix role, for example, which needs to be played out in one field of life if not in another.

She was first alerted to this ritual need while working with women suffering from anorexia nervosa. It occurred to her that something in the feminine archetype was struggling for recognition, expression and a new position in our modern-day values — an 'image darkly forming,' which is the title of her book. She sees each of us as making our own rituals, using the experiences of everyday life as our initiation ground, and oft times seeking the privacy of some self-erected transitory hut of darkness in which to face our inner selves and discover our true potential.

Her book deals with the dilemmas of five women from different age groups and walks of life. Individual paths, individual rituals, each woman dealing, or trying to deal, with her problem in her own unique way. What united them was an intensity of experience which ensured, as they each affirmed, that they would never be the same again. They had crossed the threshold, and their comments upon reading each other's stories for the first time was that they felt they had been sisters!

When change comes to a woman, Dr Shorter tells us, it is initially received and registered in the body, and only afterwards does its meaning reveal itself. We have no say in those bodily changes, such as menstruation and the menopause, which are the inevitable lot of our sex. Nor can we dictate their timing. The role of past rituals was to bring to consciousness the true meaning of these experiences: 'Psychologically,' she says, 'the progression is from rupture and division of the body and spirit to their eventual reunion in psyche/soul.'[12]

The Puberty Rites of the Bemba tribe in Africa are still said to 'grow a woman' as if from seed. If the purpose of these and similar ceremonies is to prepare the young women for their role in a dominantly patriarchal society, as well as teaching them to come to terms with their own minds and bodies, then we are surely dealing with a *gestalt* situation which is fundamental to the nature and psychology of those soul fragments that are experiencing life through the female psyche. Shorter explains that a mother cannot teach her daughter to be a woman, she can only expose her to the necessity of that experience.

Women's supposed susceptibility to limerance,* which is viewed by some men as a character weakness, is frequently used as an excuse to debar them from certain areas of activity in the material, religious and metaphysical worlds. It should be emphasized, however, that the limerant mode is not exclusive to the female sex and does not therefore merit use as a weapon of female invalidation.

Another point to be borne in mind is that her role as creatrix is not limited to the maternal mode. The notion that every woman should be a mother is based on the myth of the maternal instinct. Many biologists, psychologists, psychiatrists and sociologists are now of the opinion that the wish to become a mother is a socio-cultural conditioned response and not, as was previously believed, a biological need. In plain words, it has been pro-grammed into the female gender as a social convenience. This

*See Glossary

ritual commences in childhood with toys specially designed to accustom the girl child to the fact that she will be expected to reproduce at a later date and should therefore familiarize herself with the idea as soon as possible. It is followed in school with the encouragement of more 'feminine' studies as against the sciences, and reinforced by parents and peers, while the medium of advertising hammers it home at every possible opportunity. Those women who do not conform are viewed as either 'oddballs' or just plain selfish human beings. Tricia Stallings, writing in the *Guardian* (December 15th 1987) caps it beautifully in her article 'Nature Never Meant us to be Mothers' with the comment:

> Nowhere else do we find such a thorough and complete conditioning process. Yet we are told the desire to reproduce is based on 'maternal instinct'. The ultimate tyranny of a social dictate is the acceptance of that dictate having its origin in nature. This is the case with the so-called maternal instinct.

Many primitive Women's Rites were orientated towards mother-hood because the primary aim of the tribe as a whole was that of survival, and as there was little else for women (or men for that matter) to pursue in the way of self-expression or creativity, the maternal mode offered a solution to both of these social consider-ations. In today's world there are no such excuses, and women should be free to pursue the lifestyle to which they feel drawn, be it motherhood or otherwise.

In my counselling days I encountered far more cases of women who had followed the collective and produced children, only to find themselves frustrated and cheated of self-realization, than I did of women who had pursued their chosen careers and later regretted their lack of parenthood. The latter phenomenon, which may occasionally manifest during the early stages of the menopause, soon passes.

In spite of all the freedom and equality noises one hears lauded throughout the liberal media, the role of women is still a subser-vient one and anything that can help to make that burden easier to bear would, one supposes, be welcomed by many. As Jung affirmed, we do not make images but are made by them, and when we lose the security of our contact with those images we have formed during certain development stages in our lives, we lose something of ourselves which needs to be replaced and re-established on a new and more adult basis.

The abduction of Persephone and the story of Demeter's search for her daughter constituted the basis of the Eleusinian Mysteries which lasted for over a thousand years. These were basically feminine mysteries, and yet they were open to both men and women. So, as I see it, in the final analysis there is no real need for the sexual distinction as far as the transcendental quest is concerned; we may all worship, aspire and tread the Path together. The sexual superiority theme, when seen from either angle, is spiritual child's play, indulged in by those younger souls who are eager to seize any opportunity to express the domination principle through whichever avenues are available during any given time in history. And much as it may distress certain factions in our midst, the truth is that we all have to grow up some day!

Endnotes:

1. *The Paradise Papers* Merlin Stone, p. 241.
2. *Memories, Dreams and Reflections* C G Jung, p. 193.
3. *Rites and Symbols of Initiation* Mircea Eliade, pp. 41–42.
4. *Ibid.* p. 43.
5. *Ibid.* p. 43.
6. *Ibid.* p. 44.
7. *Ibid.* p. 45.
8. *Ibid.* p. 46.
9. *Ibid.* p. 79.
10. *Daughters of Copper Woman* Anne Cameron, pp. 61–62.
11. *Touch The Earth — A Self-Portrait of Indian Existence* compiled by T C McLuhan, p. 125.
12. *An Image Darkly Forming* Bani Shorter, p. 73.

Part 3
Rituals of the Nuclear Age

Chapter 19

THE AGE OF THE CULT

Many of those rites which we have been examining in preceding chapters have originated and developed in the Piscean Age and earlier. They have, to an extent, been coloured by the solar ages in which they manifested. Piscean Rites, for example, lean towards Sacrificial and Emotional forms of expression, while their Arien predecessors tended to accentuate the Severity Code.

Tracing back the history of the rites even further, astrological authorities inform us that the Leonian Age, which is placed somewhere around 10,000 BC, gave birth to much pomp, regality and creative art, with lion and sun motifs frequently appearing in architecture and religion. According to arcane sources this was the latter period of the Atlantean era, which was doomed to destruction by the earth's axial change which brought about the Cancerian Flood. The Age of Cancer, estimated to have commenced around 8000 BC, spawned the numerous matrist cults with their associated Lunar Rites, and there is a tradition which ascribes to the belief that many of these emerged as a result of a change in the moon's position in relation to earth. The Geminian Age, about 6000 BC saw the birth of the Twin Cults, many of which filtered through to later times via the Twin God Rites. Sacred pillars dedicated to pairs of gods have been found in Babylonian, Assyrian, Grecian and Samothracian temples. The Taurean Age — 4000 BC saw the emergence of bull worship, as manifested in the Minoan culture and later in Egypt and surrounding countries.

What we are now faced with is the Aquarian Age, and this means a gradual change from the more collective forms of Piscean expression to the individualization that must and will result from the Aquarian influence. When any Solar Age commences, or more especially during the death throes of the preceding Age, there is a period of chaos which inevitably takes its toll on established patterns in all forms of expression. The approximate date given by astrologers for the commencement of the Aquarian Age is around the year 2000, although by astronomical computation a more precise figure of 2740 is given.[1]

This change of astrological emphasis on the planet, in general, will engender a corresponding change of attitude and approach towards the Rite. This has already started to manifest, much to the consternation of those stalwart traditionalists of the Piscean era who see it as posing a threat to their security. But change is ever the pattern of the universe, and those soul fragments that are entering incarnation with Aquarian expression in view will naturally eschew the Piscean collectives, having been pre-programmed for a different approach!

During the early onset of the Aquarian influence, fluctuations are bound to occur which will naturally result in cross-rhythms. Piscean rites will find their way into Aquarian camps, where they will naturally be out of place, and many who entered life ostensibly to experience in the Piscean mode are likely to find Aquarian mental techniques somewhat disquieting. People who have not been pre-programmed to handle Aquarian sensitivity could well experience frustration if they find themselves unable to emulate those altered states of awareness that are destined to form part of the Aquarian mental inheritance. This frustration may cause them to turn to drugs and questionable rites and practices which forcibly project them into 'trips' for which they are not psychologically prepared. Older souls are better able to handle transition periods than their younger brethren, which is why, during times of major change or 'quantum jumps' in the evolutionary cycle of a planet such as earth, there is usually an influx of old soul (or more mature soul) fragments.

There are many schools of esoteric thought concerning the subject of soul age, and I have no intention of becoming involved in a philosophical disputation. Suffice it to say I do not concur with the concept of straight line or linear evolution through 'inner time' — although this may be much easier for many to grasp than the 'fragmented hologram' theory which is much favoured by those who like to combine metaphysical considerations with the scientific approach. This view conceives of a state of 'outer time' which exists beyond the confines of the inner time we see on our clocks, although the environmental time circuits of the latter obviously appear valid to all who function within these wavebands. In certain frequencies which exist beyond the frozen energy of our own planet, therefore, the past, present and future are all one, and the various incarnations of the soul or psyche (I prefer the term 'Essence') are but fragments of the Whole essence which, like the broken hologram, each retain the characteristics of the original picture.

We experience some lives as young soul fragments; others, in intermediate or mature modes. Making contact with the so-termed 'Higher Self' therefore consists of contacting a more mature fragment which can handle and transmute energies which we ourselves are unable to compute while encapsulated in this time zone we call the present. As far as the Rite is concerned, mature soul fragments may well choose to express themselves via the faiths of modern-day collectives (as no doubt mature soul fragments have ever done in the past) in order to fulfil their chosen roles of sacrifice or service to the community. Strap-hanging on set dogmas, either religious or social is not, however, the hallmark of spiritual maturity. The real nature of Truth is both abstract and fluid, and our understanding of its principles adjusts naturally as we progress, which implies that none of us is truly cognizant of its entirety.

I fully realize that the foregoing will leave a lot of question marks regarding time and soul age, but these have been taken care of in my book, *The Lion People*, and I have only mentioned the subject here inasmuch as it affects the nature and observance of the Rite in this, the Age of Change.[2] Older soul fragments will feel the need to explore the universe mentally and spiritually, and although those journeys into the abstract may be right for them, they could constitute a danger for their younger brethren.

Philosophers and metaphysicians tell us that in this day and age the gap between soul ages on this planet is unnaturally wide. This divergence, of course, results in a gross variance in ritualistic expression ranging from the evangelical and fundamentalist movements of Christianity and Islam to the broader Aquarian approaches, many of which incorporate magical and psychic practices. The Aquarian Age allows for individual expression. In other words, we are each free to choose our own path to enlightenment and initiation, accompanied by whichever rites we may find appropriate to that quest. The truly Aquarian approach would therefore be one of tolerance towards the beliefs and rites of others although, sadly, this would not seem to be the case.

Aquarianism is, of course, a double-edged sword in that it can either manifest as a balanced assumption of individual responsibility, or a hedonistic fling at the expense of society. One should also remember that, astrologically speaking, Aquarius is ruled by Uranus, the 'Great Awakener'. There is nothing sentimental, sloppy or even vaguely Piscean about Great Grandfather Uranus, who is nothing if not enquiring, inventive, far-seeing, original, progressive, unconventional, reforming, strong-willed, unusual, outspoken, magnetic and cosmically inclined; on the negative side he is also changeful, detached, eccentric, perverse, rebellious, willful and dangerous (with due acknowledgement to astrology!). Computers, astrophysics, technological advancements, self-help systems, genetic engineering and those rites which reach beyond this earth for the answers to its problems — these are Uranian things. The first flurry of Uranian freedom saw the 'love-ins', 'flower power', women's liberation, the feminist movement, and the 'back to nature' craze of the 1960s and 70s with their resultant mental and somatic side-effects. The 1980s have witnessed, among other things, an increasing awareness of the oneness of all life, and many new approaches to illness, self-discovery and self-discipline. Certain sections of the world's population are starting to pull together, as may be evidenced in such mass global rituals as Band-Aid, other collective efforts in aid of African famine relief, and the Harmonic Convergence observance in 1987.

The nature and expression of the Rite may appear to be changing — but is it really? I think not; the principles are still the same. It is only the approach and enactment that have altered. Like the ouroboros (the snake swallowing its tail), the past has finally caught up with the present. Old rites from centuries past are resurfacing to be enacted in modern language, with modern colours and up to date themes. Aquarians are reaching backwards as well as forwards in their search for cosmic roots, while many are also reaching outwards, beyond the confines of earth, earthly religions and god concepts. There has been a great resurgence of ancient religions and their associated ceremonial. Books on ancient Egypt, Celtica, Shamanism, Amerindian and Far Eastern Rites sell side by side with popular novels. The new eco-religion, with its ritualistic association with ley lines and power centres, has survived its birth pangs and is now gaining weight! Its voice is to be heard crying aloud both in politics and the personal expression of faith. Old stone monuments, monoliths and barrows once more host worshippers as they did in days of old, while the Solitary Rite has never been more popular.

Many people today either indulge in these practices themselves, have relatives or young folk in their families who espouse such causes or, if they are opposed to them, speak out in disgust about: 'those strange people across the road who troop off to Stonehenge or the Rollrights for some dreadful pagan ceremony — it ought to be stopped!' or, 'I don't allow my family to go to *that* house, they have tarot cards, astrology books and other such works of the Devil lying about!' But we must be patient, the fishes who swim downstream to join the big ocean of the universal unconscious will, no doubt, eventually return upstream to spawn in the new waters of the future.

What a rosy picture this Aquarian Age presents us with! Or does it? After all, we are dealing with a double-edged sword and now we come to the snags.

New Age thinking appears to have brought with it a host of dependencies, which is not really Aquarian at all if you care to think about it. The Cult of the Guru, for example, which has flourished over the past twenty or more years, in spite of its ecletic overtones is nothing more than an extension of the Piscean principle with the guru replacing the local parish priest, parson or minister — although the guru usually fares better by worldly standards! From a psychological standpoint, dependencies are not good for one in the long run, however comfortable they might seem to some. Too many of those who espouse the cause of some teacher or master do so because they wish to rid themselves of personal responsibility on the one hand, or as a social convenience on the other.

Of course the same can be said of any religious or social collective. Many people regularly visit this or that church or political gathering, not because they believe for one minute in what is going on, but as one young couple put it: 'We have such a smashing time, and the food is good. We just nod off when they start talking about all that other stuff.'

The use of the Rite as a social convenience is by no means limited to the present, there have ever been spiritual 'women's institutes' and their male equivalents, and no doubt many of those who danced along behind the Eleusinian procession in ancient Greece, or cast their garlands at the statue of the Goddess in the Egyptian Rites at Bubastis were, to coin a modern phrase, 'only here for the beer!'

Then there is the negative aspect of the 'back to nature' movement, many who espouse completely free and natural expression having failed to observe the fact that nature herself is nothing if not disciplined. When her ecological balance is not disturbed in the name of economic necessity or desecrated by opposing hedonistic factions, she manages to keep her affairs in good order. Were we to observe the natural rhythms of nature and live according to Cosmic Law, we too could avoid a great deal of suffering both personal and global. Therefore, those rites which imitate these rhythms — Seasonal Rites, Earth Rites, and the rituals of natural or cosmic phenomena — are usually beneficial to all, as the ancients well knew.

Strangely enough, the late Carl Jung himself has become something of a cult figure, and there are groups and institutes in many countries which accord a biblical-type veneration to his works. This he would no doubt disapprove of were he still around to voice his views. It is not so much his life itself that stands as a shining example to many, but his open and enquiring mind that was ever ready to acknowledge the close relationship between the outward expression of the psyche and its inner, transcendental needs.

Ritual today has become very much institutionalized, in that both establishment and non-establishment collectives indulge in ritual displays as social statements. For example, those wishing to identify themselves with a particular cult, school of belief or way of thinking tend to dress alike, and the explanations given are frequently quite comical. Some months ago I engaged in conversation a group of young people who were all dressed identically in black, with the same ornamentation, hairdo's and make-up (both male and female!) They thought me frightfully 'square' and hastened to say so. I asked them why and one of them replied, 'Well, look how you dress, just like all the rest of them'!

I surveyed the passers by in the street with an air of mystified confusion — not a single lady around was wearing a coat like mine to start with, so I drew this fact to the attention of the young lady who had made the remark. Then I pointed out how absolutely alike *they* all were, whereupon they all had a good giggle before finally nodding their heads in assent.

There are those who do feel the need to don the ceremonial robes of their cult and parade down the high street in colourful garments as a form of ritual social statement, but such behaviour usually constitutes part of the unspoken rites of modern puberty, and most of us pass through this or a corresponding phase at some time or other in our youth. The fact that the rites of popular cults are out in the open is psychologically good. It is when they assume a covertness which has power complex undertones that the necessity for caution arises.

One of the dangers of living in a free society is that many people do not feel sufficiently supported morally and ethically. Old established ways of behaviour are now considered *passé* and the tendency, especially amongst the young, is *not* to be seen to be 'different' which in view of the Aquarian leaning towards individuality is something of a dichotomy. During my counselling days I frequently encountered young men and women who were being pressured by their peers to indulge in sexual and social practices which they personally found to be morally and ethically unacceptable, and the resulting mental conflict frequently affected their health. It takes a strong mind to hold out against the collective, but it can be done and many have survived it intact. A psychological danger, therefore, lurks in group social rituals which do not accord with the individual conscience, and people of all ages — the young in particular — should pay heed to this if they wish to avoid problems in later life.

Those who are aware of their own inability to handle too much freedom tend to turn to collective groups and rituals for support. The commune, for instance, can offer security to people who wish to carry out an alternative lifestyle in an environment which is free from the ever critical voice of conventionality. Safe within its confines, they can practise their rites and indulge in constructive debate on their beliefs and ideals. There are also many people who employ the Rite as a means to express their own collectivity, attending evangelical meetings, group rallies, rock festivals or other religious and social occasions. If one feels the need to state one's sense of belonging to the family of Homo sapiens in a public or collective way, then fair enough. Not all of us are ready to stand alone, the process of individuation being a painful one. The danger however, lies in the condemnation of those who do choose a different form of expression.

Many people are totally unhappy if exposed to the rites of faiths other than those to which they have chosen to adhere. A close friend of mine, who is a pagan, was recently coerced into attending a Christian service to please another person, knowing full well that she would never reciprocate by observing one of the rites of his faith. It does not do to submit to the will of another if it results in a sense of guilt and spiritual unease. This is the sort of stuff of which neuroses are born and the same applies conversely should you be the Christian in the case.

Modern life imposes a triple programming from transpersonal, genetic and environmental sources — each of which needs to be carefully weighed and balanced against the other until, from somewhere among the mental and spiritual confusion, we find our true selves. In the prevailing social and environmental climate the cosmic quest for life's *raison d'être* is by no means an easy one, but the gnosis is never completely denied — it may always be accessed via the Rite.

Endnotes:

1. *The Modern Textbook of Astrology* M E Hone, p. 279.
2. *The Lion People* Murry Hope, Chapter 2.

Chapter 20

INTERPLANETARY AND INTERSTELLAR RITES

The total dissatisfaction with existing social structures and systems of belief has given rise to a series of alternatives. These can be condensed into two main streams which could be broadly classified under 'past' and 'future'. The former involves looking back into the past of this planet for inspiration, transcendental guidance and spiritual security and has already been explored in the preceding chapter. The latter looks forward into the future and outward into the cosmos for the answers to life's enigmas. Many in fact successfully combine the two, noting references to interplanetary and interstellar exchanges in ancient writings from the distant past which are conveniently interpreted to suit the space age of the future.

There is a whole psychology behind the UFO phenomenon and those schools of belief which have arisen from it (which Jung wisely noted), and although these noumenals are eschewed by psychology's more materialistic stalwarts, it is not really out of keeping with the normal evolutionary pattern of Homo sapiens. After all, without that spirit of adventure, of wanting to know, to explore, to understand, our ancestors would never have left their caves, and viewed in the microcosmic/macrocosmic light our planet is, in a sense, a cosmic cave or moving spaceship, from which chrysalis we must ultimately emerge into universal flight.

There is nothing wrong with looking forward and outward.

The spirit of adventure, tempered with reason, practicality and factual observation is always healthy. It is only when the belief or ideal becomes a prop for personal inadequacy, self-delusion, escapism or ego inflation that there is cause for concern.

One of the simplest approaches to the acknowledgement of external influences on the human psyche has been the resurgence of popular astrology. Newspaper horoscopes have never enjoyed such an enormous readership, and although professional astrologers may throw up their hands in despair at what they feel to be a travesty of a legitimate science, there are millions whose lives are literally ruled by their daily or weekly 'stars'. Reading the horoscope has become a ritual for them to the extent that they are uneasy if some event such as a newspaper strike occurs to deprive them of their regular dose of planetary placebos.

Astrology also features in ritual itself, being the deciding factor in many rites as to the time, date and conditions of the enactment. However, the content of this chapter is aimed towards another interplanetary or interstellar field of enquiry. It involves the belief that there are beings somewhere 'out there' who are interested (or the reverse) in what is taking place here on earth, and with whom communicatory links can be forged or established to the benefit of both parties. Many of these channelled communications have given birth to a whole new set of rites which, at first glance, appear to differ considerably from the rituals of the past both in content and intent. But do they? Observation and study force me to conclude that they all add up to the same principle, albeit on a different octave.

Many mystics, psychics and occultists are of the opinion that the Sirius factor holds the key to the future of this planet, and that its energies are somehow destined to play an important role in the evolutionary quantum jump — much beloved of the eschatologists (the science of the end of things) and frequently forecast of late — which will provide the proverbial melting pot or sorting-out time for the denizens of this planet.

The Sirius Ray is believed to represent the essential polarity of anima/animus, yin/yang, receptive/projective, which principle is being sorely tested by the conditions of the Age in which we live. Those who are unable to handle Siriun energies frequently find themselves experiencing a sexual identity crisis which can put them at odds both with themselves and society at large. It is also believed that the abuse of the physical energy and mental freedom that these energies engender in the human psyche has been responsible for the rapid spread of sexually transmitted diseases on the one hand, and the rise in cases of psychopathic behaviour and crimes of violence on the other. Rites are therefore needed which counteract the negative effect of the transmutatory qualities of this binary star. There are, to my knowledge, several private groups already working along these lines, although I am also aware that many followers of the Sirius or Sothian cults prefer to dispense with ritual and work in Mind Magic.

How do we know all this? The information has come from many sources all over the world, for example the Hopi Indians, for whom Sirius forms an important part of their most secret teachings and who know it by the name of 'The Blue Star Kachina'. According to their most ancient tradition, beings from planets in the Sirius system visited our earth some 250,000 years ago and deposited time capsules some of which, they believe, are due to be triggered off from now (1988) onwards. In addition to these old legends and prophecies, many people have experienced recollections of a life or lives in the Sirius system, while psychiatrists and psychotherapists are starting to uncover similarly related memories among students engaged in experimental work, (as against those who are actually receiving treatment for psychological disorders, for whom the delusion factor might well apply). This brings us back to the subject of channelling, the Law of Synchronicity and the collective unconscious.

We have already discussed the problems of channelling in Chapter 5, and the not unwarranted prejudice against it which is strong among certain occult traditions. The shamans, on the other hand, seem only too happy to indulge in preternatural activities, effecting the ecstatic state at will, which would appear to grant them access to the minds of other life forms on this planet, and probably elsewhere in the cosmos if the truth were known. The main pitfalls of channelling would appear to lie in self-delusion, lack of good imaging ability and inadequate terms of reference. People also tend to make things fit their own pet ideas and theories rather than opening their minds to new concepts. I recall an instance many years ago when I was invited, along with two others, to the home of a well known medium for 'advice'. She was sweet, elderly soul and every inch the devout Christian. Her guide, she informed us, was none other than John Wesley himself, who would put us straight on a few good Christian points. The fact that she was a very fine medium may be evidenced from the ensuing events.

After we had settled down and the Rite of Preparation — which involved several prayers and readings from the Bible — had been observed, she entered the trance state and assumed the booming voice of an evangelical preacher. Both my friends and myself knew enough at that time to challenge the entity, whereupon the persona changed completely and the voice assumed a softer, more disciplined tone. Having received an 'identifying sign' that I could recognize, I then addressed him and asked why he found it necessary to masquerade as a Methodist preacher. He replied that the woman herself was an excellent channel, and good channels were few and far between. However, she was greatly prejudiced in favour of Methodism and refused to allow entry to any intelligence that did not conform to that school of belief. The Wesley persona, therefore, allowed him access to help her personally and also render a broader understanding of the world and its problems to those for whom she regularly executed the trance state. No, he was not at all proud of the deception, but he had weighed it against the good work he could do and the number of people who could benefit as a result, and the two seemed to balance out.

A sad state of affairs when our personal prejudices can so effectively block our progress; but then there is, one supposes, a right time for everything both for the individual and the world at large.

The interplanetary and interstellar cult has given birth to a whole new line of gurus, many of whom have enormous personal followings. Although some of these cults lack the backing of logic or scientific fact, they would appear to supply an emotional need and are, therefore, in their way no more destructive or injurious to the human psyche than many of the emotionally orientated popular religions of the day.

There is a belief among some metaphysicians and mystics that very young soul fragments veer towards the instinctive in their rites and beliefs. Although they are often unable to logicize those tenets which they observe, they are in fact nearer to the ways of the old soul than the middle stages of spiritual evolutionary development, which frequently feature either emotionally orientated or rigidly logical approaches. All four states — instinctive, emotional, logical and intuitive — eventually combine in the truly mature soul fragment, but having passed through the former stages, the old soul is careful never to condemn his or her youthful associates. Prejudice, intolerance and hatred of any kind can be counted among the hallmarks of spiritual immaturity. An interesting corollary to the aforesaid may be evidenced in the way that children and young people are frequently closer to their grandparents than to their mothers and fathers, and vice versa.

The rites of guru-orientated 'space age' groups usually assume a similar pattern in that they may or may not require personal participation. So, while large or small gatherings are sometimes convened, the fellowship may involve no more than a 'tune-in' for members at set times of the day, plus the regular receipt of a news sheet or appropriate literature. These tune-ins usually involve a short ritual which follows a pattern of preselected imagery that may be designed purely to connect the followers with the guru, or in the case of channelled work with the guiding entity. Or it could have wider connotations, as in the case of the 1987 Harmonic Convergence. The rites of some space age gurus can involve long periods of meditation, the repetition of mantras, and the execution of body movements designed to increase sensitivity or open up certain psychic centres. Exactly the same dangers apply here as are outlined in Chapter 10, and the fact that the whole practice is executed under a pseudo-scientific flag does not preclude its participants from the normal consequences of meddling with heightened states of awareness without due forethought, knowledge, correct preparation and protection.

Much channelling is purely the result of dipping into the collective unconscious. The danger in this practice lies, among other things, in ignorance of the true facts, as in the case of the medium who wrote copiously about early Egypt but managed to get her deities hopelessly mixed up. A little study of the Egyptian god-forms, their associations, triads, and the periods of Egyptian history in which they were best-known would have saved her a lot of later embarrassment. Knowledge and inspiration should always walk hand in hand, one without the other inevitably giving rise to problems.

Those who indulge in the type of space age rite that requires voluntary movement forward or backward in time should beware of the time trap — our ability to transcend the barriers of space and time being decided by our soul age. The situation could be likened to a small child who is anxious to cross a main thoroughfare because on the other side of the road there is the best sweetshop in town. If he tries to cross alone and unaided there is every likelihood of a fatal accident, because he has not yet learned the highway code. As in the case of civil laws, ignorance of Cosmic Laws does not protect one against the consequences of breaking them! Now that child can seek the help of an experienced adult who will either take him across the road or go over to the shop for him, or he can make do with the sweetshop next door to his home and venture further afield when he is older.

Unfortunately, young souls, like young people, frequently think that they know all the answers, and their egos are badly bruised if it is suggested to them for one minute that they are not yet ready for this or that mystical or magical adventure. The Rite inevitably has its chapter of accidents. However, as it has ever been the way of man to struggle forward in his search for knowledge, and the pages of history are strewn with the casualties of this quest. So, we cannot judge — we can only forewarn.

Chapter 21

THE ROLE OF RITUAL IN EVERYDAY LIFE

Ritual observances are by no means limited to metaphysical modes of expression. If we care to analyse it, they occupy a large part of our everyday lives. How many of us, for example, carry out a set morning routine, which is followed by the regular journey to our place of employment. Our lunch period is probably taken up doing almost the same thing every day and when we arrive home in the evening we pursue a similar ritual which will be dictated by our age group, taste, hobbies or responsibilities. The discipline of regularity is a good thing as long as it does not become an end in itself. There are people who are so frightened to vary their daily rituals that when they are forced by circumstances to do so, they become highly stressed or even ill as a result. This tells the psychiatrist that the routine or daily ritual had developed into a compulsion neurosis; in other words, it has become an obsession.

Exactly the same happens to those who practise religious or magical rites to the extent that the Rite itself, rather than the reason for its enactment, becomes the dominant factor (see also Chapter 3). There is a wise old Buddhic parable about a man who went searching for God beneath a stone, but in the process of lifting the stone he became so absorbed with its quality and beauty that he forgot his initial reason for raising it. No Rite, be it religious, secular, magical or social, should ever be allowed to control one's life. Rituals are simply tools for the discipline of the mind, body or spirit, which having a liminal content, can also allow access to other dimensions of consciousness, archaic resonances or energy levels external to those upon which we normally function.

Many people carry out quite meaningful rites without knowing why. Simple superstitions, for example, have often originated in more serious modes of ritual expression. In a recent television series people from all walks of life were interviewed in the street and asked why, for example, they always avoided walking under ladders, threw salt over their left shoulder or carried mascots. Many were unable to give an explanation although one man stated quite emphatically that he thought it to be a load of rubbish. The interviewer then asked him, in view of this remark, whether he would still continue to do it, to which he replied: 'Yes, I suppose I always will.' 'But why?' the interviewer persisted. The man shrugged his shoulders and was obviously quite confused over his own attitude. 'Because, one somehow feels one *has* to,' was his response.

This kind of inurement to habitual ritualistic practices might not be traceable to present life environment, but could be psychically inherited from the collective unconscious of the race or group soul, or a former existence (time zone, in my terminology).

Today's social rites constitute one of the most powerful conditioning factors in modern life, rituals of sport and entertainment in particular demonstrate the power of the Rite in collective programming. The media, therefore, stands as the most influential agent in the manipulatory game, its voice assuming an almost divine authority to many. The world of advertising, ever awake to this fact, never misses an opportunity to exploit it commercially. I knew an old lady, now deceased, who, after seeing an advertisement for a particular brand of soap powder repeated several times on television, hastened to her local shop to purchase the product. The shopkeeper asked her why she felt the need to change from her usual choice, to which she replied in all sincerity: 'I have to, my dear. It says so on the telly'!

That was a simple matter of choosing an alternative household commodity, which might appear harmless enough to many, but it is the principle behind it which gives cause for concern. Programmes attacking or ridiculing the beliefs of certain minority groups, for example, can have disastrous effects on the lives of the people who practise those faiths. As so much of what is covered by the media is taken by many as 'gospel', it is little wonder that broadcast or televised rites effect such a powerful sway over the populace at large.

There is a saying that materialism and science are the gods of today. If so, when faced with the choice between these and the dogmas of old established collectives, it is little wonder that the more discerning, or spiritually orientated, are turning to alternative faiths, cults, therapies or ideologies. The deities of materialism and science, in keeping with all worshipped principles, also have their rites and sacraments. Scientific sacerdotalism, for example, has simply exchanged the priestly robes of the past for the laboratory white coat, while the idols of materialism stand aloft on their gilded pedestals, greedily devouring the adulation of their fans from the worlds of 'pop', sport, politics, the arts — any area of life, in fact, in which the personality cult flourishes. Pop concerts, political rallies, mass sporting events, soap operas — these are their rites, and well attended they are too!

Why, then, should this be so? Because, for the majority, these act as substitutes for the gratification of day-dreams, outlets for undisciplined energies, or channels through which they might live out their fantasies. Contrary to what many might think, things have not changed all that much over the centuries. A Roman centurion visiting a modern football match would see little difference between the behaviour of the fans and the reactions of the old Coliseum crowds to the performance of the gladiators! No doubt 'gladiatorial' hooliganism was just as much a problem to the good citizens of Rome as its football equivalent is to the more peaceful elements in today's society.

Those among us who consider ourselves civilized decry the ancient rites of sacrifice and torture, and look back at our ancestors who indulged in these practices as cruel and inhuman barbarians. And yet, how many of us experience a sense of guilt when we watch the enactment of those very same rites of violence and horror in the media as part of our programme of daily 'entertainment'? Seated in a comfortable armchair in front of the television set, we may indulge our cruel and sadistic fantasies to our heart's content in the safe knowledge that no one will ever know for what we are actually compensating. But unfortunately, it doesn't stop there. The energies of the Rite can reach and penetrate the mind via the signals of the broadcasting media, and their effects on the human psyche are identical to those experienced by the participants of in-group or solitary rituals. This may be evidenced in the increase in all kinds of violence — maltreatment of children, vandalism, drug abuse, and so on — in fact, the whole gamut of today's social ills.

Of course, the eternal dualism of light and darkness, knowledge and ignorance has always manifested in some form or other down the ages. Jung once remarked to the effect that every town or city had both its respectable parts and its red light areas, and as long as these remained in balance then well and good. But should one start to invade the territory of the other, or impose its statutes by majority rule or force, the right of the individual to effect a choice would become jeopardized and serious problems would arise.

Age-old magical and religious dualisms are still enacted in the arena of modern life but how many would recognize them? Old evils re-emerge under new names; salacious literature masquerades under the protective banner of social comment, while in the world of the occult 'chaos magic' is logicised as an excuse for hedonistic licence. Legitimate mystical sciences are perverted in the name of experiment, and discipline has become a dirty word! One could go on. As to the harvest to be reaped from these questionable seeds, we only need to look around us or observe the news headlines to become aware of the truth.

Yet, from among all this confusion and doubt, there emerges a glimmer of compassion and reason — the caring attitude of people at large towards the victims of major accidents, disasters or famines and the work of those who regularly perform those rites which encourage the energies of Love, Peace and Light.

Chapter 22

SECRET RITES

There have been secret rites since man first organized himself into distinct tribal or cultural groups. Initially, these acted purely as a form of demarcation between the ruling or priestly castes and the remainder of the tribe, but as time progressed they assumed initiatory significance on the one hand, while suggesting a source of hidden power or 'know-how' on the other.

Many of the earlier secret rites — the initiation rituals of shamanism, for example — were hereditary, being passed from father or mother to son or daughter, in the same way that they were (and in some cases still are) in the Craft of Wicca. This was believed to maintain the pristine quality of the art and guard against corruption — the 'blood is thicker than water' idea guaranteeing the unblemished continuity of the original gift. Celtic Druidism, which had shamanic origins, also functioned in this way for many centuries before finally succumbing to social pressure following the advent of Christianity.

In ancient Egypt, secret rites which concerned such practical matters as the erection of buildings, sacred geometry and architecture, and the remnants of scientific know-how that had somehow managed to survive the Flood, gave birth to the old Orders of Masonry, of which the god Ptah — the Master Builder and Architect of the Universe — was the patron. Although certain elements in modern Freemasonry still believe their Cult to have had its origins in those far distant times, others among them staunchly deny any connection with magic, ancient or otherwise, claiming that their organization is purely a charitable one, the rites of which are designed to encourage integrity, self-discipline and group co-operation.

As the ages rolled by there emerged another valid reason for the existence of the secret rite: persecution. Inasmuch as many of the deities of earlier civilizations were comfortably interchangeable there was little cause for religious intolerance, but with the emergence and growth of those monotheistic faiths which claimed to be the one and only truth, fear spread among all who felt they could not in conscience embrace these new doctrines, and the rites of many older religions and minority groups went underground. Sometimes these were kept alive by secret Orders, such as the Knights Templar, where they were conveniently hidden beneath an exterior of religious convention. But as inquisition after inquisition broke the power even of the learned, wealthy and well born, these Orders withdrew deeper into the safety of anonymity, taking their rites with them.

There is, however, a third and highly questionable kind of secret society. Unscrupulous charlatans down the ages have ever been wise to ways of making a quick profit, and during those periods of history in which occult and allied studies have particularly flourished or been in vogue, they enjoyed a heyday. This they could never have accomplished were it not for the egos of those who saw themselves as being something special, apart from or above most ordinary people, a privilege for which they were prepared to pay handsomely. Certain of these Orders, therefore, instituted sub-divisions which were supposedly reserved only for the highly initiated and specially gifted who were also, needless to say, very rich. Each man (women were seldom featured in this strategy) was handled separately and kept well apart from the others on the pretext that he, and he alone, had been chosen for some high occult rank, which was usually blessed with a suitably impressive Latin title. The best-known of these was probably the Scottish Knights, an offshoot of Adam Weishaupt's infamous Illuminati. Each 'knight' believed himself to be the one and only Grand Master of the Order, for which privilege he parted with large sums of money, land or worldly goods. We can read the same story over and over again in today's Sunday press, and I have personally come across several cases of people who have suffered similar wrongs, but who have been too embarrassed or frightened to come forward and report them.

Numerous apologies are rendered for the secrecy of occult or magical rites, many of which are perfectly valid. Some of these will be obvious from the dangers I have already highlighted. Many people, however, both within and without the occult world, feel that it is time for magic to come out of the closet and face world opinion. This is all very well if the perils attached to its malpractice and the side-effects which can result from the unskilled use of its rites are also made quite clear.

There are aspects of the secret society code which call for psychological qualification, however. These involve: (a) those so-termed mystical 'schools' which are nothing more nor less than private religions; (b) intellectual occult groups which cast disdainful glances at all and everything that is not included in or approved by their own smug little cliques; and (c) the 'Union', or magical closed shop into which one cannot or may not be permitted to enter unless one is part of that set.

Let us commence with (a). Private religious groups are all very well as long as there is nothing subversive in their activities. In using the term 'subversive', I am not implying national or political ethics, but rather those powerful holds over the minds of people which are frequently effected by collectives of this kind who think nothing of splitting families, homes or lovers in their efforts to maintain control over the individual and ensure that they do not stray from the fold. I shall refrain from mentioning names here, but I am sure that most of my readers will know the sort of organizations to which I am referring.

The persuasive methods employed by such cults can be compared with similar practices in earlier times, while many of them are not averse to utilizing modern inurement techniques to gain their ends. Their rites and practices are geared to the control theme, which is easily recognizable by the limiting nature of its precepts. We are thinking creatures, gifted with a degree of freewill which, sociologists may argue and rightly so, is to an extent limited by our personal psychological make-up and environmental background. But we should be allowed some manoeuvrability within that limitation (which has frequently been karmically imposed by the Higher Self anyway), preferably within a structured framework of self-knowledge and self-discipline.

Category (b) embraces everything which could vaguely be classified under the heading of spiritual or intellectual snobbery. Here we have a classic example of the inferiority complex manifesting in a superiority thrust, a sense of power through being on the inside, or knowing something (or thinking one does) which no one else knows or understands. This is a real psychological trap and one into which the aspiring occultist is particularly likely to fall! From time to time we all like to think that we have something concrete to contribute to society, as well as to our own personal development and wholeness. It cheers us up, does our egos good, and makes us feel special. But, in truth, this is a child's game in which the players must eventually submit to the reality of spiritual maturity.

Nor is this category limited to occult or magical circles. There are just as many groups who fly the banners of sanctity who are guilty of that very unholy practice known as 'spiritual snobbery'! One is tempted to recall the biblical parable of the Pharisee and the publican: while the latter was full of humility and only too aware of his own shortcomings, the former addressed his Maker with the words, 'God, I thank thee that I am not like other men, extortionists, unjust, adulterers, or even like this tax collector . . .' (Luke 18: 10-14). When we lose our sense of proportion to that extent, then we are truly psychologically and spiritually disorientated. Fanaticism of any kind constitutes a mental imbalance, and this includes extremes of both faith and scepticism. The emotional approach to religion engendered by the media in some countries, for example, can be extremely harmful in that it casts aspersions on those who are not followers of that particular cult or system, which in turn, produces persecutions and inquisitions, both private and public.

Finally we come to the 'closed shop' or select clique. Forming cliques would appear to be a facet of human nature — albeit an undesirable one — but nevertheless a fact of life. We are all entitled to select our friends, company or associates in accordance with our personal views and aspirations, and our general feelings about and attitudes towards the world in which we live. The laws of physics and chemistry attest to the fact that all elements do not mix happily and harmoniously, and those same laws also apply to all living creatures. Two positives clash, two negatives end up getting nowhere. Hence the value of understanding the Law of Polarity. Then there are the various levels of cultural, somatic and spiritual development to be taken into account, plus our personal psychological make-up and unique individuality. Bearing all this in mind, it is little wonder that many people find it difficult to effect harmonious relationships with their fellow human beings.

As I see it, there is no harm in forming private groups with one's own kind, as long as the situation is kept in proportion and one does not begin to see in that clique an élitism which distinguishes its members from, elevates them above, or renders them power over, others. As any genuine occultist or mystic knows, there are transcendental moments of sublimity, enlightenment and spiritual awareness which can only be shared with the few, or in some cases with no one at all. To expose such sensitivities to the irreverence of the uninitiated would be sacrilegious in the extreme — *not* because one is any better, wiser or more gifted than one's fellow men, however, but because one has the right to express in a personal way, that spark of the Creator which is unique and individual to oneself. There is certain knowledge that one simply cannot pass on to everyone and anyone, any more than one would hand a dangerous device to a small child as an amusing toy. This has nothing to do with feeling better, greater or more powerful than one's fellow human beings, but simply being more aware. Through one's own initiations, one has learned to love all life, and therefore has no wish to cause it any harm. That is all.

Sometimes the need for secrecy is a legitimate psychological requirement, as Jung observed during an instructive encounter with the Pueblo Indians in which the hidden nature and inaccessibility of their religion came up for discussion. Long conversations with their Elders convinced him that their secret rites were essential to the good order and psychological well-being of their people, and that they experienced great suffering on account of the efforts on the part of the American authorities to stamp out their rituals and forbid their dances. The dignity and sorrow of these Indians greatly impressed the psychiatrist, and left him questioning European rationalism and all that it implied.[1]

To be or not to be secret would, in the final analysis, appear to be very much a question of the proportion, intention, and right of the individual to simply be him or herself.

Endnotes:

1. *Memories, Dreams and Reflections* C G Jung, pp. 235–237.

Chapter 23

NEW AGE INITIATION

In previous chapters we have examined the various methods for crossing the initiatory thresholds which have been devised by numerous cultures down the ages. Sometimes the barriers to be passed, or the difficulties to be overcome, are social or psychological ones which relate to the individual and his or her role or status in the community. At other times the quest has been a magical one in which the aspirant or neophyte has embarked on a journey of spiritual discovery to find not only his or her true cosmic identity, but also to make contact with those Higher Energies or Essences which have been designated by mankind as 'divine'.

Although we may read about or listen to the accounts of those who claim to have received some form of divine revelation or communion with the Infinite, what could constitute a valid mystical experience for one might hold no subjective reality for another. Over the years I have heard many such descriptions which have varied according to the faith or persuasion of the narrator, none of which impressed me personally however. Some pursuants of the mystical path are frequently heard to say: 'Oh, how I wish that Jesus/Isis/Cernunnos/the Archangel Michael, or whoever, would suddenly appear to me in their full glory, then I would *know* for sure!' (One is reminded of the story of Zeus and Semele.[1]) This expectation is no doubt based on the premise that the successful initiation culminates in an ecstatic vision or the manifestation of some form of paranormal celestial phenomena, a view which is frequently reinforced by the experiences undergone by shamans, saints, mystics and visionaries of various kinds.

While it would be presumptive to reject this possibility out of hand purely on rational grounds, it should not be accepted as a canonical fact; the reaction to both the initiation itself and the comprehension that follows in its wake is uniquely personal, and naturally will vary according to the psychological make-up of the novice. It would be useless, for example, to subject a person who is thoroughly adept in the ways of the material world to a series of tests in situations which would not normally constitute problem areas for him or her. Likewise, those among us who are comfortably at home in other dimensions are hardly likely to be frightened by the rattling of chains under the bed! What happens is, we are hit where it hurts the most, and the fact that we exist in a modern world in which there would appear to be no obvious transcendental realities, in no way precludes us from being subjected to the rigours of initiation through those channels of suffering afforded by the conditions rampant in that world.

Most of us (and I am generalizing here as this will not apply to everyone) meet our monsters, our Symplegades, our insurmountable obstacles and our moments of madness in the ordinary occurrences of everyday life — just as our vision of the divine may equally shine from the petals of a flower, the ripples of a stream or the eyes of a child, animal or loved one. Experiencing supraphysical phenomena is not an essential prerequisite to wisdom, and not all psychic events necessarily qualify for classification as 'enlightening'. Remember what the Gnostics had to say about the Hyle, Psyche and the Pneuma? (See Chapter 3.)

Returning once more to the realms of ritual magic, there are Initiation Rites which are religiously observed by those groups, cults or systems, of whose liturgy they form an essential part, many of which involve elaborate rituals and ranks akin to those of Masonry. The fabled Order of the Golden Dawn, for example, maintained a complex ranking system, through which the neophyte could hopefully ascend to adepthood, and from thence become a magus should that be his or her destiny. These ranks are frequently featured by fiction writers endeavouring to add a little mystique to their plots, sometimes with disastrous results for the readers. There are those people who, as a result of reading the works of the late Dennis Wheatley, labour under the misapprehension that a secret army of occult Adepts, ruled by a mysterious evil Ipsissimus, controls the workings of our planet and therefore exert a baleful influence over their lives.

Now I am not questioning the feasibility of there being power- ful minds at work among the hierarchies of nations, but I doubt very much whether they adopt such fancy titles. The occult does not necessarily work this way, real power often being far removed from the ceremonial chamber. Nor should scholarship be equated with occult prowess. With due deference to those who believe literacy to be the memory bank of culture, anyone with a retentive mind can read a book and quote from it, and the danger in biblicizing any system lies in the fact that its adherents can become so bound up in the supposed authenticity of their ancient volumes, that they fail to observe the practical magical results which are being achieved by the less erudite in the real world. As past experience has shown, sophisticated ranking systems can also present an ever-open door to the ego-tripper and social climber with a good memory. We should take heed of this and learn from it.

The Craft of Wicca also has its Initiatory Rites, which appear to me to be eminently more realistic than the aforementioned. These are known as The Three Degrees. The first degree initia- tion, to quote Janet and Stewart Farrar;

> . . . makes you a rank-and-file witch. But, of course it is more complicated than that.
>
> As every experienced witch knows, there are some people who are natural witches from birth — often maybe from a past incarnation. A good High Priestess or High Priest is used to spotting them. Initiating one of these is not 'making' a witch; rather it is a two-way gesture or recognition and acknowledgment — and, of course, a ritual of welcome to a valued addition to the coven.
>
> At the other extreme there are the 'slow starters' — often good, sincere and hard working people — who the initiator knows very well have a long way to go, and maybe a lot of hang-ups and false conditioning to overcome, before they can be called real witches . . .
>
> Second degree initiation promotes a first-degree witch to be a High Priestess or Priest; not necessarily, of course, as the leader of her or his own coven . . . A second degree witch may initiate others — only, of course, of the opposite sex, and only to the first or second degree . . .
>
> The third degree initiation elevates a witch to the highest of the three grades of the Craft.[3]

Here we have examples of initiations carried out under the

auspices of experienced practitioners who are able to keep a close
watch on their pupils and give them a helping hand along the path
until the point is reached where the assumption of individual
responsibility becomes part of the test. A wise teacher may take
his or her pupil so far, but there inevitably comes a point where
the novice must face the inevitable, alone. After all, one repays a
teacher badly who is always a pupil!

Many of us, however, may not be afforded the opportunity of
joining a good coven, temple or lodge. Perhaps we live in some
remote area which is not served well by public transport, or we
may have domestic responsibilities which ties us for long hours to
our homes or places of work. This in itself may well provide
initiation material through which we must inevitably plough in
order to reach our karmic goal. However, Dolores Ashcroft-
Nowicki has provided just the tool to enable such people to
pursue the magical path should they so wish. In her *Ritual Magic
Workbook — A Practical Course of Self-Initiation*, she provides
safe guidelines for the loner who is either unable to work in the
group situation or has a preference for the solitary path — while
the organization she represents, The Servants of Light, provides
special seminars and postal courses.

All initiations, however, are not of the magical variety. Many
involve character-building in everyday existence, and we are
faced with those same transitions for which the civilizations of
the past had their Rites of Birth, Puberty and Departure. Psychiatrists like Bani Shorter have voiced the view that we are mentally
impoverished without these, because: ' . . . they were devised to
contain "liminality", liminality being the realm of rudimentary,
archaic hypothesis.'[3]

In a world where life's initiations are constantly failed by
many, the psychological debris which is the aftermath of the
battle is left for the doctor, psychiatrist, counsellor or alternative
therapist to clear up. Few of us, if any, escape completely and
those who do have either earned that right from a former life, or
are too insensitive in the first place to respond to the pressures
which constitute the weapons of the affray.

Dependencies are built, some seemingly harmless enough
while others, like narcotics, are decidedly insidious. Many kick
the habit only to replace it with another dependency — the 'Jesus
instead of drugs' syndrome, for example, which is more acceptable to society as a whole. Whether or not it really helps the
dependant is another thing, of course, but we must assume that if

one's Quest is a genuinely transcendental one and not just a prop, then an initiation has been achieved.

People often ask whether there is some psychological factor which determines our ability (or otherwise) to tread the path of Initiation. Let us take a look at a few facts which are known to psychologists and psychiatrists concerning the human personality, in the light of which we might find it easier to decide whether or not the Path is for us.

The main personality types are outlined as follows:

1. *The Hysterical Personality*. Contrary to popular belief this occurs in both males and females. Such people have an immature quality about them and a low tolerance threshold, which inclines them to sudden swings of mood and irrational outbursts. Much to the consternation and perplexity of those around them, they soon recover from these tantrums and proceed to act as though nothing untoward has occurred. In spite of being difficult and childlike they are never dull and often give a great deal of themselves to their friends and those they love.

2. *The Obsessional Personality*. Obsessive types are conscientious, tidy, critical, punctual, pedantic and repetitive. They do not like change of any kind or alterations in their routine and they are reluctant to show their emotions. As they have difficulty in adapting to new ideas or concepts, they are best suited to avenues of expression which are of a regular nature.

3. *The Schizoid Personality*. This personality type lacks emotional warmth and friendliness, preferring his or her own company. Such people are not interested in others and are therefore unsociable, preferring to be left alone to do their own thing. They can make good careers for themselves, however, and frequently do well in research science and computer studies.

4. *The Paranoid Personality*. Paranoics are touchy, oversensitive, humourless, and incapable of accepting criticism. Included in this group are those who feel that the whole world is out of step with them. Such people are difficult and almost impossible to work with, but under suitable social conditions they are capable of rising in the world through their own

efforts, and may often be seen leading new groups or sects, Adolf Hitler being an example.

5. *The Depressive Personality*. I think we have all met those pessimists who turn every statement into a negative. If one tells them, for example, that one has a bad knee, they will inform one that *both* of *their* knees are bad — also their shoulder, tummy and a few other parts of their anatomy. Likewise, if one makes the mistake of mentioning to them that one is broke or having emotional problems, one's woes are inevitably 'topped'. A sense of inadequacy is, of course, the problem here.

6. *The Cyclothymic Personality*. These people react to life's situations with emotional excess, fluctuating between joy and despair, depression and elation, pessimism and euphoria. They are seldom, however, on a regular even keel. Like the depressive personality, they are plunged into deepest gloom by loss or failure, although their reaction to success is one of wild joy and abandonment.*

7. *The Anxious Personality*. People of this personality type are inevitably apprehensive, believing disaster to be lurking around every corner. These are the people who, if all *is* going well, will search out for something to worry about and if there is nothing on the immediate horizon, then they will create it or foresee its possibility in the future. Strangely enough, when faced with real difficulties, the anxious personality is often competent and decisive, but it is when he or she feels him or herself to be stagnating that the problems start.

8. *The Narcissistic Personality*. Here we have a person who is unable to separate his feelings and needs from the people he encounters. All must reflect him or herself and his/her own needs and wants. Narcissistic people are prone to Mirror Complexes, in that they see their faults or idiosyncrasies in others rather than in themselves. Such people love the lime-light, and are able to achieve much in wordly status as long as their preoccupation with the self is well catered for. Hence they are to be found among the celebrities of the entertainment

---

*It is interesting to note that recent research into cases of manic depression as related to genius (the two frequently go together and are generally included under the cyclothymic heading) can be traced to a certain gene. In other words, the gift of genius and the personality discomforts that would appear to accompany it, in many cases, are inherited!

Introverted

Passive	Quiet
Careful	Unsociable
Thoughtful	Reserved
Peaceful	Pessimistic
Controlled	Sober
Reliable	Rigid
Even-tempered	Anxious
Calm	Moody

———— STABLE ———— UNSTABLE ————

Leadership	Touchy
Carefree	Restless
Lively	Aggressive
Easy-going	Excitable
Responsive	Changeable
Talkative	Impulsive
Outgoing	Optimistic
Sociable	Active

Extroverted[4]

and political worlds, or any sphere of life which caters for the ego-conscious.

From the aforegoing it must be obvious that some personality types are better suited to magical and mystical pursuits than others. The anxious personality come off quite well, and the schizoid type may well feel comfortable in solitary rites. One is obviously likely to find plenty of narcissistic types in the cult world, while the hysterical types may be observed moving from group to group in true butterfly fashion. Cyclothymic personalities could survive as long as their swing is not too violent, but obsessionals, paranoics and depressives would be well advised to look elsewhere in life for their intellectual or transcendental outlets. Very few people represent any one of these groups *in toto*, most of us being somewhat of a mixture, although they may help us to recognize more obvious personality traits which could aid the assessment of our strengths and weaknesses.

Finally the Introvert-Extrovert complex, which is defined by consultant psychiatrist Peter Dally as follows:

While it is natural for us all to swing between stability and instability from time to time, those in whom the latter trait predominates should avoid any form of expression which is likely to accentuate their problem. As we have already seen, initiation does just this, and while we may not all be heroes or 'godlings' obliged to fight for our sanity in order to prove our worthiness to the state of enlightenment, there are plenty of times when the edge of the proverbial precipice looms too close for comfort.

Endnotes:

1. *Practical Greek Magic* Murry Hope, p. 47.
2. *The Witches' Way* Janet and Stewart Farrar, pp. 9, 21, 31.
3. *An Image Darkly Forming* Bani Shorter, p. 62.
4. *Psychology and Psychiatry* P. Dally and Mary J Watkins, p. 132.

Chapter 24

MODERN HEALING RITES

Over the past few years the field of healing has, in addition to
resurrecting many age-old treatments and ancient medical practices, opened its doors to a motley collection of therapies, many
of which constitute rites in themselves. These can be broadly
classified into three categories:

1. Revivals of older knowledge: acupuncture, herbalism, Reiki,
   naturopathy and chromotherapy, for example, plus the many
   forms of psychic healing which are embraced by the metaphysical aegis.

2. Newly inspired psycho-physical methods that are calculated
   to be in keeping with the problems and illnesses of today's
   world: radionics, reflexology, crystal therapy and Bach
   flower remedies, to name but a few.

3. Innovations in the worlds of psychiatry, psychology and
   fringe medicine: rebirthing, primal therapy, encounter
   groups, *gestalt* therapy, biofeedback, neurolinguistics, and
   cymatics. One could go on.

Add to these the practices, ceremonial or otherwise, of the
numerous cults which have mushroomed of late and we find
ourselves faced with a veritable array of healing alternatives,
some of which, one might add, are not without their side-effects.
   As we have already seen, Rebirthing has much in common with

some of the old Initiatory Rites. While it can help in certain cases, some people have found it to be a frightening and thoroughly traumatic experience, which has left them with even greater problems than the ones they originally set out to correct. We come back once more to the question of individuality — the therapy which is right for one may not be so for another.

Diet also features strongly in modern therapies, and recent research has produced positive evidence of strong links between dietary components and, for example, diseases such as arthritis and cancer to the extent that a modification of the diet can help to delay the onset of the disease, slow it down or even avoid it completely.

Aerobics, muscle building and similar exercise regimens are another form of ritual in modern society. Although many of these were ostensibly designed for health and slimming purposes, the recent over-emphasis on the social aspect of physical conditioning is, according to some medical experts, causing both psychological and somatic pressures on the participants which are giving rise to concern in the therapeutic professions.

One of the problems frequently faced by the fringe practitioner or purveyor of alternative medicine is the 'Butterfly Syndrome'. There are certain people who delight in trying out everything, sometimes just for the fun of it! Like butterflies they flit from flower to flower, tasting the various nectars but never settling anywhere for very long. Strangely enough, they usually appear to find the necessary finances to do so (from the State or otherwise!) much to the chagrin of the plodders who are hard pushed to pay for their National Health Service medicines.

While the 'butterflies' may be seen moving from course to course or seminar to seminar, always remaining students, they contrast widely with the other extreme — those people who attend a couple of weekend workshops, read a little literature or a book which takes their fancy, and then set themselves up as 'experts'. Such people are, I am assured, the bane of both the orthodox medical profession, as well as those who have undergone recognized training in therapeutic techniques, mainly due to the fact that the unqualified practitioner could be the cause of a patient neglecting a serious disease in an early recognizable stage, and only reporting for professional diagnosis and help when it has passed the point of no return. This has been much evidenced by doctors working at the new cancer clinics. Reputable healing associations, such as the Confederation of Healing Organizations, advocate that their practitioners always request medical affirmation of a patient's condition.

One has to accept, of course, that there are born natural healers, many of whom are prevented by circumstances from embarking on long, arduous and expensive training courses. But even an inspired or psychic healer should learn something about the nature and potentialities of their calling, and none of us should ever be too proud to take advice and direction from those who have been in practice for many years. Neither all the books in the world, nor all the guidance from 'above', can compensate for good, honest field work.

Aside from the aforementioned there are other groups who undertake therapeutic work. Many Wiccan covens regularly perform rites to aid the sick and suffering with first-class results. Healing Rites are also enacted with regularity by orthodox religious bodies, those churches concerned favouring either prayer sessions or the 'laying on of hands'. Any recoveries that might result from such activities are usually ascribed to the intervention or power of the 'Holy Spirit', whose identity the cynic might well question. Some researchers are of the opinion that many so-called healing miracles are effected by a transference of psychokinetic energies between healer and patient, while others see the whole phenomenon as a game played in the arena of the mind. The same criteria apply to those spiritualist healers who claim to be overshadowed by the soul of a deceased doctor, Indian medicine man or Chinese sage. The empirical views on these and allied phenomena have been dealt with in Chapter 5.

In the final analysis, it is the end result alone that must be the deciding factor as to the efficacy of a practice. Any therapeutic method, be it orthodox, psychological, psychic or religious, which can effect a clinically established cure or alleviate suffering, constitutes a valid contribution to the world of healing and should not be discarded out of hand. What we must watch out for are the dangers which result from ignorance, malpractice, and those grasping moneymakers who never miss an opportunity to cash in on whatever promises a fat reward.

The solitary Healing Rite is, in many ways, one of the safest in that the self-healer assumes personal responsibility for his or her own actions. Providing the technique is a good one, a great deal can be achieved through self-healing, as one frequently discovers a great deal about one's real self and one's hidden potential during the process. This is why I see the Huna *Ha* Rite, and similar self-

programming techniques as highly beneficial, as they encourage
self-reliance, and veer away from those mentally limiting dependencies which have become so much a part of the analyst-patient
relationship in psychology, and the 'redeemer carry all' concept
in religion.

The one inherent danger in the practice of self-healing lies in
failing to acknowledge one's somatic limitations. So while it is
possible to programme oneself to negotiate a particularly difficult
passage in life, using what most people would describe as sheer
will-power, there comes a point when a price has to be paid and
the delayed shock sets in. This is why people who appear to sail
easily through periods of intense stress and tribulation frequently
suffer some form of collapse when the crisis has passed.

From the special study I have made of self-programming,
several interesting factors have emerged. We can programme
ourselves either consciously or unconsciously. I have witnessed
instances of the former in sports persons, singers, dancers and
dedicated students who have focussed their undivided attention
on their chosen avenue of expression to the exclusion of all else.
This has achieved exactly the same results as those effected by the
person who makes a special ritual effort — mental or otherwise
— to master some gift or quality, the only difference being that
the former usually takes longer.

When one is initially conditioned to believe that the enactment
of certain rites alone will achieve the desired results, a dependency on those rites is effected. 'Imaging', 'visualization' or
whichever title one chooses to attach to the principle and practice
of self-inurement (or reprogramming, as some prefer to call it, the
inference being that we must first clear our minds of all previous
negatives) can, if handled in a disciplined and correct manner,
take us a goodly way along the path to that cosmic realization
which is the essential prerequisite of release from the wheel of
birth and rebirth in the realms of dense matter.

Techniques for encouraging self-reliance and self-healing have
recently come in for criticism from psychiatrists and social
workers on the grounds that they favour the strong minded, at
the possible expense of those of insufficient strength of character
to master them. As with all such considerations, this contains an
element of truth. The ability to assume individual responsibility
should not therefore be used as an excuse to look down on, or
refuse help to, those who are less able to cope. The assistance
rendered, however, should be in the way of helping them to help

themselves, rather than supplying a permanent prop on the one hand, or a placebo to keep them happy on the other.

In conclusion, I would like to refer to a view I encountered recently which suggested that there should be a special rite for aborted or miscarried children and the mothers who have undergone the associated experience. It was pointed out that the body registers a degree of discomfort at the abrupt cessation of the cycle which it had been programmed to set in motion, and that this alone is trauma-inducing without taking into account the emotional factors involved. In primitive tribes elaborate rites were carried out to ensure that the spirit of a miscarried or naturally aborted child was helped on its way with love and understanding, while the mother was also given appropriate therapy. In view of the current abortion figures we might be well advised to devise a Placatory Rite for the soul of an unborn child who is unceremoniously despatched for social convenience, plus a special Ritual of Adjustment which would take into consideration the possible feelings of guilt, loneliness, resentment and sense of loss suffered by the woman herself.

Chapter 25

COLLECTIVE POWER RITES

In previous chapters we have discussed the missionary mode, the expression of which includes all forms of indoctrination — social, political and religious — as being psychologically indicative of personal or emotional insecurity. The need to belong to a power collective which imposes its will on the majority, and from which one may in turn draw strength, is based on the delusion that 'might is right' or that the greater the number of people who follow a given doctrine, philosophy or *Weltanschauung*, the more likely it is to be the best, the most accurate or the most divinely inspired!

As a consequence of this erroneous and illogical doctrine, minority groups down the ages have suffered persecution in varying degrees, their rites being viewed in terms of being 'dark', undesirable or socially offensive. There is little one can do about this other than to set an example, although even that does not work at times. Good and conscientious healers I know have frequently been accused of 'trafficking with the Devil' by those who should know their own Bible better, as it states:

> But when the Pharisees heard it they said, 'It is only by Beelzebul, the prince of demons, that this man casts out demons.' Knowing their thoughts, he [Jesus] said to them, 'Every kingdom divided against itself is laid waste, and no city or house divided against itself will stand; and if Satan casts out Satan, he is divided against himself; how then will his kingdom stand? And if I cast out demons by Beelzebul,

by whom do your sons cast them out? Therefore they shall be your
judges. But if it is by the Spirit of God that I cast out demons, then the
kingdom of God has come upon you. (Matthew 12:24–28)

The inference here is surely that those who are doing good works
are automatically tuned into the forces of Light, whatever their
doctrinal persuasion; the concept that the powers of Light manifest through the powers of Darkness is both self-defeating and
utterly ludicrous! But then religious dogma has long served as a
convenient peg upon which to hang one's robes of personal
prejudice.

Let us leave aside those doctrinal conflicts which have afflicted
our planet for the past few centuries, and glance for one moment
at the new groups, cults and collectives which are fast taking the
place of established orthodoxy. There is a psychology behind the
formation of many of these which involves the struggle for
personal power: the 'big fish in a small pond' syndrome. Most
groups I have come across, barring those whose hierarchies are
kept strictly under the auspices of one family, appear to suffer
power struggles from time to time. Some of us, myself included,
are best suited to the lone path, although we are usually obliged
to put in a few years of public or group service in order to learn
our social, psychological and magical 'trades'.

What does constitute a source of anxiety to many analysts,
psychotherapists and genuine spiritual seekers is the need felt by
some to exert power over others. If orthodox channels do not
afford such people the opportunity to indulge their power complexes, they are likely to initiate new orders, groups or collectives
wherein they, as founder members, can claim full authority. The
motives behind the formation of all groups and collectives —
spiritually orientated or otherwise — should therefore always be
open to question, while the nature of and intention behind their
rites also merits scrutiny.

Although the liberal-minded among us are happy to support
the freedom and right of expression of minority groups, we must
ensure that we ourselves do not fall into a similar trap, albeit on a
different level. Racism and equal rights should not be limited to
the dimensions of this planet, but applied cosmically.

I was quite shocked recently to hear a man, whom I had
believed to be enlightened, comment regarding some channelled
communications which had purportedly come from another
planet. The content, he said, was both profound, scientifically

logical and spiritually illuminating, but he could not accept the fact that such wisdom had issued from non-hominid aliens. His view was that had these teachings been dispensed by an earthly master, angelic being or a cosmic teacher in the hominid image, that would have rendered them acceptable. With this sort of prejudice firmly programmed into the human psyche, what chance do we have if and when (and I firmly believe there *will* be a 'when') we do finally venture beyond our own world into the dimensions of space and timelessness, for which journeys we are already being subconsciously programmed. Each evolutionary forward thrust has its avant-garde, and it is always wise to remember that today's science fiction may well become tomorrow's science fact, as many scientists of the older schools are rapidly discovering to their chagrin. After all, an open mind is hardly a costly affair, either in terms of stability or self-esteem.

The new eco-religion calls for an acknowledgement of the oneness of all life and the equality of all genotypes, whether they look like hominids, trees, plants or pussycats. Centuries of dogma which have taught that Homo sapiens is the dominant species in the universe, which alone carries the image and likeness of the Creator, need to be ritually broken and reassessed in the light of new revelations, both scientific and metaphysical. The rites and traditions of the very earliest peoples acknowledged the Universal Family, while the Dogons, ancient Egyptians, Sumerians, Chaldeans, and shamanic cultures experienced no difficulty whatsoever in conceiving of a deity, deities or other life forms of equal (or superior) intelligence to themselves as existing within the great expanse of the cosmos.

The Gaia hypothesis, which is now gaining credence in established scientific circles, proposes that the Earth is a living, breathing entity in her own right, and as such she will follow the normal course of self-preservation which is the genetic inheritance of all life. British geochemist James Lovelock, who first proposed the Gaia concept in 1970, predicts that the Earth, if stretched to her limits, will respond by initiating a new environmental condition which could result in the elimination of many current species.* This view is obviously being seriously considered in scientific circles — the American Geophysical Union met in San Diego, California in 1988 to consider methods for

---

*The 'Greenhouse Effect', now an established fact, could represent one such Gaia response.

testing Dr Lovelock's theory. The Gaia concept must be present in the collective unconscious, as it has been making its appearance in documented channelled communications and clairvoyance for some years.

This refreshing change of direction by a branch of the scientific community bodes well for the future of this planet and the lifeforms thereon, as any attitude which places a limitation on creative thinking implies the domination principle, which may manifest in all walks of life and experience — scientific, medical, political, social, religious, or occult. We must be allowed to think for ourselves, to be able to move forward and outward into the universe, to explore and to be mentally and spiritually free, but within a framework of *self-imposed* discipline.

As Einstein once remarked; 'Imagination is greater than knowledge', and whatever you can imagine, *is*.

Chapter 26

ETHICS AND SELF-DEFENCE

As Chapter 14 of this book features two Protection Rites, the question which constantly arises in relation to religious, occult and transcendental pursuits is: From whom or what does one need to protect oneself? The answer to this will depend, of course, on one's personal concept of good and evil, or the established dogmas on the subject that are held by the persuasion to which one has elected to adhere. Dualism is a popular belief among many esoteric traditions, while others see evil as existing only in the minds and hearts of men. A third faction denies its existence completely, either as an ethical concept or an organized force, which would seem to suggest the absence of any moral guidelines.

I do not intend to stand by any existing dogma or doctrine concerning the nature of evil — or 'negative thought' as some prefer to call it — but I will offer an alternative theory which some may accept and others may not.

That which is generally termed 'evil' is nothing more nor less than misplaced or disorganized energy which has come adrift from its natural time zone. Standards of ethics are relative to periods of evolutionary development. Those conditions we see as social evils in today's world were not viewed in such a light as recently as one hundred years ago, just as our present ethics will no doubt be decried as barbaric by future generations.

There would appear to be a very definite set of Cosmic Laws which function regardless of how we might feel about them here on earth in any particular period of time. This may come as something of a disappointment to those who are seeking excuses to give vent to their destructive or negative tensions. Just as the effect of combining certain chemicals can be guaranteed, so it is with Cosmic Laws, which are constant throughout all zones of time. 'Time' is, in fact, the keyword here as 'time warps' are usually involved in those energy misplacements which are inevitably lumped together under the devil's umbrella!

Undesirable force-fields are built up by tensive energies that are set in motion by those intelligences in both Inner and Outer Time which operate outside the wavebands of Cosmic Law. There are techniques for avoiding these which involve side-stepping, or changing to a time zone or frequency wherein they are unable to function or are negated by counter forces. Many rites are built around this premise, especially the very early ones, although the original reason and logic behind them has become lost along the corridors of linear time.

A parallel to this concept would be the instances of certain diseases that existed in centuries past, which have since been conquered by science so that the evil they represented in their time no longer poses a threat.

Evil is misplaced or misdirected energy that is out of its correct time sequence, but as there are many forms of evil, to simplify it this way might well give the idea that its existence is being denied. This is far from the truth! Of course evil exists, but only as relative to time. Anything that transgresses Cosmic Law could loosely be labelled 'evil'. Those who choose to run counter to the cosmic flow automatically set in motion a series of contra-energies that assume form as they gather momentum, eventually becoming a collective identity which feeds greedily on all that is around it. This misplaced force-field can be utilized by intelligences that have chosen to abandon temporarily the ways of Light and Love, and adopt the path of Chaos. Thus, what are broadly referred to as 'evil forces' assume personalities according to the philosophical inclinations prevalent in the Age in which they first manifested. However, as science has already explained (see Chapter 5), chaos is eventually self-organizing, so for all their rebellion, stray energy-fields and their accompanying intelligences eventually find their way back to the matrix.

Of course there will always be those tensions which form part and parcel of the lessons offered by each time zone, which usually result from the group or collective experience of the race or planet in question. This observation has given rise to the aforementioned concept of dualism, or the idea that the forces of good and evil are in constant counterbalance. In one sense this is a fair assessment, for each time zone or period of history does present relative tensions against which those functioning within that circuit can push or thrust. It is only when the accumulated potential of that tension mode becomes out of control, or out of balance, that the resulting force-field lends itself for utilization by energies incompatible with Cosmic Law. Some believe this to be the problem with our planet today.

Certain errant energies can only operate within given wave-bands or frequencies — poltergeist phenomena, for example, which result from an involuntary release of PK energy. Mis-placed or misdirected energy is by its very nature destructive, unless it is negated by its opposing force or 'anti-zone' — which brings us back into the realms of High Magic.

Another point to take into consideration is incompatibility. The fact that all energy patterns or frequencies are not necessarily compatible does not make them evil. One may effect a Banish-ment or Cleansing Rite to disperse elements which are not in harmony with oneself or those with whom one is working. Most of us have at some time or other in our lives entered a house, shop, office or whatever, and felt uncomfortable or slightly ill at ease. It is the same with the people one meets. This is a basic law which operates via one's chemistry and one's psychology. There will always be those people and those places with whom, or in which, we do not feel fully at ease. It is for this reason that most occultists plant their own special 'ray', which is sometimes referred to as 'erecting the temple' when they take on a new house or sanctuary.

The same applies in cases of exorcism. In my exorcising days I was always taught never to leave a vacuum, or, as the Bible wisely informs us, 'seven more will enter.' My normal procedure was therefore to ascertain the basic nature of the inhabitants of the place which one was clearing. Let us say there was a family with small children, in which case I would effect a working which would invoke the Isis Ray, or her equivalent in other pantheons. For the Christian-orientated family it would be Mary, of course. On the other hand, a young, artistic man living alone would probably be more comfortable with the frequencies of Apollo, Baldur or Horus.

Not all exorcisms, incidentally, call for the banishment of evil forces. Many simply involve either the relocation of lost souls who are unaware that they have passed over and who need to be helped to their correct time zone, or the dispersal of magical energies which have been evoked and not correctly dismissed. For the benefit of those who cannot differentiate between evocation and invocation, to *invoke* is to 'call in' or 'call down', while to *evoke* is to 'call forth'. Anything that the magician sees as being of a higher order is therefore invoked, while aspects of the self, nature spirits, those energies which inhabit inanimate objects and the denizens of the Elemental Kingdoms are evoked.

Having established that we do have something negative to contend with, even though it may not be 'Old Nick' himself, how do we go about defending ourselves from its influence? Several factors are involved here: the deity you believe in (or don't believe in as the case may be); the strength of your mind; and your dependency (or otherwise) on the power of a collective, to name but three. There is a whole psychology behind the protection theory, which is based on the premise that fear can only exist if the mind allows it to.

There is also a mistaken belief that only the archetypes of the major world religions can afford one protection, which is nonsense. Each individual has the potential within him or herself to effect his or her own protection by coming to terms with the Creative Spark within. In fact, what we are dealing with here is a situation in which might is not right, but *mind* is! The African who has been cursed by his witch-doctor cannot be saved by Jesus or Western medicine, unless his faith in either of those is stronger than his belief in the efficacy and power of his witch-doctor. It is all a question of who or what one believes in. The barriers are self-erected within the mind but the Law of Equalities inevitably triumphs.

What, then, is this Law of Equalities that has received frequent mention throughout this book? It is one with which every aspiring magician should acquaint him or herself as early as possible in his or her studies. It is the Cosmic Law which stipulates that when two equal forces meet in opposition one will eventually give way to the other, and the winner will then increase in status as a result. This law is re-echoed in the natural laws of science and may be clearly evidenced in particle physics. If, on the other hand, you are faced with an energy field which is more than you can handle, and you acknowledge this fact, there are ways in which you can seek external help both ritually and otherwise, until such time as you have learned to march under your own personal banner which is, after all, what initiation is all about.

Fear is really the basic enemy when it comes to facing the unknown. Note how, when a few people are gathered together late in the evening and the conversation gets around to ghosts and hauntings, an eerie atmosphere starts to prevail so that the slightest noise assumes unnatural proportions. This is because the minds of those present have unconsciously built up a pocket of PK energy, which in turn commences to affect the autonomic nervous system. Result — one's pulse quickens and hearing becomes more acute. What was *that* at the back door? Fear has reared its ugly head!

Too much nonsense is talked about supposed occult attacks. People suffering from varying degrees of paranoia frequently relate incidents of fictitous occult encounters, and tend to blame 'magic' for events which would probably take place in their lives anyway as a direct result of their own mental malfunctions or practical mismanagement. They need qualified help which is available to them free of charge, in this country anyway, while there are also numerous alternative therapies to which they can turn for guidance.

The likelihood of being attacked by any really powerful force or group is extremely remote unless one goes out of one's way to court that kind of trouble. Petty squabbles between rival occult factions do occur, of course, and these frequently constitute part of the learning process for the people concerned. However, it takes two to make an argument, so if one does not wish to become involved, one can always remove oneself from the sphere of influence or activity!

There are also other factors against which we need to defend ourselves, however. The manipulatory techniques of social programming, for example, which may be evidenced in a recent experiment undertaken by psychologist Dr Laura Pendleton, as reported in *The Times* on 31 December 1987. Dr Pendleton invited a group of people to a party at which champagne, vodka and a wide variety of other alcoholic beverages freely flowed. After an hour or so most of those present exhibited some symptoms of inebriation ranging from the mildly happy to the boisterous. Dr Pendleton then informed them all that the liquor they had consumed contained *no* alcohol whatsoever, so their performance was purely psychological! In other words, like Pavlov's dogs, we are ritually conditioned to relax or let go of our inhibitions when we drink alcohol, whereas we could in fact do so at any time by the power of our own minds without recourse to the bottle. One interesting aftermath of the experiment was the anger and resentment expressed by those present who felt they had been cheated of a good time and immediately sobered up. What puppets we are!

At the purely practical level, there is nothing imaginary about a burglar or mugger, as the ancient Egyptians — who were past masters at the art of ritual magic defence — well knew. In later dynasties, as spiritual values were replaced by materialism, the power of the priesthood waned and the old skills were forgotten. In spite of this there is still a great deal of power in Egyptian symbology, especially when it comes to protection, as the following true story (related to me first-hand) will illustrate.

A lady was returning home from a visit to Manchester on a long-distance coach one winter's evening in 1985. At the time she was not a firm believer in the occult but her husband, a dedicated Freemason, was, and he had persuaded her to carry a talisman of the Egyptian god Anubis, Patron of Travellers, in her handbag. The journey was, a long and tedious one, the evening was dark and the lady, like most of the other passengers, was quietly dozing. Suddenly she became aware of a movement on her lap, which brought her round. Her handbag seemed to have given an involuntary jump. She immediately opened it to find that the Anubis card had managed to work itself up from where she had laid it at the bottom, as though it had a life of its own. Fear being ever a first class demolisher of barriers, she remembered what her husband had told her and looked round to see if anything was wrong. All seemed calm enough until she noticed that the driver had also dozed off to sleep and the coach was perilously plotting its own path along the motorway! Horror stricken, she hastily roused the man sitting in front of her who immediately stepped forward, grabbed the wheel and awoke the driver. To this day she is convinced that the Egyptian god Anubis saved her life and the lives of the other passengers on that coach. This is but one of many tales I could relate about the efficacy of ancient Egyptian magic, which seems to work just as well at a certain level for the 'person in the street', who is in no way involved in the occult, as it does for the practising ritual magician.

I have written a small book entitled *Practical Techniques of Psychic Self-Defence*, so rather than repeat a lot of what is covered therein I will refer the reader to it for further study. As it also contains several tested and reliable Protection techniques. Banishment Rites and prayers are also available from other religious, mystical and magical sources for those who prefer to work ritually, and any good occultist or witch will, I am sure, be only too happy to point the seeker in the right direction.

Chapter 27

CONCLUSIONS

I wonder how many people have ever considered the comparisons between the microcosm and the macrocosm as they apply to the everyday things of life? I mention this as it has frequently struck me that we design rites specifically to effect contact with our Higher Self, the gods or some exalted or sublime force, which we may see as having a degree of power over us — either for devotional or supplicatory purposes — without perhaps fully appreciating the power we ourselves have over lesser life forms. In other words, we pray for this and that, we hope that our luck will change, or our health will improve, or that some benign Essence will see fit to smile on us as a result of our acknowledging its existence, but do we accord the same courtesies and blessings to other life forms?

One day I saw a small spider busily spinning its way from ceiling to floor, and my natural reaction was to remove it. Then it suddenly struck me; what absolute power I had over the destiny of that tiny creature! Was it performing a rite to me to ask for its life, and if so, what right had I to thwart its destiny? I gently removed it by its own thread and placed it in a safe place from which it could retreat outside or make its home under the floor boards as it so wished. In others words its life was once again its own.

After that experience I started to apply this logic to other living things over which I appeared to have power. I have always talked to plants and flowers, so that was nothing new, but the idea that many of these life forms may see us humans as their gods, and offer to us their Rites of Homage and Beauty, became more strongly entrenched in my thinking. It reminded me of the biblical tale of the man who sought forgiveness from his master for an error he had made, which the master in his charity granted; but afterwards the man promptly beat his own servant mercilessly and had him imprisoned for the same offence. (Matthew 19:23)

Our brains may assume god-like proportions to the many minute life forms that we host, as well as the organs and chemical constituents of which our bodies are composed, which is another good reason for taking care of our physical vehicle and treating it with respect.

Perhaps the next time we perform our rituals we should remember these things, and think of the ancient Egyptian Funerary ritual of the Negative Confession. If, when we come to face our respective Osiris after death, we can say to our Assessor: 'I have duly observed the Rites to the Gods, and I have also graciously accepted the Rites paid to me by other creatures . . . ', that just might help balance our misdeeds against Maat's Feather of Truth.

Although I am not affiliated to *any* orthodox school of belief, occult or otherwise, I do acknowledge that there is a grain of truth in the ancient literature, myths and legends of many cultures. It is a great pity that we cannot draw on the Rites practised in what I like to call the 'Old Country', meaning Atlantis, because although many of us remember these in our hearts, this is not sufficient to warrant their inclusion among established ethnological and anthropological facts. Perhaps at some later date there will be a book about Atlantean memories, or even memories of other cosmic pasts far removed from this planet. But a little at a time, as it is psychologically bad to break down old mental programmes too quickly; this has to be achieved gradually, always effecting a suitable replacement for that which is removed.

Contrary to opinion, each and every one of us *does* acknowledge a form of deity to which we accord appropriate rites. Those who worship the god of materialism acknowledge him through the Rites of Acquisition and Temporal Power; the god of politics is worshipped at the party altar with sacrifices of economic strategies and appropriate manifestos; while for science and technology, the empirical rituals of methodology are guaranteed to produce eventually the required proof for which the Rite was designed.

Mankind always has and always will employ the Rite in one form or another. Rituals, whether they be of the mental or practical kind, would appear to be part of the universal order of things. And we are not alone in this practice; it may be observed throughout all kingdoms — minerals, insects, fish, birds, plants, trees and animals. Each one abides by the regular cycles of death and rebirth, growth and display, maturation and withdrawal which are deftly enacted according to the nature of the species. The whole cosmic scene is represented at one level or other within the context of these ritual dramas. So when we are unsure as to our own role or purpose in the universal scheme of things, we would do well to take a few tips from the ritual practices of those other life forms with which we share this still volatile globe.

It has ever been the nature of people to debate their beliefs, views and philosophies, which in itself constitutes part of the learning process. In the final analysis, however, we would surely be better employed in applying our literary and verbal skills to the construction of rituals of peace and brotherly love among *all* life forms on this planet and throughout the universe.

Appendices

A QABALISTIC PATHWORKING

A Self-Exploratory Rite which could fit into either the Analytical or Contemplative Codes, although pathworkings as such are really a class unto themselves.

(From *The Shining Paths*, Dolores Ashcroft-Nowicki, pp. 116–122.)

TIPHERETH TO CHESED

The twentieth path is that of the Hermit, or Wayshower, the Adept. It leads from the sphere of the sun to that of the Master Teachers. On this path all those who have brought knowledge and teachings to mankind have their place. This includes those named in the Bible as the Sons of God as well as the Lord Buddha, Jesus of Nazareth, Lao Tzu, and beings of the stature of Melchisadek, Enoch and Moses.

Tiphereth is called the 'Mediating Intelligence', whilst Chesed is named as the 'Receptive Intelligence', so on this path we have a near perfect balance of giving and receiving. The fact that the Hebrew letter is that of *yod*, the hand, the prime symbol of both giving and accepting confirms this. This Hebrew character is also used to symbolize the beginning of something, or, in its capacity of the male seed, someone. On the twentieth path we have the opportunity placed before us to *become* a new person. We travel from the sphere of those who are born into a new way of life.

What is more the road we take is under the sign of the Virgin, the prime receiver of the life giving *yod*.

The Hermit is also a pilgrim, a traveller who is nearing the end of his journey. On one level it is the approach to the grade of Adeptus Exemptus who will no longer need a physical body in which to work. On another level it is the Night of the Vigil, the approach to full knighthood, a time of silence, prayer, and preparation for the day of renewal.

On the twenty-first path we saw the grey pilgrims at their work, and became aware that we had an opportunity to join their ranks. On this path the option is taken up and we are prepared for the work ahead. We must also take into account the path leading from Hod to Tiphereth, and through it to the twentieth. Then we need to travel through the dark night of a mind in thrall to illusion, to learn a new way of thinking. Now we sit quietly in the darkness to re-assess what we have learned and to make certain we are in the best possible condition to go on.

These two paths comprise a night, a day and another night, of testing and preparation. *Ayin* and *yod*, the Eye and the Hand, now working in harmony bring about co-ordination of mind and body. It is this co-ordination that constitutes the new person born on this path.

You can also align the twenty-fourth and the twenty-second paths in this way, being the path of death, then a journey in the solar boat to the Hall of Judgement. This is the way to use the Tree of Life to its fullest extent, seek out for yourselves the way in which one path can underline another, and you will find a lifetime's work ahead of you.

One can look on the paths exiting from Tiphereth to Geburah, Daath/Kether and Chesed, as continuations and extensions of those leading into it from Hod, Yesod and Netzach. I can assure you that it is not a coincidence that lines drawn across the Tree following these paths, form the symbol known as the Chi Rho, or Labarum.

On the path of the Hermit it should be understood that on a higher level you are taking on a spiritual commitment, on a lower level you are saying, 'I am ready to accept change in my life'. For this is what the twentieth path amounts to, acceptance! The hand outstretched to receive the communion wafer, the sword and helm of knighthood, the rod of power, or the lamp of the Hermit ahead of you, who is now ready to hand over the symbol of his authority to one who has been trained to receive it.

The sign of the path may, in the context of the student or traveller, be seen as the 'newness' of the soul to this higher condition of self. A virgin self as yet untried, but willing to accept its destiny and bear whatever may come as a result of this decision. In the Christian aspect this means becoming as 'a little child', the symbol of Tiphereth. In other traditions it can mean the offer of oneself to the Great Mother, the Virgin from the beginning of the world.

The Hermit is on this path to throw light onto the condition of the soul self and its intention, and when it is ready, to light its path ahead. All spheres are grails, each sphere is a finer more intangible version than the one before, though all are and remain Holy Grails. Kether is the ultimate Grail, for it contains all the others as well as those who seek them.

THE TWENTIETH PATH

The temple is empty and silent when it forms around us, and as we walk across the tiled floor the central door opens slowly. We pass between the pillars and go through onto the misty path leading to Yesod. We walk on until we see the gleam of the silver Moon doors ahead. They open and Gabriel waits for us. We are welcomed and drawn into the temple. The archangel appears to us as a young man in a Greek tunic, a friend we know and love. He smiles and having opened the door gives us a gentle push on to the winding rainbow road. The temple of Tiphereth calls us and we hurry towards the great arch of light.

Tall shadowy figures crowned with light wait for our coming. We cannot see them clearly, but know them for the Malachim. One day we will see them as they are. We join Raphael at the altar and with the Kings he robes us in the clothes we need for this journey. For the men, feather light chain mail, with a white surcoat emblazoned with the letter *yod*. The women have robes of deep blue girded with amber stones and a white veil, and a cloak of gold with the *yod* embroidered on the shoulder. We are taken to one of the doors in the south-east wall, and Raphael summons the tarot card.

The Hermit faces to one side, the lamp held high before him, we step through and on to the road he guards. It is nearly sunset and ahead of us is a castle, we walk across the drawbridge and enter the courtyard, here many people wait for us, and heralds in coloured tabards sound a fanfare as we go through into the inner part of the castle. Here there is a chapel and we are directed to enter. Set over the door is the sign of Virgo. We enter in procession and walk down the nave.

It is much bigger than it looks from the outside and down each side are placed small alcoves with a curtain across them. Here we will make our vigil from sunset to sunrise. Each is conducted to their place, we may neither eat, drink nor sleep until the heralds come for us again. The alcoves are fitted according to the traditions we follow, here all faiths are one. Whatever we hold sacred is here.

We take our place, from now on we are silent. During this time we will look back on the paths we have taken and assess what we have learned, we will go back in memory through the experiences we have undergone. The curtains are drawn and we are left with our thoughts. The footsteps of the heralds die away and silence builds around us. The vigil begins, at dawn we will have the opportunity of taking the oath of service to the King. By doing so we place ourselves at the service of mankind.

We remember the cave of Hecate, the Styx and Charon the ferryman. We must go back and keep our promise to help the wraiths left without passage to the Mother, we will keep on returning so that those lost in darkness at the moment of death may be helped. We see again the laughing face of Persephone, and feel the warm breast of the Moon Mother. We stand beside the elders, and watch Hephaestus strike the chains from the limbs of Prometheus and help him to rise, the eagle swoops for the last time and settles on his arm. Titan and bird look at each other with love, each has obeyed without question the destiny laid upon them. We remember the Garden of Eden, the city and library of Alexandria, and understand the reality of its knowledge, still held on the inner levels, to which we will have access as soon as we can use the knowledge safely.

We watch once more the leap of new thought that paved the way for love between a neanderthal man and his son, and see the animals waiting in the garden of Aphrodite for the fulfilment of her mating with Pan. We see the power of love in all its aspects and understand that pleasure in loving is no sin but a priceless gift. The only real sin is envy in all its forms. We stand outside the Chapel of the Grail and watch the gods and the sidhe take part in the Mass within, we see Lucifer weep and know the enormity of what he has given up.

We remember an unfinished task on the twenty-seventh path, and promise ourselves to go back as soon as possible. The lesson of that path rises in us and we wonder how we have been guarding our tongues lately. We break again the mirrors of illusion, and watch the Devil turn into the Sun King, and know that never again will illusions have a hold on us. A dull ache on the heel reminds us that the power of healing lies within, ready to be used.

For a moment we are back in the stillness of the chapel as we hear the cry of an owl in the distance, then we sink again into memory. The feeling of coldness as we lay in the pyramid returns, we went back over the paths then. We realize that we must constantly reappraise our progress, striving towards a better understanding of old experiences, certain paths call for this reliving of events. What seemed to be a dull path may turn out to be one of the most profound.

We see again the kiln of Khnum and feel the sign with which he marked us burn for a second. Ahead lies an even greater burning out. But we have been well prepared and know that each time lessens the amount with which we have to deal at the end. In the darkness the face of Maat takes shape and she speaks:

> This path is one of the giving of self, and the receiving of that self by those you call the Masters. Under their guidance you will be called to the service of man, through whichever tradition you work, the only requirement is Love. You have a choice to take the oath or not, you may not feel ready to give too much, if you do, you will be called upon to uphold it or to answer for a broken promise, think well.

The vision fades and the sound of the returning heralds wakes us fully. The curtains are drawn back and dawn fills the chapel. We rise to numbed feet and stumble out into the courtyard. The place is filled with people, some we recognize from the paths. On a raised throne sits the King carrying the sceptre and orb. From the chapel comes a procession of knights and ladies, and lastly a figure of great presence wearing a blue robe and carrying the Grail from the temple of Tiphereth. Each is called by name and comes to either give or not, the oath of service. Those who do are asked to place their hand upon the Grail as they swear, they are then accounted as Knights and Ladies of the Grail, and invested with its insignia. Then the blessing is pronounced on all present.

Across the door of the chapel we see the tarot curtain, and the Hermit turns and beckons us through. We come into the temple of Tiphereth and Raphael and the Malachim help us to disrobe, they tell us that these robes are here for us when we need them. This path must be fully earthed before we walk the next one, it will work on us very subtly Raphael tells us. We thank him and take our leave, passing under the arch and crossing the winding rainbow road.

As always Gabriel has a warm welcome for us, and after hearing what has happened he escorts us to the road down to Malkuth, waving as we depart. The Ashim wait at the door of the earth temple, like children waiting at the window for a friend. We stay with them for a while and watch them as they dance, then we allow the physical world to enclose us.

AN ANCIENT EGYPTIAN BALANCING RITE

Dedicated to the Cat Goddess Bast

A Recollective Rite in the Intellectual Code.

(Excerpts taken from *The Book of the Dead*, translation by E A Wallis Budge, pp. 4–7, 94–95, 102–104 and 539–541.)

No more than nine persons should normally take part in an ancient Egyptian Rite, but as this is a Balancing, Twinning or Polarizing Ritual the numbers must be even — so groups of four, six or eight would be suitable. These should include the roles of Celebrant, Scribe or Recorder, Protector, Scryer, and Keeper (the one who is responsible for the sacred instruments, altar layout, and so on). The following archetypal god-forms are suggested as being suitable covers for these roles, depending on the number of people involved:

Celebrant	— Isis, Osiris or Horus.
Scribe	— Thoth, Anubis or Maat.
Protector	— Anubis, Hathor or Sekhmet.
Scryer	— Nephthys, Tefnut or Bast.
Keeper	— Ptah, Shu or Horus.

The Celebrant should allot the roles appropriate to the deities (see

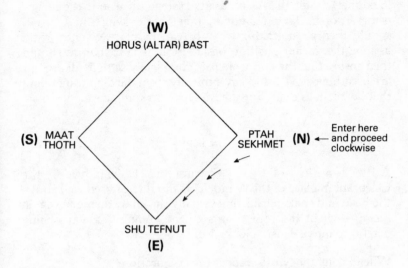

Practical Egyptian Magic, Chapters 12, 13, 15 and 16) and all preparations must be observed as laid down in Chapter 11. Let us feature eight participants in this particular Rite: Shu and Tefnut, Horus and Bast, Thoth and Maat, and Ptah and Sekhmet, making eight roles in all. The predominant colour should be turquoise, which is Bast's colour, with gold rather than silver ornamentation. Flowers should be orange or blue, and incenses sandalwood or lavender. The Rite should be orientated to the west, which point of the compass should accommodate the altar.

Archetypal roles have been allotted as follows:

Celebrant	— Horus (twinned with) Bast
Scribe	— Thoth (twinned with) Maat
Protector	— Sekhmet (twinned with) Ptah
Scryer	— Tefnut (twinned with) Shu
Keeper	— Ptah (see Sekhmet)

The altar should be pre-set and the placings arranged as shown in the diagram which represents the double pyramid. Assuming that all the correct preparations have been taken care of, including the cleansing of the ritual area, the participants should enter in the following order: the Celebrant (Horus) with Bast; the Scribe with Maat; the Scryer with Shu; and the Keeper alone. The Protector

(Sekhmet) should then effect a ritual safeguard around the group, using an open flame (candle or taper), after which he (or she) should then enter (taking care to seal the place of entry) and assume the vacant position beside Ptah. The Celebrant should then ensure that the atmosphere is completely settled, all present are breathing slowly and rhythmically from the diaphragm, and that he or she is ready for the Rite itself to commence.

The Rite

As this is a Rite to Bast, the Sistrum must be employed by the Celebrant in place of the Wand. This should be raised well above the head and shaken four times facing the altar, then once again facing each of the four points of the compass, always being careful to move deosil (clockwise).

When facing the North, repeat the conjuration:
> *Hapi, who is Lord of the Spirits of the North, deign to honour us with your presence and the presences of those of your kindred.*

To the West:
> *Imsety, who is Lord of the Spirits of the West, deign to honour us with your presence and the presences of those of your kindred.*

To the East:
> *Qebhsnuf, who is Lord of the Spirits of the East, deign to honour us with your presence and the presences of those of your kindred.*

To the South:
> *Duamutef, who is Lord of the Spirits of the South, deign to honour us with your presence and the presences of those of your kindred.*

The Celebrant then faces the altar, replaces the sistrum thereon, and turns to face the group, after which he or she raises his/her hands upwards in supplication for a moment of silence, before lowering them to read (or recite) aloud the following:

> *A Hymn of praise to Ra, when he riseth in the Eastern part of Heaven. Behold, Osiris, it is I, _____ (Celebrant's*

mystical or Lodge name), *who saith:*

Homage to thee, O Thou who hast come as Khepera; Khepera as creator of the Gods. Thou risest, thou shinest, thou makest light in thy mother the goddess Nut; thou art crowned King of the Gods. Thy mother Nut doeth an act of homage unto thee with both her hands. The land of Manu receiveth thee with satisfaction, and the goddess Maat embraceth thee both morn and eve.

May He, Ra, give glory and power and triumph and a coming forth as a living soul to see Heru-khuti, who is Horus of the two horizons, to the double Ka of Osiris.

Hail all ye gods of the Temple of the Soul, who weigh heaven and earth in the balance. Hail Tatunen, thou One, thou creator of mankind and Maker of the substance of the gods of the South and of the North, of the East and of the West. O come and acclaim ye Ra, the Lord of Heaven, the Prince of Life, Health and Strength, the creator of the Gods, and adore him in his beautiful form at his rising in the Atet boat.

They who dwell in the heights and they who dwell in the depths worship thee. The god Thoth and the goddess Maat have written down thy course for thee daily and every day. Thine enemy the serpent hath been given over to the fire. The serpent fiend Sebau hath fallen down headlong and his legs hath Ra hacked off from him. The children of impotent revolt shall never more rise up. The Temple of the Aged One keepeth festival, and the voice of those who rejoice is in the mighty dwelling.

The gods exult when they see Ra as he riseth, and when his beams flood the world with light. The Majesty of the Holy God goeth forth and advanceth even unto the land of Manu; he maketh brillant the earth at his birth each day: he journeyeth on to the place where he was yesterday.

O be thou at peace with me, and let me behold they beauties.

Scribe:
Who, then, did slay the serpent Apep, enemy of the Divine one?

Maat:
I, Truth, say that it was the Cat that fought by the Persea Tree.

Solar Cat slaying the Serpent of Darkness

Scribe:

And who, then, is this Cat who is the Champion of the Divine Ra?

Bast:

I am the Cat which fought hard by the Persea Tree in Annu, on the night when the foes of Neb-er-tcher were destroyed.

Scribe:

Who, then, is this?

Celebrant:

The Male Cat is Ra himself, and He is called Mau, by reason of the speech of the God Sa, who said concerning him: 'He is like unto the noise he hath made, which is Mau, or as others say, 'It is the God Shu who maketh over the possessions of Seb to Osiris.' As concerning the fight by the Persea Tree in Annu, it concerneth the children of impotent revolt when justice is wrought on them for what they have done.

Bast:

I am the Twin of the Divine God, the sister of Mau. We are as one, and together did labour to destroy the serpent Apep, the enemy of Light.

Celebrant:

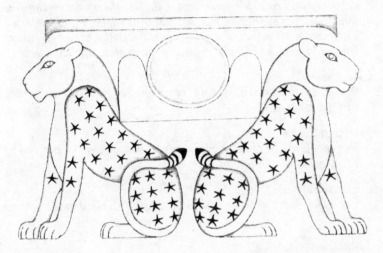

The Twin Lion Gods of Yesterday and Today

Ra spake unto Osiris: Lo, that this may be said unto me in Amenhet. I am the Divine Soul that dwelleth in the Divine Twin-Gods.

Maat:
As concerning the Divine Twin-Gods, they are Heru-netch-hra-tef-f and Heru-khent-an-Maati or, as others say, the double Divine Soul which dwelleth in the Divine Twin-Gods is the soul of Ra and Osiris; or, as others say, it is the Soul which dwelleth in Shu and Tefnut, and these are the double Divine Soul that dwelleth in Tattu.

Scribe:
Who, then, are the Twin Lion Gods of yesterday and today?

Shu and Tefnut together:
We are yesterday. We are also the eternal today, which is known as the future.

Scribe:
Who then is this?

Shu and Tefnut:
Yesterday is Osiris, and today is Ra on the day when he shall destroy the enemies of Neb-er-tcher and when he shall establish

as prince and ruler his son, Horus, or, as others say, on the day when we commemorate the festival of the meeting of the dead Osiris with his father, Ra, and when the battle of the gods was fought in which Osiris, the Lord of Amentet, was the leader.

Celebrant:
Speak forth, those present who are twinned, and say the nature of your virtues.

Ptah and Sekhmet:
We speak forth, change and renewal being ever the pattern of creation in the Divine Eyes.

Shu and Tefnut:
We speak forth, past and future being ever united in the Divine Eyes.

Thoth and Maat:
We speak forth, Wisdom and Truth being ever united in the Divine Eyes.

Bast and Horus (Celebrant):
We speak forth, harmony and strength being ever united in the Divine Eyes.

Celebrant (to Bast):
Come forth, therefore, my Lady, and take this thy symbol. (He hands her the sistrum.) *Invoke the forces of Harmony and Strength, the forces of Change and Renewal, the forces of Wisdom and Truth and the forces of Past and Future.*

Bast steps forward into the centre of the group, raises the sistrum high above her head, and repeats the following Invocation:
Energies of the spheres of polarity, Energies of the Creator of the Universe, Energies of the Single Mind made Manifest in the dual qualities of outgoing and incoming, who breathest out and in with the cosmos, whose breathings create both the worlds of matter, and the subtle spheres which are known only to the Gods. We beseech you to envelop us with those energies so that we may each find our own true state of balance, and in thus finding, realize more of the nature of your creations. And we also beseech that you cast the rays of enlightenment upon this planet which is called Earth, that all who dwell thereon in All life forms, animate and inanimate, may also benefit from

this understanding, and thus benefiting become more harmo-
nious amongst themselves.

The Blessing:
> *I am She who is The Lady of Joy, Harmony, and True Love. I*
> *am She who calleth down the Turquoise Ray of peace and*
> *tranquillity.*
> *I am She who is ever cautious of the presence of the spawn of*
> *Apep. I am She who is sister to the Sun God, and daughter of*
> *the Divine Mother and Father.*
> *My blessings I bestow upon those present and all who acknow-*
> *ledge my name and those Principles which I represent.*

Bast then raises her sistrum and shakes it in the direction of each
member of the group, turning clockwise as she does so. She
then faces front again to give her final Benediction:
> *May the Divine Law of Polarity be ever manifest, And the*
> *Divine Law of Equipoise ever victorious.*

With that she returns to her own place to the left of Horus
(Celebrant) and hands the sistrum back to him (her).

Celebrant:
> *You who are Tefnut, Lioness of Tomorrow, what instructions*
> *or guidance do the Old Ones have for us for the present and the*
> *future?*

Scryer (who has been overshadowed by Tefnut or one of the gods
or goddesses of Prophecy):
> *The gods speak thus: . . .* (as inspired).

Celebrant:
> *The Lion Goddess be thanked. So shall her statutes be observed*
> *and her warnings heeded.*
> *And so also are the thanks of those present offered humbly*
> *to the Great Ones who have honoured us with their presence*
> *and assisted in our Rite this hour.*

The Celebrant then offers the final prayer:
> *Homage to thee, O Sekhmet-Bast-Ra, thou mistress of the*
> *gods, thou bearer of wings, lady of the Anes bandlet, queen of*
> *the crowns of the South and of the North, only One, sovereign*
> *of her father, superior to whom the gods cannot be, thou*
> *mighty one of enchantments in the Boat of Millions of Years;*
> *thou who art pre-eminent, who risest in the seat of silence,*
> *mother in the horizon of heaven, gracious one, beloved,*

destroyer of rebellion, offerings are in thy grasp and thou art standing in the bows of the boat of thy divine father to overthrow the Fiend. Thou has placed Maat in the bows of his boat. Thou art the fire goddess Ami-seshet whose opportunity escapeth her not.

Praise be to thee, O lady, who art mightier than the gods and words of adoration rise to thee from the Eight gods. The living souls who are in their chests praise thy mystery. O thou who art their mother, thou source from whom they sprang.

Utchat of Sekhmet, mighty lady, mistress of the gods is thy name, who maketh souls strong and who maketh sound bodies, and who delivereth them from the abode of the fiends which is in the evil chamber.

The goddess saith with her own mouth, 'They shall never be fettered, and I will do according to what ye say, O ye Tchaui of the divine son.'

The Celebrant then dismisses the Spirits of Hapi, Imsety, Qebhs-nuf and Duamutef to their appropriate points of the compass, and effects the full and meaningful thanks of those present. The Rite is then brought to a close (according to the normal procedures employed by the group in Egyptian Magic), and the participants are dismissed in the order in which they entered until the Protector (or Sekhmet) alone is left. The Protector then extinguishes the candles, ensures that the atmosphere is well earthed, and adds a final prayer of protection and clearance for the whole area in which the Rite has been performed to ensure that all energies have been returned, in rightful order, to their respective spheres and that nothing untoward remains:

By the strength of the Lion, the Keen Eye of the Hawk, The Cleansing Waters of Hapi of the Nile, And the Power of the Sacred Obelisk of our Ancestors, So shall this place be freed of all that is not of the Light of the Gods.

He (she) then follows the others out and the Keeper is free to return to remove the sacred instruments and dismantle the Temple.

A TRIPLE GODDESS RITE

A Celestial Phenomena/Devotional Rite in the Instinctive Code according to the Wiccan tradition.

(From *The Witches' Way*, by Janet and Stewart Farrar, pp. 72–76)

THE THREE GODDESSES RITUAL

The Farrars originally enacted this Rite on a private island in a clearing screened by thick trees and within the sound of running water. They assure us that it can, however, be adapted to an indoor working.

The Preparation

The Circle is set up in the normal way, but with a bonfire in the centre (indoors, the Cauldron with a candle in it). Outside the Circle, preferably in the North-East, is an avenue of three pairs of inflammable torches (candles indoors), ready for the three Goddesses to ignite as they approach between them. Means for igniting them must be available, and also some means for the Crone to extinguish them as she leaves; for flaming torches, we used a can open at one end and nailed across the end of a stick.

A reasonably loud bell, gong or cymbal is ready on or by the altar.

Three women witches are chosen to enact the Maid, the Mother and the Crone. If they are robed, the traditional colours are white for the Maid, red for the Mother and black for the Crone. Even if the ritual is skyclad, the Crone alone should be robed in black, preferably with a hood or headscarf draped like a hood. Imagination should be used in adorning the Maid and the Mother — whether skyclad or robed — to bring out the spring-time freshness of the Maid and the summer ripeness of The Mother.

The High Priest conducts the ritual; and since the High Priestess is likely to be one of the Three, we refer to his working partner for the occasion simply as 'the Priestess'.

Suitable Goddess names should be chosen for the Maid, the Mother and the Crone, according to the Coven's own background or tradition. Here we use three Irish ones — Brid (pronounced 'Breed') for the Maid, Dana for the Mother, and Morrigan for the Crone. Brid or Brigid, Goddess of inspiration, is the one most often referred to as triple — the 'Three Brigids' in Irish mythology, and has a springtime air about her; Dana is the predominant Irish Mother-Goddess name; and the Morrigan, Goddess of battles and destiny, is the most powerful of the dark Goddess aspects.

The Ritual

The High priest casts the Circle, with everyone inside it except the Maid and the Mother, who are at the outer end of the avenue (out of sight if possible). The elements are carried round and the Lords of the Watchtowers summoned.

The Priestess stands with her back to the altar. The High Priest and the crone face each other between the altar and the bonfire, the High Priest carrying the wand. The rest of the coven stand around the perimeter of the Circle facing inwards but leaving the inner end of the avenue free.

The High Priest walks round the Crone once, deosil, faces her again and says:

Within each man and each woman lies the mystery of the Dark Mother of all creation, the ruler of the oceans, the still centre to which all must return as their prelude to rebirth. Let her come to us this night, but so as to create no imbalance in this our Priestess _____ [witch name] who shall represent her; for no human can bear the undiluted power of the Great Mother in her dark aspect; whereas in the balance of her Three Aspects, all are safe. Do thou, _____, therefore represent her dark aspect without fear, knowing that her other aspects are also present within our Circle. With this wand do I protect and fortify thee for thy task.

The High Priest then gestures ritually towards each of the thirteen openings of the Crone's body in turn with his wand. He then uses the wand to open a gateway in the Circle in front of the avenue. The Crone leaves the Circle along the avenue to join the Maid and the Mother, and the High Priest closes the gateway with the wand. He replaces the wand on the altar.

The High Priest then gives the Priestess the Fivefold Kiss (but Drawing Down the Moon is not enacted, and the Charge is not given). He then delivers the *Bagabi laca bachahe* and *Great God Cernunnos* invocations.

High Priest, Priestess and coven circle to the Witches' Rune.

The coven return to the perimeter.

High Priest and Priestess consecrate the wine (with only a little wine in the chalice). The Priestess holds up the chalice and says:

Dana, old Earth of untold summers, beloved Earth and womb of the golden corn, warm beating heart of the greenwood, nourishing within us thy warmth and thy love; Lady of the Harvest and Mother of us all — hold us now close to thy breast, and fill us with thy bounty, thou who art the source of all life.

She then empties the chalice onto the ground in front of the altar.

The High Priest refills the chalice and replaces it on the altar.

The High Priest then faces the avenue and invokes in a clear voice:

Brid, of the waxing Moon, daughter of Spring, sweet Goddess of the Flowers, we call to thee. Come to our Circle and bring to us the breath of Spring. Fill us with thy joyful music and laughter. Let blossom rise from beneath thy feet, and the singing of water be thy voice. Come to our Circle, Brid of the waxing Moon.

The Priestess strikes the bell three times.

The maid approaches the Circle along the avenue of torches,

and lights the pair nearest to the Circle. She then walks deosil outside the Circle and stands behind the East candle.

The High Priest, still facing the avenue, invokes:

Dana, of the full Moon, thou Great Mother, most wonderful Lady of the Lands of Summer; we call to thee. Come on the Summer wind, bringing unto us ripe grain and sweet fruits. Fill us with the joy of maturity; teach us the wisdom of fulfilment; bathe us in the reflected glory of thy consort, the Sun. Come to our Circle, Dana of the full Moon.

The Priestess strikes the bell seven times.

The Mother approaches the Circle along the avenue of torches, lighting the middle pair. She then walks deosil outside the Circle and stands behind the South candle.

The High Priest, still facing the avenue, invokes:

Morrigan, of the waning Moon, thou most secret face of the Goddess; we call to thee. Bring to us the knowledge of the Wheel of Death and Re-birth; grant us thy power, and the wisdom to use it rightly, for we know that to use it wrongly is to poison the soul. Teach us to use it, not to harm, but to heal. Come to our Circle, Morrigan of the waning Moon.

The Priestess strikes the bell nine times.

The Crone approaches the Circle along the avenue of torches, lighting the final pair. She then walks deosil round the outside of the Circle and stands behind the west candle.

When the Crone is in place, the High Priest fetches the wand and opens the circle beside the East candle. He says:

Brid, Maiden-Goddess of the waxing Moon — be welcomed into our Circle.

The Maid takes three paces into the Circle, and the High Priest closes the Circle behind her. He then kisses her on the lips, takes her hand and leads her to stand in front of the altar at its Western end.

The High Priest goes to the South, opens the Circle beside the South candle and says:

Dana, mother-Goddess of the full Moon — be welcomed into our Circle.

The Mother takes three paces into the Circle, and the High Priest closes the Circle behind her. He then kisses her on the right hand and, still holding her hand, leads her to stand in front of the altar at its centre, beside the Maid.

The High Priest goes to the West, opens the Circle beside the West candle and says:

Morrigan, Crone-Goddess of the waning Moon — be welcomed into our Circle.

The Crone takes three paces into the Circle, and the High Priest closes the Circle behind her. He then kisses her on the right foot, takes her hand and leads her to stand in front of the altar at its eastern end, beside the Mother.

The High Priest lays the wand on the altar and takes up the sword. He walks deosil round the bonfire and faces the Triple Goddess across it. He salutes them with the sword (hilt in front of face with point upwards, sweep downwards and outwards to the right front, hilt in front of face again with point upwards). He then reverses the sword so that its point is on the ground just in front of his feet, and rests both his hands on the hilt (or one hand only if he has to read the script). He says:

Behold the Three-Formed Goddess;
She who is ever Three — Maid, Mother, and Crone.
Yet is she ever One;
For without Spring there can be no Summer;
Without Summer, no Winter;
Without Winter, no new Spring.
Without birth, no life;
Without life, no death;
Without death, no rest and no re-birth.
Darkness gives birth to light,
Light to darkness,
Each needing the other as man needs woman, and woman man.
So it is
That were she not Maid, Mother, and Crone,
The Goddess herself could not exist —
And All would be nothingness,
Silence without beginning or end.

Behold the Three-Formed Goddess;
She who is ever Three — Maid, Mother, and Crone.

Yet is she ever One;
She in all women, and they all in her.
Behold her, remember her,
Forget not one of her faces;
With every breath, hold these three in your heart —
Maid, Mother, and Crone;
Look on these Three, who are One, with a fearless love,
That you, too, may be whole.

The High Priest then walks deosil round the bonfire till he reaches the avenue, where he opens the Circle with his sword. He says to the Three:

All hail, and blessed be.

The Maid leaves the Circle along the avenue, followed by the Mother, followed by the Crone. The High Priest bows to each as she passes, and finally closes the Circle behind them.

The Maid and the Mother continue up the avenue, out of sight if possible. The Crone extinguishes the torches as she passes them, and then follows the Maid and the Mother.

Meanwhile High Priest and Priestess have returned to the altar, where the High Priest puts down the sword, and they both stand with their arms raised until the Three have disappeared into the darkness. Then they and the coven link hands and circle deosil round the bonfire in silence.

When the Three are ready, having removed their adornments, they come back down the avenue, in their normal role as witches, and wait on the edge of the Circle. The High Priest breaks away from the circling coven long enough to open and close the Circle to admit them. All rejoin the others, and the circling become joyous.

AN OLD CELTIC HEALING RITE

A sympathetic magic Healing Rite in the Instinctive Code.

The timing for this Rite is important, as it will be most effective if performed at the full Moon, the idea being that as the Moon wanes, so will the ills outlined in the ceremony also wane and finally disappear.

Situation: The ideal situation for the performance of this Rite would be near a fast-flowing stream or river, which is preferably unpolluted and where one is not likely to be disturbed. The participants must stand on the bank so that the water is flowing downstream from *right to left*, and not the other way round. The Rite may be addressed either to the *genius loci*, or one of the deities of healing. The following Rite is addressed to the Great Goddess in her Healing aspect, while also requesting the good offices of the spirit of the river or stream.

Time of Day: The evening, preferably around 7 p.m.

Requirements:
1. Small effigies carved from wood, preferably oak, but if this is not available then any other real wood will do. Plastics or man-made fibres should *not* be used, however. These figurines need not be works of art but simple representations of the sick person,

with an exaggerated portrayal of the affected limb or organ. For example, a stomach ulcer may be shown as a dark or reddish patch in the abdominal area, and a headache as a tight band around the forehead. In the case of eye trouble, one would simply black-out the affected eye, and so forth.

2. A small gift for the Water Spirits. This can be something as simple as a sprig of flowers or small object which has held some sentimental value to one of those present. Water spirits are also rather partial to perfume, so a few drops of essential oil (no synthetic stuff, please!) sprinkled on the waters, usually pleases them. Another idea is a small piece of virgin parchment on which each participant has written a message of love to the Great Mother and the eco-forces of nature. Such sentiments are always acceptable to the Ondines, who resonate to that aspect of the human psyche which governs the emotions.

This Rite may be worked in the solitary form, or if with others in threes or multiples thereof, in honour of the triple aspects of the Goddess.

Prepare a small patch of ground by the river or stream by marking out a semi-circle with leaves or branches, preferably of ash, willow or apple. This should be of sufficient size to accommodate those participating in the Rite. Let us work our Rite around the number of three, in which case the positioning would be thus:

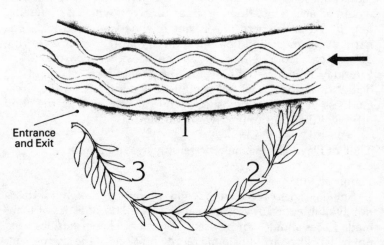

Entrance
and Exit

No. 1 represents the Celebrant or whoever is conducting the ceremony.

The branches and leaves of the semi-circle should be laid around numbers 2 and 3 by the Celebrant, starting at the right hand side and working deosil (clockwise). As he or she finally steps into the semi-circle the last branch should be laid into position, thus closing the group and effecting a protection. The Ondines of the stream will provide the completion of the circle.

Prayer to be repeated while laying the leaves and branches:

> *Spirits of the Trees, friends of our ancestors,*
> *You who house the birds of flight and reach upwards towards the heavens,*
> *Stand as sentinels to our Healing Rite.*

Once within the semi-circle the Celebrant then says the following, which must be repeated after him (or her) in litany form by the others present:

> *Spirits of our ancestors, who taught us the Rites of nature:*
> *Hear our plea.*
> *Spirits of the Old Ones, who were before the time of man:*
> *Hear our plea.*
> *Spirits of the elements of fire, air, water and earth:*
> *Hear our plea.*
> *Spirit of this flowing stream (river), who conveys the energies of the waters to the great ocean beyond:*
> *Hear our plea.*
> *Great Mother, whose divine touch can heal all ills:*
> *Hear our plea.*

The small effigies are then taken one at a time by the Celebrant, dipped into the water, and withdrawn. All three present then move forward, place their hands on each figurine one at a time, and repeat together three times for each effigy:

> *As the Moon wanes, and the Great Goddess withdraws her light,*
> *So may these afflictions be withdrawn from those who suffer.*

The two in attendance then step back to their original positions while the Celebrant proceeds to the water's edge. He (or she) casts each figure, one at a time, into the moving waters so that they are carried away downstream to his (or her) left — this is most important! As he (or she) does so, the following prayer is repeated:

> *Spirit of the river (stream) we ask of you that your waters cleanse our suffering friend* _____ (name of the person who is represented by the figurine), *and as this effigy is swept down to the sea, so may his (her) affliction be also washed away, the guilt which has caused it becoming absorbed in the great ocean of the unconscious, wherein dwell the spirits of our ancestors. May this sickness therefore be exorcised by your good offices, in the name of the Great Goddess* _____. (Use whichever name you know Her by.) *In anticipation of your kind aid we offer you this gift, with love and acknowledgement.*

The gift should then be cast into the water. There should be a pause for meditation and focussing between the dropping of each figurine, and after the last one has been given to the charge of the *genius loci* a period of quiet should be observed, preferably three minutes. One minute should be devoted to the maiden aspect of the Goddess, one to her Maternal aspect and one to her Crone aspect. During the first minute the development of the world's illnesses should be considered, how these have come to be deserved by breaking Her Laws, and so on. During the second, thought should be given to their manifestation in the many diseases that afflict all life forms today, and during the third, the gradual decline of these conditions, to be aided by the magical offices of the Wisdom aspect of the Goddess.

All three present should then form a line at the water's edge and repeat the following Thanksgiving, which is intoned or spoken aloud by the Celebrant:

> *Spirits of the Trees, we thank you for your kind vigilance.*
> *Spirits of the elements of fire, air, water, and earth,*
> *We thank you for your participation in our Rite.*
> *Spirits of our Ancestors, we thank you for hearing the small voices of your brethren.*
> *Spirits of the old Ones, we thank you for hearing our plea.*
> *Spirits of the flowing stream (river), we thank you for conveying the suffering of our brethren to the great ocean for cleansing.*

Great Mother, we thank you for hearing our prayers.

The Celebrant may then remove the last branch he (or she) placed in the semi-circle thus breaking the power and leave through the exit followed by the other two participants; after which the remaining branches and leaves should be stacked together and set alight, so that they are not profaned by later visitants to that spot. The following few words may be repeated while the latter is taking place:

> *Spirits of Fire:*
> *Accept this gift of these holy leaves and branches which have been the walls of our Temple this evening.*
> *Transform their energies to a higher sphere, so that they may return anew as the green buds of the spring;*
> *For which we thank you.*

The participants may then dismiss, but a small repast or drink, taken together, is suggested to aid the earthing process.

AN OLD ROMAN CATHOLIC PROTECTION RITE

A Protection Rite in the Emotional Code.

Requirements: Holy water which has been recently blessed. Four white candles which have either been blessed, or present in a Church during the performance of the Mass.

Location: A private room. As this Rite takes up very little space it is ideal for solitary use.

The Rite should be performed facing south if possible, and the candles set up at four corners to create a square. Make the sign of the Cross and light the candles one at a time, starting with the candle that stands to front right and working clockwise. The holy water should then be sprinkled between each lighted candle, using the same order and direction of movement, thus effecting a fire/water protection.

Face the first lighted candle and repeat aloud:

Holy Michael, the Archangel, raise your flaming sword to protect me against the forces of darkness.

Facing the second candle:

Holy Gabriel, protect me against the wrath and evil doings of my fellow men.

Facing the third candle:

Holy Raphael, protect me against the diseases and afflictions of this Earth.

Facing the fourth candle:

Holy Guardian Angels, guide my steps through the paths of righteousness, and be thou ever by me,so that the powers of evil may not afflict me, either by day or by night.

Prayer:

Michael, Archangel, defend us in the day of battle, that we might not perish in the dreadful judgement. The sea was shaken and the earth trembled when the Archangel Michael came down from heaven.

Gabriel, who was chosen to announce the mystery of the Incarnation of The Lord, bring unto me the Light of the Blessed Mother and her Divine Son, in which I may bathe and so be freed from all evil.

The Archangel Raphael took and bound the devil — great is the Lord and great is His power.

Bless the Lord all ye his angels: you that are mighty in strength and execute His word, hearkening to the voice of His orders.

Kneel in the centre of the square and recite the following prayers, preferably in Latin (both versions are given here, but the Latin is said to carry the stronger power):

Pater noster, qui es in coelis: sanctificetur nomen tuum: ad veniat regnum tuum: fiat voluntas tuas sicut in coelo et in terra. Panem nostrum, quotidianum da nobis hodie: et dimitte nobis debita nostra, sicut et nos dimmitimus debitoribus nostris. Et ne nos inducas in tentationem. Sed libera nos a malo. Amen.

Our father, who art in heaven, hallowed be thy name. Thy kingdom come, thy will be done on Earth as it is in heaven. Give us this day our daily bread, and forgive us our trespasses, as we forgive them that trespass against us. Lead us not into temptation but deliver us from evil. Amen. (The minor doxology is omitted in this Catholic version.)

Ave Maria, gratia plena: Dominus tecum: benedicta tu in mulierbus, et benedictus fructus ventris tui, Jesus. Sancta Maria, Mater Dei, ora pro nobis peccatoribus, nunc et in hora mortis nostrae. Amen.

Hail Mary, full of grace. The Lord is with thee. Blessed art thou amongst women, and blessed is the fruit of thy womb, Jesus. Holy Mary, Mother of God, pray for us sinners, now and at the hour of our death. Amen.

Gloria patri, et Filio, et Spiritui Sancto. Sicut erat in principio, et nunc, et semper, et in saecular saeculorum. Amen.

Glory be to the Father, and to the Son and to the Holy Ghost. As it was in the beginning is now and ever shall be, world without end. Amen.

To Conclude: *And so shall the spirits of the Holy Angels and Archangels, our Blessed Lady and our Lord Jesus Christ watch over me and protect me from henceforth.*

In nomine Patris, et Filii, et spiritus Sancti. Amen.

In the name of the Father, and of the Son, and of the Holy Ghost. Amen.

The candles may then be extinguished, one at a time, in exactly the same order in which they were lighted, and the person who has carried out the Rite is advised to finally bless him or herself three times, with the holy water.

THE HAMMER RITE

A Protection Ritual in the Severity Code according to the Norse/
Teutonic tradition.

(From Futhark, *A Handbook of Rune Magic*, by Edred
Thorsson, pp. 91–95.)

This example is written in a northward orientation, and appropriate changes of course should be made in the order of *galdrar* in rites of an eastward orientation.

1. With the rune wand in the right hand, face the North Star.
2. Beginning with *fehu* in the north sign, send the runes of the futhark in a ring around you at the level of the solar plexus as far out as the circle on the ground or floor, always 'with the sun' in a clockwise direction. The runes should form a complete band ending with *othala* next to *fehu* in the north.
3. Stand in the cross *stadha* and visualize an equilateral cross lying horizontally in the plane of the rune ring and your solar plexus, with that point as the center of the cross. The arms of this cross should end at the points where they intersect the rune band. Imagine a surrounding sphere of shimmering blue light with the red rune band as its equator. Then visualize the vertical axis coming through your length from the infinite space above and from the infinite space below.
4. Feel and see the force flowing into your center from all six

directions as it builds a sphere of glowing red might. The colour may be altered depending on the ritual intention (see section on solar symbolism).

5. The vitki should touch the hinder part of the wand to the breast at the center of power and thrust it forward, projecting the force from that center to a point on the inside face of the outer sphere. Then the runester should sign the hammer ___ from the mass of magical might. The sign should be traced as shown below:

During this process intone:

Hamarr í Nordhri helga vé thetta ok hald vördh![3]

(Hammer in the North hallow and hold this holy-stead![4])

Then, turning 90° to the right, send and sign another hammer sign vibrating.

Hamarr í Austri helga vé thetta ok hald vördh!

(Hammer in the East hallow and hold this holy-stead!)

Hamarr í Sudhri helga vé thetta ok hald vördh!

(Hammer in the South hallow and hold this holy-stead!)

And in the West:

Hamarr í Vestri helga vé thetta ok hald vördh!

(Hammer in the West hallow and hold this holy-stead!)

Returning to the north, direct your attention overhead, there send and sign the *hamarsmark* on the 'ceiling' of the sphere, saying:

Hamarr yfir mér helga vé thetta ok hald vördh!

(Hammer over me hallow and hold this holy-stead!)

And then project the hammer sign below to the 'floor' of the sphere (*not* the ground or room floor) and intone:

Hamarr undir mér-helga vé thetta ok hald vördh!

(Hammer under me hallow and hold this holy-stead!)

6. Now, strike the cross *stadha* again and sing:

Hamarr helga vé thetta ok hald vördh!

---

[3] A literal translation of this phrase would be 'Hammer in the North hallow this sacred enclosure and keep watch (over it)!'

[4] This version is poetically more effective and therefore better for those wishing to use English in their rites.

(Hammer hallow and hold this holy-stead!)

Turning in the center of the *vé*, repeat this once for each of the other four directions and once for the vertical axis. The visual effect should be one of axes connecting all six shining red hammers to your personal center, all engulfed by a field of sparkling deep blue light and surrounded by a band of bright red runes.

7. Finally, center all the forces of the *vé* by folding your arms from the cross *stadha* in toward your center, with your fingertips touching at the solar plexus, and saying:

Um mik ok í mér Ásgardhr ok Midhgardhr!

(Around me and in me Asgardhr and Midhgardhr!)

This ritual may be repeated at the end of a working or exercise, and the entire sphere may be drawn into the personal center, or the walls of the globe may be split with the knife allowing the collected energy to flow to its goal.

The basic form of the rite given here is intended to shield the consciousness of the vitki for magical or meditational work. Modifications in the rite, such as the ones already suggested, may be worked out so that this ritual form may be used as an active magical tool. The runes on the face of the sphere may be drawn from, or projected through to, the outside in order to create magical effects. It is up to the runester to discover the further powers of the hammer rite lying beyond these instructions.

The Opening Ritual

In important ritual work the vitki may wish to recite an invocatory *galdr* into which the hammer rite may be incorporated. Such a *galdr* would serve to invoke divine forces or simply act as a general invocation to the runic powers, or both. The knowledgeable vitki will compose his or her own rite and *galdr*, for this would be a great deed of runecraft! Note how the hammer rite is interwoven into this example:

1. Standing in the middle of the *vé*, face north or east, in the *stadha*, and intone:

Fare now forth
mighty Fimbultýr[5]
from heavenly homes all eight
Sleipnir be saddled,

[5]'The Awesome God' (Ódhinn).

hither swiftly to ride:
Galdrsfadhir,[6] might to give and gain.
Holy rune-might flow
from the hoves of Hangatýr's[7] steed;
in streams of steadfast strength—
through staves of stalwart standing!

2. Go to the northern (or eastern) rim of the *vé* and with the wand trace the circle in the direction of the sun, from left to right. During this process sing:

The rune-might is drawn
'round the holy-stead,
unwanted wights wend away!

3. When the circle is complete return to the center and facing the original direction, perform the rune-ring portion of the hammer rite. When this is complete say:

The worrisome wights
now wend their way
eastward toward etin-home;
hallowed be the hall of Hroptatýr,[8]
with the help of Hrungnir's slayer![9]

4. Now perform the rest of the hammer rite.

5. After which, if the ritual calls for a brazier, the fire should be enkindled. If the vitki knows it, and the ritual needs it, this fire may be enkindled by the need-fire friction method; but normally, the runester will light the fire-pot with a previously prepared flame. Also necessary at this juncture are containers of salt and brewer's yeast; a pinch of each should be added to the flame at the point indicated in the *galdr*. Lighting the brazier, sing:

Endless light of life
give thy living gift
fill the night of need;
to the hearth of this hall
bring thy boon so bright
to quicken this salt
and yeast all so cold
together live long and well
in the hearts of Hár's [10] sib.

[6]'The Father of Incantation (Magic)' (Ódhinn).
[7]'The God of the Hanged' (Ódhinn).
[8]'The God of Hidden Things' or 'The Hidden God' (Ódhinn).
[9]Thórr is the slayer of the giant Hrungnir.
[10]'The High One' (Ódhinn).

6. Once the fire-pot is enkindled, the vitki also may add leaves, thin strips of wood from trees, or herbs that correspond to the intention of the rite to be performed (see Appendix D). The body of the magical ritual may now begin in a 'loaded' atmosphere.

The Closing Ritual

When a rite has been begun with an opening formula, a closing rite is in order.

1. Face north or east in the ↑ *stadha* and intone:
   Now is done the holy work
   of word and deed
   helpful to godly children
   hurtful to etin-churls
   hail to (him/her/them) who speak(s) them
   hail to (him/her/them) who grasp(s) them
   needful to (him/her/them) who know(s) them
   hail to (him/her/them) who heed(s) them.

2. At this point the hammer rite (without the rune ring) may be performed, although this would be optional.

3. If it is not *totally safe* to allow the brazier to burn itself out, extinguish it by placing a cover over it with the words:
   Fire that glows without
   forever be kindled within
   by the might of Ódhinn-Vili-Vé.

4. If the energy built up by the entire operation is to be internalized, then draw the collected energies into your personal center by standing in the cross position, and while deeply inhaling, draw your arms in so that your fingertips touch your solar plexus. Turn in all four directions and repeat this action, each time visualizing the sphere being drawn into your center. If the energy of the rite has been sent abroad, then you may simply split the sphere with your hand or knife and step out of the circle.

AN ENOCHIAN ANGELIC RITE

An Invocatory Rite in the Intellectual Code.

(From *Enochian Magic*, by Gerald J Scheuler, pp. 31, 72, and 86–94.)

The following gives only the outline and diagrams of the Rite. As the lists of angelic nomenclatures required are too lengthy for inclusion in this book, the student is advised to refer to the complete work before attempting this ritual.

HOW TO INVOKE THE ARCHANGELS AND ANGELS

The Kerubic Angels, Archangels and Lesser Angels are all invoked using the appropriate Calls from Table VII, together with the Pentagram Ritual. Each Angel is attributed to the element of the corresponding Watchtower. The Archangels and Ruling Lesser Angels are attributed to Spirit, the element of the Tablet of Union.

A pentagram has five points and each corresponds to an element, and therefore to one of the Holy Tablets. During the ritual, a pentagram is drawn for a particular Angel or Archangel by beginning it at the appropriate point. The pentagram is shown opposite. The four lower points correspond to the Watchtowers,

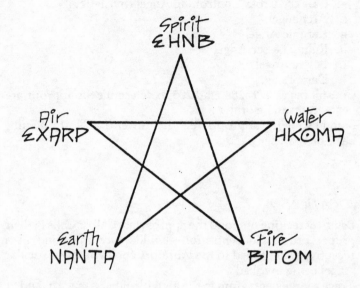

Pentagram for Invocation and Banishment of Angels and Archangels

and above them is Spirit which corresponds to the Tablet of Union.

Invocation of Archangels and Angels: Step by Step

PREPARATION.

1. Select the Archangel or Angel to be invoked. This will depend upon the motive or purpose for the invocation.
2. Determine the corresponding Watchtower, Angel and Element.
3. Determine and be familiar with the appropriate Calls, from Table VII.
4. Memorize the pronounciation of all names involved. The order of the Enochian Hierarchies is:
   a. Great Holy Name
   b. Great King
   c. Six Seniors
   d. Calvary Cross Angel (six letters)

    e. Calvary Cross Controlling Angel (five letters)
    f. Archangel
    g. Kerubic Angel
    h. Ruling Lesser Angel
    i. Lesser Angel
    j. Demons
5. Consult pages 279, 284 amd 285 to determine the appropriate pentagrams to be drawn.
6. Stand facing the appropriate Watchtower (*i.e.* North, South, East, or West see page 283).

INVOCATION.

1. Begin by reciting out loud the appropriate Call or Calls in their proper order. Concentration should place the mind in a receptive state, tuned to the vibratory forces of the particular Angel being invoked.
2. Trace a large pentagram in the air with either a magic wand or rod.
    a. Begin at the point of the pentagram shown on pages 284 and 285 depending upon the corresponding element. There are two pentagrams for the Tablet of Union, one for E and B (both are active) and another for H and N (both are passive).
    b. Trace the pentagram in a single unbroken line. Begin in the direction shown in the figures by the arrow and continue until returning to the starting point.
    c. Imagination is important here. As the magician traces the lines in the air, he imagines that a pentagram is actually being drawn. He must be able to see it very clearly in his mind. The color of this psychic construction is as follows:

If the starting point is:	Then the color of the pentagram is:
Spirit (E, B)	bright purple
Spirit (H, N)	deep purple
Air	sky blue
Water	sea green
Earth	amber
Fire	bright fiery vermillion

   d. To further tax the imagination, after any pentagram is drawn, imagine the following symbol at the center of it, shining with the same color:

Spirit	⊕
Air	△ (with bar)
Water	▽
Earth	▽ (with bar)
Fire	△

3. As a general rule, pronounce the Holy Name while tracing the pentagram and the Great King's name while constructing the inner symbol. Then pronounce the names of all six Seniors while concentrating on the pentagram.

4. Continue calling out the names of the angelic hierarchy in their proper sequence until naming the Angel to be invoked. While speaking outwardly, the magician vibrates the name inwardly, mentally filling the universe with it. If done properly, this will have the effect of clearly visualizing the locality of the invoked Angel and his exact relationship with the watchtower. In other words, it will establish a psycho-magnetic link between the magician and the Angel.

5. If successful, he will appear in the pentagram in some form and will converse with the magician. If partially successful, the magician may catch an idea or thought from him.

6. Success or failure is not measured by requiring that an Angel physically jump out of the Aethyr at the magician. It is measured only by the degree in achievement of the original motive. Success or failure may not be known for days or even months after the operation.

BANISHMENT.

1. Every Angel invoked, must be properly banished after the operation. If unsure whether the invocation was successful or not, use the banishment ritual anyway. It is a psychological necessity to banish these foreign impulses and forces from one's consciousness lest they influence one unconsciously (which is a form of possession).

2. To banish an Archangel or Angel back to his region, simply make another pentagram in reverse, as shown on pages 284 and 285.

3. As the banishing pentagram is drawn, imagine that the colored lines previously traced are being erased (this may take some practice at first). Imagine that the central symbol disappears simultaneously. When the banishing pentagram has been drawn properly, the magician will no longer see any pentagram at all. He should feel that a great distance once again separates him from the Angel.

An Invocation of a Lesser Angel.

Suppose, for an example, one would like to increase his capacity for knowledge. Perhaps he has a poor memory, or is slow to learn new things. In order to ease this problem, he decides to call on the assistance of ABMO, the highest of the Lesser Angels in the subquadrant Earth of Air.

As part of his preparation, the magician finds that ABA can mean 'to bend' or 'to come down' and that OM means 'knowledge' or 'understanding.' AB-OM can thus mean 'the coming down of knowledge,' and the Angel AB-MO (where MO is an anagram for OM) is 'he who brings down knowledge.' He also calculates the gematric value of ABMO to be 131 and uses this number to find an equivalent Enochian word or phrase. He knows that he will be working on the Watchtower of Air, so he reviews the Governing Angels of this quadrant and the two pentagrams to be used (one for invoking the other for banishing).

The magician begins by casting aside all distracting thoughts and concerns. He should be alone, or at least without distractions or interruptions. Once such operations begin, any interruption could be disastrous.

The magician stands with arms outstretched facing the East and recites Call no. 3 and then Call no. 8. The meanings of these Calls must be clear. Their symbolism should lead to a vibratory feeling for the subquadrant Earth of Air.

Then the magician speaks the Holy Name, *Oh-roh Ee-bah Ah-oh-zod-pee* and vibrates it in his mind while tracing a large light blue Air Pentagram. He should be able to see the blue pentagram shining in the air before him.

He then sees a light blue symbol for air(▲) in the center of the pentagram while he simultaneously vibrates the five-syllabled name of *Bah-tah-ee-vah-heh*, 'he whose voice seems to have wings.'

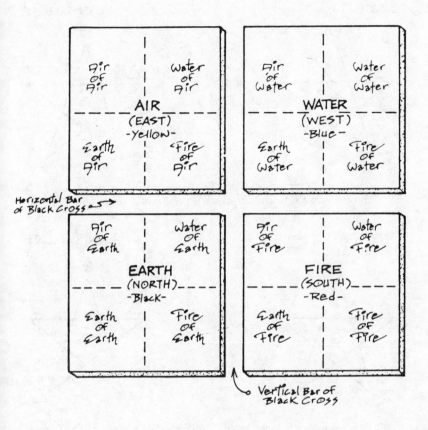

Major subdivisions of the Enochian Tablets

As he looks at the completed pentagram, he slowly vibrates the names of the six Seniors:

> Hab-bee-oh-roh
> Ah-ah-oh-zodah-eefeh
> Heh-teh-noh-rah-dah
> Ah-ha-oh-zodah-pee
> Ah-veh-toh-tah-rah
> Hee-poh-teh-gah

INVOCATION   BANISHMENT

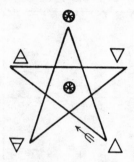   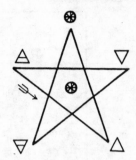

Pentagrams for Invocation and Banishment of Angels and Archangels
Whose names Begin with the E(XARP) of Air and the B(ITOM) of Fire.

INVOCATION   BANISHMENT

Pentagrams for Invocation and Banishment of Angels and Archangels
Whose Names Begin with the H(KOMA) of Water and the N(ANTA)
of Earth.
Pentagrams for the Element of Spirit.

By now the magician should be in good rapport with the Watchtower of Air. A psycho-magnetic link should be clearly established. He is now ready to proceed to the proper subquadrant. He
begins by saying:

'Ahee-ah-oh-ahee, who stands upright at the great Cross, be
within me, and grant my request.

Ohee-ee-ee-teh, who expands outward to control the mighty
Cross, be within me and without me, and grant my request.

INVOKING   BANISHING

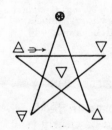

Invoking and Banishing Pentagrams for Angels and Archangels of the Four Elements

O Mighty Archangel, Eh-ten-beh-rah, who guards over the Earth of Air, manifest my request; make my inner desire for knowledge to be an outer reality.

Table VII. When to use the eighteen calls.

Call No.	When To Use call
1	Use first for all angels associated with the Tablet of Union.
2	Use second for all Archangels of EHNB of the Tablet of Union as well as for other angels.
3	Use third for all Ruling Lesser Angels of (E)XARP. Use first for Lesser Angels of the Watchtower of Air. Use first (only) for all angels of Air of Air beginning with IDOIGO.
4	Use third for all Ruling Lesser Angels of (H)KOMA. Use first for all Lesser Angels of the Watchtower of Water. Use first (only) for all angels of Water of Water beginning with NELAPR.
5	Use third for all Ruling Lesser Angels of (N)ANTA. Use first for all Lesser Angels of the Watchtower of Earth. Use first (only) for all angels of Earth of Earth beginning with ABALPT.
6	Use third for all Ruling Lesser Angels of (B)ITOM. Use first for all Lesser Angels of the Watchtower of Fire. Use first (only) for all angels of Fire of Fire beginning with RZIONR.
7	Use second for all angels of Water of Air beginning with LLAKZA.
8	Use second for all angels of Earth of Air beginning with AIAOAI.
9	Use second for all angels of Fire of Air beginning with AOVRRZ.
10	Use second for all angels of Air of Water beginning with OBGOTA.
11	Use second for all angels of Earth of Water beginning with MALADI.
12	Use second for all angels of Fire of Water beginning with IAAASD.
13	Use second for all angels of Air beginning with ANGPOI.
14	Use second for all angels of Water of Earth beginning with ANAEEM.
15	Use second for all angels of Fire of Earth beginning with OPMNIR.
16	Use second for all angels of Air of Fire beginning with NOALMR.
17	Use second for all angels of Water of Fire beginning with VADALI.
18	Use second for all angels of Earth of Fire beginning with VOLXDO.

O mighty and merciful Kerubic Angel, Ten-beh-rah, may my inherent capacity for knowledge be made manifest in this life. O Ten-beh-rah, may a balance be made between ignorance and wisdom.

O kindly presiding Angel, Rah-beh-moh, may knowledge of all things come easily to me.'

The magician has now worked his way down to the Angel who is to be invoked, ABMO. Consciousness which was first expanded in all directions (*i.e.* blank), has been guided to the great Watchtower of Air in the East, and then to the subquadrant Earth of Air, and then to the specific squares of that subquadrant where the Lesser Angel ABMO dwells. All the while the original goal is kept firmly in mind and the Air Pentagram still sparkles in the air before the magician's eyes. He is now ready to invoke ABMO:

'O Ah-bem-oh, who governs over the three Lesser Angels Nah-koh, Oh-ken-em, and Ess-hah-el; assist me!

O Ah-bem-oh, whose number is one hundred and thirty-one, attend me!

You are ETHAMZA (Eteh-ahm-zodah) MADBESZ (Em-ah-deh Bess-zod) (*i.e.* 'you are hidden by the god of matter.' Both of these equal 131).

Ah-bem-oh, Ah-bem-oh, come to me. Make the ASr of Knowledge to be the earth of intelligence for me. Help me to fully realize my inherent ability to learn and to retain what is learned. May I be made firm in knowledge even as you are earthed in Air.

Ah-bem-oh, assist me!'

Now the magician should feel the airy nature of knowledge becoming a solid fact within himself. He imagines ABMO in the pentagram showering forth his ability to manifest the capacity for knowledge. He is now one who can learn easily and remember facts over long periods of time. His own inherent ability will now surely be enhanced.

In gratitude to ABMO, he now banishes the Angel with a banishing Air Pentagram. ABMO thus returns to the Watchtower of Air in the East and the pentagram is gone from his sight.

A successful outcome here is likely because the magician has requested that an inherent ability (*i.e.* inherent in man) be made manifest in this life. The Angel was not asked to perform an impossible mission. He was asked only to assist the magician to make a desired psychological change within himself in accordance with the Great Work. Enochian Magic is extremely powerful in this regard.

GLOSSARY OF TERMS

ABREACTION: The sudden release of long pent-up emotions induced by external means, such as psychoanalysis, hypnosis, or drugs.

ALTER-EGO: Another side of the Self or personality.

ALTERED STATES OF CONSCIOUSNESS (ASCs): Mental states in which the perception becomes divorced from normal reality. These fall into several categories, the best-known of which are:

> (a) Those induced by psychedelic drugs (see **PSYCHEDELIA** and **PSYCHEDELIC**) which are said to bend the mind 'sideways' rather than supplying it with information to which it does not already have access, so that nothing is experienced that is not already within its existing terms of reference.

> (b) Heightened states of awareness, often of a transcendental nature, induced voluntarily through disciplined practices, such as meditation, astral projection, yoga, and so on.

> (c) Those states of religious ecstasy engendered by highly emotional, and overtly devotional stimuli.

ANIMA/ANIMUS: The feminine/masculine aspects of the personality. Each person is imbued with a degree of both, the state of balance between the two being one of the deciding factors as to the mode of outward expression.

ATAVISTIC: From atavism; relating to the appearance of either a recessive or complementary gene, informally referred to as a 'throwback'. The reappearance of characteristics in a descendant of a remote ancestor after several generations of absence. A reversion to a more primitive type or earlier state of behaviour.

BIOFEEDBACK: The method of learning to control what were once considered to be involuntary bodily processes such as heart rate and breathing. Yogis have been practising this for years, but Western scientists have only recently mastered the technique in controlled laboratory experiments with the use of artificial aids.

BISEXUALITY: Sexual or emotional attraction to members of either gender.

BRAIN, (THE): A computer-like communications system which processes data from the senses. New information is constantly coming to light concerning the various functions of the brain and it would not be possible to include all medical facts in a short summary. The functions of the following sub-divisions, however, are generally considered to affect human thought and behaviour to some degree:

(a) the **Cerebellum**, which lies below the occipital lobes of the cerebral hemispheres, is responsible for the regulation and co-ordination of complex voluntary movement and balance.

(b) the **Cerebrum** consists of a large rounded structure occupying most of the cranial cavity and divided into two cerebral hemispheres which are joined at the bottom by the corpus callosum. Different regions are associated with particular kinds of mental activity, such as memory, speech, writing and abstract thought. The *left hemisphere*, being generally concerned with logic, language, analytical abilities and day to day 'factual' matters, confines itself to linear time; the *right hemisphere*, which governs creativity, spatial perception, musical and visual appreciation and abstract thought, tends to function in 'outer time', a state of timelessness. Areas of the cortex, or outer layer, receive and interpret sensory impulses and control movement.

(c) the **Hindbrain**, or rhombencephalon, the portion of the embryonic brain from which the metencephalon, myelencephalon, and subsequently the cerebellum, pons and medulla oblongata develop. The hindbrain's association with primeval development has prompted some researchers to link it with the collective unconscious, on the one hand, and certain instinctive awareness patterns, on the other.

(d) The **Hypothalamus** is a complex of nerve cells below the thalamus that controls body temperature, sexual drive, appetite, water balance and other autonomic activities, including the functioning of the pituitary gland.

(e) The **Limbic system** is located in a semicircle in the middle of the brain and governs basic activities, such as self-preservation, reproduction and the expression of fear and rage. Scientists have also observed a connection between this system and the functions of memory and dreams. Rockefeller Institute neuroscientist, Dr Jonathan Winson, writing in *Brain and Psyche*, comments: 'Our brains may be handling thoughts below the level of conscious awareness all the time', and proceeds to elucidate why new research is tending to allocate the exact location of the mind or 'psyche' within the limbic system.

(f) The **Pituitary gland** is a small, oval endocrine attached to the base of the vertebrate brain, the secretions of which control the other endocrine glands and influence growth, metabolism and maturation. Also called 'hypophysis' and 'pituitary body'.

(g) The **Thalamus** (Greek for 'hidden chamber') is referred to by some scientists as the 'old brain' or 'reptile brain'. It consists of two egg-shaped masses which relay nerve impulses from all the senses, except smell, to the cerebral cortex. Experiments carried out at the Rockefeller Institute in New York established that people who claimed to have powers of clairvoyance, telepathy and extra-sensory perception were able to demonstrate their gifts with amazing accuracy when tested under rigorous scientific control.

Psychoanalyst, Dr Eric Berne, attributes this kind

of highly developed 'sixth sense' to an exceptionally sensitive thalamus. The late Dr Alexis Carrel, a leading scientist wrote, 'Normally, the uncanny powers of the thalamus are smothered and overridden by the cortex of the brain. As science lifts the curtain on this mystery out of our primitive past we begin to understand that we are barely tapping our potentialities. And the certainty that the sixth sense exists makes the investigation of these long-dormant faculties of the mind an urgent and exciting task.'

BRAIN WAVES: **Beta Rhythm** — associated with talking, thinking and working out normal day-to-day activities.

Alpha Rhythm — takes over when the individual is relaxed with his or her attention turned inwards or concentrated on a given subject, as in meditation.

Theta Rhythm — associated with the state of drowsiness experienced prior to entering sleep state. Theta rhythms also accomodate sudden bursts of inspiration, creativity and ESP.

Delta Rhythm — the state of deep sleep.

CHTHONIC: Below the surface. In or under the earth. Designating or relating to the gods and spirits of the underworld in Greek mythology.

COLLECTIVE (THE): What some psychologists refer to as the collective relates to the group entity encompassing the majority of humanity which decrees the norm at any period in question. It should not be confused with the collective unconscious.

COLLECTIVE UNCONSCIOUS: That which belongs to the primordial past and is inherited by everyone. It concerns the storage of age old ideas and feelings which may often appear irrational but which connect with strands that reach back into distant history.

COMPLEX: Originally coined to express the combination of those facets of a person's way of thinking and acting which together form a personality type. Jung called the two extreme forms 'introvert' and 'extrovert'.

CONDITIONING: That which effects a reaction through an association between two particular things. Conditioning does not necessarily imply brainwashing, but people and animals may be programmed to react in a certain way if

292 The Psychology of Ritual

subjected to carefully selected stimuli (Pavlov's dogs, for example).

DEHUMANIZATION: The psychological process that takes place when a crowd or gathering of people assumes a group identity, as may be witnessed in the behavioural patterns of lynch/witch hunt mobs, unruly sports gatherings, and incidences of emotionally or fear-induced mass hysteria. In his essay *The Nature of Crowds* the distinguished author and scientist, Dr Lyall Watson, commenting on the views of the neglected writer Elias Canetti, states: 'Canetti regards the crowd as an organism in its own right. At one moment the street is empty save for a random scattering of individuals, and in the next, in response to a mysterious signal, there is a concerted action. People push together to form the nucleus of a crowd. Those involved in the action seldom know what has happened. If stopped and questioned, they are unable to provide any reasonable reply . . . ' As one reviewer remarked, 'This sinister dehumanization is obvious at any political rally, football match or picket line.'

DEPERSONALIZATION: A depriving of personal or individual characteristics such as can occur in cases of schizophrenia, drug abuse or unbridled religious ecstasy, where the personality suffers fragmentation.

EGO: Defined by Freud as the conscious guiding force that controls the id and prevents it from having its own way. The ego only allows the id to fulfil those desires which are not to its detriment, just as the superego, in turn, imposes upon the ego the external standards set by society. Following Freud's death, a group of psychologists led by his daughter Anna broke away from his original concept, believing that the ego had its own store of energy enabling it to satisfy its personal, social and creative needs independently of, and without constant conflict with, the id. Today the term is more generally used to denote the 'I', or unique expression of the individuality.

EGO TRIP: The over-glorification of the Self. The act of projecting the personality to the exclusion of more rational or caring considerations.

ESP: Extra-sensory perception: the sixth sense or ability to receive and transmit information mentally. ESP encompasses those gifts which are commonly labelled the 'psychic'.

EXTROVERT: One who turns to his or her environment for stimulation. Extroverts enjoy being around other people, thriving on a variety of experiences. They usually seek external attention, especially when under stress.

GESTALT THERAPY: One of the humanistic therapies developed by psychologist Fritz Perls in the late nineteen fifties, it derives from the German word 'gestalt' meaning wholeness or completeness. Very popular with encounter groups, the aim of the therapy is to put the patient in touch with all aspects of him or herself.

HYSTERIA: A neurosis characterised by susceptibility to suggestion, emotional instability, amnesia, and other mental aberrations. The term is also applied to excessive or uncontrollable fear or other strong emotion.

ID: Freud defined the personality as having three vital Strands: the id, the ego and the superego, the former being totally unconscious and the latter two a mixture of conscious and unconscious. The id, sometimes referred to as 'animal energy', is concerned with instinctive impulses and demands for immediate gratification of primitive needs or desires. As the boiling cauldron of the personality, it represents a strong force which often finds expression in fantasies. Being amoral, it has no sense of right or wrong hence its association with mankind's darker nature. Desire, aggression and greed are said to emanate from the id.

INDIVIDUATION: A psychological evolutionary process which enables an individual to become a singular, discrete and balanced being in his or her own right, the term describing a 'coming to selfhood' or self-realization. Although the process usually involves a break from the collective, the individuated person should have no difficulty in relating harmoniously to the rest of the group.

INTROVERT: One who relies more heavily on his or her inner resources for stimulation rather than on the environment. The introvert prefers quieter pursuits and withdraws into himself or herself when anxious.

LIBIDO: Freud coined this term for what he saw as the energy behind the life instinct, as most commonly expressed in sex and love. He felt it to be the strongest motivating factor in all human behaviour, being the directional force behind the quest for sexual and emotional satisfaction and the propagation of the species. Wilhelm Reich also employed the term to express the sex drive, but today sexual impetus is considered to be decided by hormone levels and is not, therefore, a personality indicator as such.

LIMERANCE: Dorothy Tennov's word coined to describe what is generally termed 'romantic love'. Limerance, Dr Tennov tells us, is characterized by involuntariness of feeling and intrusive fantasies. Non-limerants are apparently incapable of understanding the lack of logic displayed by those who are in the limerant condition!

MASOCHISM: There are two types: perverse masochism in which sexual pleasure is derived from the experience of pain, humiliation and abuse; and moral masochism where the person inevitably involves him or herself in relationships that are obviously doomed from the start. This latter type often indulges in other self-destructive acts such as smoking, excessive drinking, or drug taking. According to psychoanalysts both kinds stem from the same basic cause: lack of freedom to develop the individual identity in childhood. The term derives from the writings of the nineteenth century Austrian novelist Leopold von Sacher-Masoch.

MIND (THE): There are three main schools of belief regarding the nature and function of the mind.

> (a) *Monoism*. That it is purely the expression of the physical brain, the size, nature and internal working of that organ being the deciding factor as to what sort of mentality the individual may possess.

> (b) *Dualism*. That it is concerned with some external and to date unmeasurable energy field that exerts a programming influence over the physical brain.

> (c) the metaphysical concept that it is directly concerned with the psyche, soul, or spirit.

The fact that the brain can be altered surgically and the mind still remain strong leaves (a) open to question, while (b) could simply be a more scientific way of describing (c) without involving ethical or religious bias. Although the term would appear to mean different things to different people, according to which school of psychology, humanism, metaphysics, or religion they may adhere to, there is no doubt that mind as such, no matter what its true nature or function might be, is a force in itself that does motivate the growth and behaviour of matter. This influence may apply negatively (as with psychosomatic illnesses) or positively (through self-healing, or any beneficial mental discipline), according to the inclinations and strength of character of the individual.

NARCISSISM: Love of the Self to the exclusion of others. From the Greek story of the youth Narcissus who became entranced by his own beauty after catching sight of his reflection in a pool.

NEUROSIS: Any of various illnesses affecting the mind or emotions without obvious organic lesion or change, and involving anxiety, depression, phobia, hysteria, or other abnormal patterns of behaviour. An amusing saying goes: 'Neurotics build castles in the air, psychotics live in them and psychiatrists collect the rent.'

PARANOIA: A chronic psychosis characterized by delusions of persecution or grandeur, defended by the afflicted with apparent logic and reason. The condition may manifest initially in irrational feelings of distrust, suspicion and oversensitivity, from which a persecution complex can develop if the symptoms are allowed to worsen. Paranoia is often used too glibly in common parlance as a term of derision.

PARAPSYCHOLOGY: A scientific study of paranormal phenomena, for example, poltergeists, UFOs, telepathy, psychokinesis (PK), clairvoyance, precognition, ESP, out-of-the-body experiences, spiritual healing, Kirlian photography, and so forth.

PERSONALITY: From the Latin 'persona', meaning a mask. In Roman plays the masks signified the characters of the actors.

PLACEBOS: Biologically inactive substances made to resemble certain drugs but containing none of the drugs' properties. Sometimes termed 'sugar pills', placebos may be used to determine whether a particular active drug does what it is supposed to do, or whether it is all in the mind of the recipient.

PRIMAL THERAPY: A scream emitted by a patient during a psychotherapy session led Arthur Janov to formulate his theory of suppressed pain memory being the cause of those tensions that inevitably lead to neuroses. The aim of primal therapy is, therefore, to disclose or uncover suppressed traumatic pain experiences through the process of reliving them.

PSYCHE: The whole personality which, according to Jung, has three levels: the ego or conscious mind, the personal unconscious in which is stored all our fantasies, dreams and desires, and the collective unconscious. Freud defined its three vital strands as the id, the ego and the superego, while another threefold reference qualifies it in terms of the natural/instinctive, rational/intellectual, and creative/intuitive. The term psyche is also used among certain groups to describe either the superconscious or higher Self, or the soul or spirit which is believed by many to be the spark or intelligence that gives life to the body.

PSYCHEDELIA: from the Greek 'psyche' (soul) and 'delos' (bright/clear).

(a) The world of psychedelic drugs, those who take them, and the effects produced by them.

(b) The music, art, books, artefacts or mental disciplines that are calculated to suggest or evoke psychedelic experiences.

PSYCHEDELIC: Of, pertaining to, or generating neurological changes, hallucinations, distortions in time and perception, and occasionally states resembling psychosis.

PSYCHIATRY: The branch of medicine that is specifically concerned with the diagnosis and treatment of mental disorders. The practice of psychiatry requires a full medical degree with further specialized training.

PSYCHOANALYSIS: A practice based on the personality theories of Sigmund Freud, but later refined, modified and altered by a succession of famous analysts. It involves a lengthy process designed to bring the patient's unconscious to his conscious awareness. Psychoanalysts undergo special training, but a medical degree is not a necessary prerequisite for analytical practice. No drugs or exercises are involved.

PSYCHOLOGY: From the Greek word 'psyche' (soul), psychology literally relates to the soul or spirit, but it is more commonly a study of the mind or of human or animal behaviour. However, none of these definitions are really broad enough to encompass the full range of studies that shelter under the psychological umbrella. Unlike psychiatry, psychology is not simply involved with mental illness but with all behaviour, both normal and abnormal.

PSYCHOKINESIS: Psycho — of the mind. Kinetics — motion. Often referred to as PK, this term was originally used in parapsychology to denote the production of motion — especially of inanimate or remote objects — by mental influence alone, as popularly demonstrated in spoon-bending and similar paranormal feats. Recent research has broadened this concept to incorporate the conscious or unconscious emission of different energy frequencies which can effect control over a far wider field of human experience than was originally believed (see Professor Stephen K Braude's recent book, *The Limits of Influence*). In psychiatry, the term is sometimes used to refer to uninhibited, maniacal motor response.

PSYCHOPATH: One whose behaviour is characterized by a complete lack of guilt. In other words, someone without conscience or feeling of any kind.

PSYCHOSIS: A broad psychiatric term used to describe the abnormal behaviour of someone who has lost touch with reality.

PSYCHOSOMATIC: Combining the Greek 'psyche' (soul) and 'soma' (body), psychosomatic illnesses are physically identifiable complaints induced by states of mind. It is now being realized that many very real physical symptoms are the outcome of mental stress, as though the mind were using the body as a mechanism of protest.

REBIRTHING: Reliving birth traumas predates Janov's primal therapy, being originally employed by Otto Rank, a Viennese psychoanalyst in the 1920's. Rebirthing is an extension of primal therapy developed by American researcher Leonard Orr. But whereas primal therapy involves reliving not only one's birth pangs but also subsequent trauma-producing pains, rebirthing concentrates on recreating the actual birth process itself in the pursuit of mental equilibrium and so-termed 'bliss'.

SADISM: Derived from the name of the Marquis de Sade, a

wealthy and extremely cruel French nobleman, the term was coined by the nineteenth century psychiatrist Kraff-Ebing to describe the achievement of sexual pleasure from the infliction of pain on others.

SCHIZOPHRENIA: The schizophrenic fails to distinguish the real outside world from the private world of his own fantasies. When external realities appear threatening he retires more and more to an inner world where he feels he cannot be reached. This term does not necessarily indicate a dual personality but may also describe one that is in the process of fragmentation.

SUBCONSCIOUS: Sometimes said to be synonymous with the unconscious, although according to certain schools of thought the subconscious mind has access to all past experience and knowledge gained, much of which has been forgotten. It is said to function outside linear or chronological time and under hypnosis forgotten minor incidents stored in the subconscious mind may be recalled.

SUPERCONSCIOUS: Frequently referred to as the transpersonal or Higher Self, that lofty aspect of the psyche that transcends the purely material plane.

TRANSACTIONAL ANALYSIS: The invention of American psychoanalyst Eric Berne, who rocketed to fame with his book *Games People Play*. 'TA' postulates that people interact with each other on three levels which Berne called the Child, the Parent and the Adult. The Child manifests itself in the kind of behaviour associated with young children — the need for immediate gratification, petulance, resentment or moodiness if lacking attention, and the inability to accept responsibility. The Parent is that part of us which is entrenched in beliefs, attitudes, and values from the past, while the Adult is the self-activating or mature aspect of the personality which evaluates life's situations as they arise and determines how to act appropriately. This triad would not appear to equate with either Freud's id, ego, and superego, or Jung's conscious mind (ego), and superego, or Jung's conscious mind (ego), personal unconscious and collective unconscious, although it could broadly be related to the instinctive, rational and intuitive trinity.

TRANSPERSONAL: From Transpersonal Psychology, often termed the 'fourth force' which refers to its position as a more recent development in psychological schools of thought, the first three forces being Behaviourism, Psychoanalysis, and Humanistic Psychology. Abraham Maslow, one of the prime movers behind the Humanistic approach, in following through his theory of self-actualization, discovered that after the various layers of conditioning had been stripped away a number of people were able to transcend ordinary reality and experience mystical states. Maslow later joined with other similarly interested researchers to form an Association of Transpersonal Psychology concerned with cosmic awareness, essence, and the pervading life energy at the core of being.

TRAUMA: From the German 'traum' (dream), a painful or frightening experience which, however short-lived, has long-term ramifications. Traumas can induce deep seated fears which may result in neuroses.

UNCONSCIOUS: That part of the individual psyche inaccessible to consciousness and consisting of repressed desires and their associated ideas that disturb the course of conscious life through dreams, phobias, and so on. Freud referred to it in terms of the id. (For Jung's interpretation see *PSYCHE*.) The term was later used to cover all hidden attitudes and instinctive feelings.

WELTANSCHAUUNG: A comprehensive world view of philosophy of life from a particular standpoint, or a specific personal or racial philosophy which gives an explanation of history in general, or the purpose of the world as a whole. Attitudes engendered by such beliefs.

BIBLIOGRAPHY

Anderson, Mary *Colour Healing*, Aquarian Press, Wellingborough, 1979.

Ashcroft-Nowicki, Dolores *First Steps in Ritual*, Aquarian Press, Wellingborough, 1982.

Ashcroft-Nowicki, Dolores *The Shining Paths*, Aquarian Press, Wellingborough 1985.

Ashcroft-Nowicki, Dolores *The Ritual Magic Workbook*, Aquarian Press, Wellingborough, 1986.

Ashcroft. Nowicki, Dolores *Highways of the Mind*, Aquarian Press, Wellingborough, 1987.

Bentov, Itzhak *Stalking the Wild Pendulum*, Fontana/Collins, London, 1979.

Bligh Bond, Frederick, and Simcox, Thomas *Gematria*, Thorsons, Wellingborough, 1977.

Braude, Stephen E *The Limits of Influence*, Routledge & Kegan Paul, London 1986.

Brookesmith, Peter (ed.) *Mysteries of the Church*, Orbis Publishing, London, 1984.

Buckland, Raymond *The Tree — The Complete Book of Saxon Witchcraft*, Samuel Weiser, York Beach, Maine, USA, 1974.

Budge, E A Wallis *Book of the Dead*, Kegan Paul, Trench, Trubner & Co., Ltd., London, 1901.

Cameron, Anne *Daughters of Copper Woman*, Press Gang Publishers, Vancouver, British Columbia, Canada, 1938.

Capra, Fritjof *The Tao of Physics*, Fontana Paperbacks, London, 1983.

Cirlot, J E *A Dictionary of Symbols*, Routledge & Kegan Paul, London, 1962.

Dally, P and Wakins, Mary J *Psychology and Psychiatry: An Integrated*

Approach, Hodder & Stoughton, London, 1986.

D'Alviella, Goblet *The Mysteries of Eleusis*, Aquarian Press, Wellingborough, 1981.

Davidson, Gustav *A Dictionary of Angels*, Free Press, New York, New York, USA, 1967.

Denning, Melita, and Phillips, Osborne *The Magical Philosophy, Book V*, Llewellyn Publications, St. Paul, Mn USA, 1981.

Eliade, Mircea *From Primitives to Zen*, Collins, London, 1967.

Eliade, Mircea *Rites and Symbols of Initiation*, Harper & Row, New York, New York, USA, 1975.

Farrar, Janet and Stewart *The Witches' Way*, Robert Hale, London, 1984.

Flood, Josephine *Archaeology of the Dreamtime*, Collins Pty., Sydney, Australia, 1983.

Fortune, Dion *The Mystical Qabalah*, Ernest Benn Ltd., London, 1979.

French, Peter J. *John Dee — The World of an Elizabethan Magus*, Routledge & Kegan Paul, London, 1972.

Halifax, Joan *Shaman* Thames & Hudson, London, 1982.

Hone, M E *The Modern Textbook of Astrology*, L N Fowler & Co., Ltd, London, 1975.

Hope, Murry *Practical Techniques of Psychic Self-Defence*, Aquarian Press, Wellingborough, 1983.

Hope, Murry *The Lion People*, Thoth Publications, Sidmouth, Devon, 1988.

Hope, Murry *Practical Celtic Magic*, Aquarian Press, Wellingborough, 1987.

Hope, Murry *Practical Egyptian Magic*, Aquarian Press Wellingborough, 1984.

Hope, Murry *Practical Greek Magic*, Aquarian Press, Wellingborough, 1985.

Hope, Murry *The Way of Cartouche*, St. Martin's Press, Inc., New York, New York, USA, 1985.

Iamblichos *The Egyptian Mysteries*, Rider & Sons Ltd., London, 1911.

Jung, C G *The Archetypes and the Collective Unconscious*, Routledge & Kegan Paul, London, 1959.

Jung, C G *Memories, Dreams and Reflections*, Routledge & Kegan Paul, London, 1963.

Jung, C G *VII Sermones and Mortuos*, Watkins, London, 1967.

Jung, C G *Alchemical Studies*, Routledge & Kegan Paul, London, 1983.

Jung, C G *Psychology and the Occult*, Ark Paperbacks, London, 1987.

Larousse *Encyclopedia of Mythology*, Paul Hamlyn, London, 1959.

Maclagan, David *Creation Myths*, Thames & Hudson, London. 1977.

Maspero, Gaston *The Dawn of Civilization*, The Society for Promoting Christian Knowledge, London, 1910.

McLuhan, T C *Touch the Earth*, Abacus Books, London, 1973.

Mead, G R S *Thrice-Greatest Hermes*, Theosophical Publishing Co., London, 1906.

Mylonas, George E *Eleusis and the Eleusinian Mysteries*, Routledge & Kegan Paul, London, 1961.

Nathan, Peter *The Nervous System*, Oxford University Press, Oxford, 1983.

Pennick, Nigel *Sacred Geometry*, Turnstone Press, Wellingborough, 1980.

Ponce, Charles *Kabbalah*, Garnstone Press, London, 1974.

Schueler, Gerald J *Enochian Magic*, Llewellyn Publications, St. Paul, Minnesota, USA, 1985.

Sheldrake, Rupert *A New Science of Life*, Granada Publishing. London, 1983.

Shorter, Bani *An Image Darkly Forming*, Routledge & Kegan Paul, London, 1987.

Slater, Herman *A Book of Pagan Rituals*, Samuel Weiser, York Beach, Maine, USA, 1978.

Steiger, Brad *Kahuna Magic*, Para Research, Gloucester, Massachusetts, USA, 1981.

Stone, Merlin *The Paradise Papers*, Virago, London, 1976.

Temple, Robert K G *The Sirius Mystery*, Sidgwick & Jackson, London, 1976.

Thorsson, Edred *Futhark*, Aquarian Press, Wellingborough, 1985.

Turner, Robert *The Heptarchia Mystica of John Dee*, Aquarian Press, Wellingborough, 1986.

Waite, A E *The Occult Sciences*, Kegan Paul, Trench, Trubner & Co. Ltd., London, 1891.

Watson, J D *The Double Helix*, Penguin, London, 1968.

Watson, Lyall *Earthworks*, Hodder & Stoughton, Sevenoaks, 1986.

Winn, Denise *The Whole Mind Book*, Fontana Paperbacks, London, 1980.

Witt, R E *Isis in the Graeco-Roman World*, Thames & Hudson, London. 1971.

Zohar, Danah *Through the Time Barrier*, Paladin Books, London, 1983.

INDEX